# THE QUARRYMEN

Also by Hunter Davies:

Here We Go, Round the Mulberry Bush
The Other Half
The New London Spy
The Beatles
The Rise and Fall of Jake Sullivan
I Knew Daisy Smuten
A Very Loving Couple
Body Charge
The Glory Game
A Walk Along the Wall
George Stephenson
The Creighton Report
A Walk Around the Lakes
William Wordsworth
The Grades
Father's Day
A Walk Along the Tracks
Great Britain: A Celebration
Flossie Teacake's Fur Coat
A Walk Around London's Parks
The Good Guide to the Lakes
The Joy of Stamps
Back in the USSR
Beatrix Potter's Lakeland
My Life in Football
In Search of Columbus
Striker
Hunting People
The Teller of Tales
Wainwright
Living on the Lottery
Born 1900
London to Loweswater
Dwight Yorke
A Walk Around the West Indies
Still Crazy

# THE QUARRYMEN

## HUNTER DAVIES

**OMNIBUS PRESS**
LONDON · NEW YORK · SYDNEY

Cover designed by Philip Gambrill
Picture research by Nikki Lloyd & Hunter Davies

ISBN: 0.7119.8526.X
Order No: OP 48199

**Exclusive Distributors**
Music Sales Limited,
8/9 Frith Street,
London W1D 3JB, UK.

Music Sales Corporation,
257 Park Avenue South,
New York, NY 10010, USA.

The Five Mile Press,
22 Summit Road,
Noble Park,
Victoria 3174, Australia.

**To the Music Trade only:**
Music Sales Limited,
8/9 Frith Street,
London W1D 3JB, UK.

Every effort has been made to trace the copyright holders of the photographs in this book but one or two
were unreachable. We would be grateful if the photographers concerned would contact us.

Typeset by Galleon Typesetting, Ipswich.
Printed in the United Kingdom by Creative Print & Design (Wales) Ltd.

A catalogue record for this book is available from the British Library.

**www.omnibuspress.com**

# Contents

# Introduction

In November 1998, while working on a travel book about the West Indies, I went to Cuba. On the plane out, I met someone who asked if I was going to The Beatles Conference. I didn't know there was one, or even that the Cubans had any interest in The Beatles. "Oh yes," he said, "they're passionate, in fact this will be Cuba's Third International Beatles Conference." I'd somehow missed all three, but he persuaded me not to miss this one. He was giving a little talk, why didn't I? I said I'd think about it, but really, I was here for other things.

My hotel in Havana turned out to be pretty boring, well away from the centre, but Pete, my friend, was staying in the centre, in an old hotel. I had a drink with him one night and met Ernesto, who was organising The Beatles Conference. I was so impressed by his Beatles knowledge, his enthusiasm, that I said "OK then, I'll give a little talk." My first time at any Beatles Convention. My first talk to real Beatles fans.

I wrote their authorised biography, first published in 1968 – goodness can it be that long ago – then went on to do another thirty or so books, all on different topics, none of them connected with The Beatles. I love them dearly, always will, both them and their music, and have kept in touch with Paul all these years, but I don't look upon myself as a Beatles expert. At one stage, I did know a lot about them, about their life up to 1968, plus bits afterwards in the Seventies, based on meeting them from time to time, but that was all, really.

It was like an examination, doing their biog. I mugged it up, lived it for two years, carried it all in my head, thought about them non stop, then once I'd got it down, written the final page, it mostly went from my mind. So it seemed presumptuous or pathetic to go on talking about them, to chunter on about how I once knew them, when very soon the world became full of real Beatles experts.

Today there are Beatles Brains who seem to know everything, can tell you what they were doing on every day of their lives. Not just in Britain or the USA. The world is awash with Beatles Brains. I'd say there must be now something like 2,000 people, from Japan through Europe to the

Americas, who are living full-time on the Beatles – selling Beatles souvenirs or material, writing about them, impersonating them, organising Beatly events. Yet very few of them were alive to see and hear The Beatles in their pomp.

I agreed to give the talk feeling I was a bit of a fraud, that I'd be caught out by my lack of real knowledge, but thinking I'll get some copy out of this, I'll meet some real Cubans, pick up stuff I can work into my travel book.

The Conference was very serious, with learned papers being read out, deep analysis being discussed. Ernesto turned out to have written three books on The Beatles, in Spanish, one of which was about the effect of Cuban music on The Beatles. I rather scoffed at this, saying, "Come on, Ernesto, they never went to Cuba, they didn't play Cuban music, what are you on about?"

"I have analysed every song they ever wrote," he replied, "and have counted 28 songs which include maracas, twelve songs which use bongos, ten with cow bells and one with a guiro which is a bit like a washboard . . ."

The reference to a washboard was interesting, as of course that was how they began, as even baby Beatles Brains well know.

I gave my chat, such as it was, before a large and attentive audience. It was simultaneously translated into Spanish. When they asked me questions, I had an ear-piece which translated their questions into English. All highly organised and professional.

The Conference lasted three days and one of the events listed was a performance by The Quarrymen.* Must be a local, lookalike, bootleg Beatles type group, so I thought. There are lots of them around today. To my amazement, it turned out to be the real and original Quarrymen – the five friends whom John got together when the skiffle craze first hit his school, Quarry Bank High, back in Liverpool in 1957.

When Paul and George came along, people who could actually play the guitar well, the original five went their respective ways in life. Beatles Brains know their names today, and know about a famous photograph of them performing at Woolton Parish Church in 1957, the day Paul first met John, but the rest of the world knows nothing of them. The Beatles went on to fame and fortune. The Quarrymen became mere footnotes in their history.

---

* Is it Quarrymen or Quarry Men? The spelling has varied over the years in various books, but I'll stick with one word because this is the way it appears in the school song, from which the name was originally taken.

*Introduction*

I could see they were now senior citizens, approaching the age of 60, just like myself, just as John would have been, had he lived. Yet they were now apparently touring the world, playing the same music, on the same sorts of instruments, which they had played back in 1957. How had it happened, so late in life, that they had become pop musicians? What it was like for them, to be doing now what they had failed to do, or not gone on to do, first time round?

I had met one of them before, Pete Shotton, while writing the book. He had been John's best friend at school and still around when I used to visit John's house in 1967. I remember John telling me that he had given Pete £20,000 to buy a shop. A nice gesture, and Pete appeared to be an amiable sort of bloke when I'd interviewed him, but it seemed a bit daft. John would probably never see the money again as Pete might just waste it. "I don't care," said John. "He's my best mate. He would have done the same for me."

I never saw Pete again, or heard what happened to him, or the shop or the money. Thirty years later, in Cuba, I suddenly got a chance to catch up on his life. Which I did, if rather fleetingly. I left Havana in the morning, going on to other places.

When I got back to England, and had finished the West Indies book, I found the Quarrymen still on my mind. I was intrigued by the notion of people who had once touched shoulders with a world famous celebrity. There are lots today, as we have more and more celebrities in this age of instant fame, even if many disappear just as quickly as they arrive.

All five Quarrymen must have clear memories of the John they once knew well – probably clearer memories now than then. And clearer than John ever carried with him. That is the nature of celebrity. The non-celeb remembers exactly what the celeb has long forgotten, or was not even aware of at the time. Over the years, they dig out detritus from the back of their brains, half forgotten incidents and images and yes, some of it is mere fluff, trivia which they build up, turning what was at the time something ordinary into something memorable. All the same, they were there, at a vital stage in John's life. How did they react afterwards? What did they think when Beatlemania happened and they were not part of it? How did their brush with history (pop music division) affect them personally?

Most of all, what about their own personal lives? I wanted to know exactly what each had done over the last 40 years.

I saw their story as a slice of social history as much as musical history. And of my history. Being of the same age, similar background, gone to a similar school, I'd lived through similar times, felt similar things, shared

ix

and nursed similar memories. It didn't really matter what it was they'd gone on to do – I just wanted to know about it. Ordinary lives can be just as interesting as the extraordinary and just as valuable to record.

So I decided to follow the lives of the six original Quarrymen over the last forty years – the five 'ordinary' members, as well as John. I soon found that John was not the only one to whom some extraordinary things had happened. As you will see. . . .

Loweswater, October 2000

# THE FORTIES

# 1

## Primary Functions

John Lennon was born on October 9, 1940, in Oxford Street Maternity Hospital, Liverpool, during a period of heavy bombing raids on the city. His Aunt Mimi, sister of his mother, Julia, saw him twenty minutes after he'd arrived into this world and insisted that he be called John. A middle name Winston was added, a patriotic gesture by his mother.

His father, Fred, was not around, and continued to be hardly around during the next few years. He was a seaman, who continued at sea when the War was over, working as a ship's steward. He sent Julia money when he could, when he had any, when other things did not conspire to stop him sending money, such as spending it all or ending up in prison for three months after breaking into the ship's cargo and stealing some whisky. Allegedly. It wasn't his fault, so Fred maintained when I met him in 1967. He told me a long and complicated story explaining how it had happened, but he didn't hide his conviction and gave me a snap of himself in prison uniform which clearly showed his prison number. He looked remarkably like John.

Fred reappeared in John's life when John was about five. He was allowed to take him off for a short holiday to Blackpool during which time he decided upon a mad scheme to emigrate with John to New Zealand. Before this could happen, Julia appeared and took John back to Liverpool.

By this time, Julia herself had found another partner, and soon started a new family. Aunt Mimi took in John, as she had always wanted, bringing him up as her own son. She and her husband George had no children of their own.

Mimi was determined to give John as good a start in life as possible, hoping he would not turn out as feckless as Fred, whom she never talked about, or as fun loving and reckless as Julia. Mimi was keen on discipline, good manners, and very aware of what she thought was her social position in life. She told me, for example, that George, her husband, owned a dairy, but in reality he was little more than a milkman, one who was very fond of gambling.

They lived in the quiet suburb of Woolton, to the south of the city, which still thought of itself as a village, with rural overtones, a parish church, old-fashioned shops which had been there for decades, several parks and some old sandstone quarries. Many of the older buildings had been made from this sandstone but around the outskirts were some newer, semi-detached houses built in the Thirties, popular with the more up-wardly mobile Liverpool working classes who wanted to bring their children up in a leafier, cleaner environment.

Mimi and George's house was a pre-war semi-detached, 251 Menlove Avenue, a rather busy, broad road, but their house did have its own name, Mendips. Mimi liked to give the impression that she and George were quite well off, but they also took in lodgers from time to time, medical students, to help with their finances.

John went to Dovedale Road Primary School where the headmaster was very impressed by him, so Mimi said. "He told me 'this boy's as sharp as a needle. He can do anything he chooses to do. He won't do anything stereotyped.'"

John was reading and writing well by the age of seven, as could be seen from his own little books and creations which Mimi had carefully kept. She showed me one called *Sport and Speed Illustrated. Edited and Illustrated by JW Lennon*. It contained jokes, drawings, pasted-in photographs of film stars and footballers. It had a serial story which ended each week with "If you liked this, come again next week, it'll be even better."

John loved reading *Just William* books, *Alice In Wonderland, Wind In The Willows*, when he wasn't whistling and singing along to jolly songs on the radio, such as 'Let Him Go Let Him Tarry'. He went to Sunday School each week with his best friend Pete at St Peter's in Woolton, the parish church. Not forced, said Mimi. He went of his own free will and was later confirmed, without any pressure from her.

All true, all later agreed to be true by John, who had clear memories of all these childhood delights in this idyllic semi rural setting. Mimi said she never heard him swear as a boy, he never did nasty things like stealing, and insisted in my book that I quoted her as saying John was "open and sunny natured . . . as happy as the day was long".

But of course there were other truths, other things going on in John's life and in his mind which today could suggest a disturbed childhood, the effects of being abandoned by his parents at an early age. On the other hand, you could say that was the way he was, how he had been born.

"I fought all the way through Dovedale." That was John's own memory. "Winning by psychological means if anyone looked bigger than me. I threatened them in a strong enough way that I would beat them up, so they thought I could.

"We used to ride on the bumpers of the tram cars in Penny Lane and ride miles without paying. I'd be shitting myself all the time, I was so scared.

"I was the King Pin of my age group. I learned lots of dirty jokes very young. The sort of gang I led went in for thieving apples and pulling girls knickers down. When the bomb fell and everyone got caught, Mimi was the only parent who never found out.

"Other boys' parents hated me. They were always warning their kids not to play with me. I'd always have smart Alec answers if I met them.

"As I got older, we'd go on from just stuffing rubbish like sweets in our pockets from shops and progressed to getting enough to sell to others, like ciggies."

Aged eleven in the summer of 1952, John sat the Eleven Plus, as every child did in those days, and passed for Quarry Bank High School.

John's first image on his first day was of the size of the school. "I looked at all the hundreds of kids and thought Christ, I'll have to fight my way through this lot, having just made it at Dovedale. . . ."

★　★　★

Pete Shotton, John's best friend, a thin, tall boy with incredibly blond, flaxen hair, lived round the corner from John at 83 Vale Road, in the same road as two others in John's gang, Ivan Vaughan and Nigel Walley.

Pete's father, George, was originally from the North East but had left to join the merchant navy, ending up as a chief engineer. He got married to Bessie, also from the North East, left the sea and found a shore job in Liverpool, working for Tate & Lyle in their offices where he became a draughtsman. Bessie did market research for Gallup Poll, stopping people in the street and asking questions.

Pete remembers childhood holidays in Sunderland with his grandparents, not far from Roker Park. Like John, he never became a real football fan, though if asked, Pete said he followed Sunderland FC.

Their house was semi-detached, like all the others, with an air raid shelter in the back garden, left over from the war. At one end of Vale Road were council houses. Somewhere in the middle was an unspoken, unwritten socio-economic demarcation line. Pete doesn't remember being told about this division, or being warned not to play with the council house kids, but he grew up aware of it. "The council house kids did strike me as being rougher, tattier. We kept ourselves to ourselves, in our own territory."

Pete's house was in fact rented, which Pete didn't realise till he was older. The tale in the family was that they could have bought their own house, but at the vital stage, when they could have managed a mortgage, Pete's grandmother – his mother's mother – wouldn't lend them the £25 they needed.

Pete was born on August 4, 1941. He had an older sister, Joan, an older brother, Ernest, and later a younger brother, David.

His first gang consisted of Ivan and Nigel. He considered himself the leader of this little trio of neighbours, even at the age of six, till the big bad John Lennon appeared from the next street. He did seem big to Pete, being ten months older, as well as stronger, more aggressive, more worldly wise, despite his funny looking spectacles. John had been born with poor eyesight and had specs from an early age but wouldn't wear them, unless he had to, wanting to look hard, as we'd say today, or not be called Speccy Four Eyes, as they said then.

Pete and John enjoyed attending Sunday School together, one of the attractions being the collection money they were always given. It was John, says Pete, who first suggested what they should do with it – spend it in the sweet shop instead, usually on bubble gum. So they'd chew away, in class, till spotted by Mrs Clark, the Sunday School teacher, who would hold out her hand for the offending items. John would take out his sticky, stringy gum and press it as hard as possible into Mrs Clark's hand, hoping to stick her fingers together.

At the beginning of Sunday School, each child had had to give his full name, which was how Pete first discovered John's middle name, and quickly realised how it embarrassed him. John had tried muttering it to Mrs Clark, but was asked to speak up. Naturally, at moments of rivalry between them, or arguments, Pete would yell out "Winnie" and John would go mad. It ended in fisticuffs one day while walking home over a stretch of waste ground. John threatened that if Pete mentioned it once more he was for it. So Pete did. John jumped on him, threw him to the ground, pinned him in the chest with his knee, till Pete begged for mercy, promising never never to say the word Winnie again. Once he was allowed up, and safely ten yards away, Pete ran like hell for home shouting, "Winnie, Winnie, Winnie." And so began a lifelong friendship, interspersed by the occasional bust-up.

Together, they managed to be naughtier, rowdier, than each might have been on his own. One egged the other on, to be daring or defying, and comforted the other when caught. They spent a lot of their time wetting themselves with laughter, convulsed by their own naughtiness, their own silliness. Harmless enough stuff, for kids aged six or seven in the Fifties. There wasn't all that much scope for being truly wild, especially in their law-abiding, semi-detached, socially conformist suburban environment.

Amongst themselves, their language was unusually rich. Pete says they would call each other a cunt, tell the other to fuck off, which from my memory was unusual for the period. Boys from their nice homes did not use such words. Even boys from the lower classes, in the council houses, which was where I grew up, did not use such words, even in private. And in public of course, in the street or buses, you didn't hear foul language.

Pete went to Mosspits Lane Primary School, not Dovedale, but outside school, they remained inseparable. Aunt Mimi considered him a bad influence on John, just as Pete's mother maintained John was badly influencing Pete.

Pete liked Uncle George, Mimi's husband, who died in 1953 when John was thirteen. He remembers him as less of a disciplinarian figure than Mimi. He taught John his first rude poem which Pete can recall to this day.

> In the shade of the old apple tree
> Two beautiful legs I can see
> And up at the top there's a little red dot
> It looks like a cherry to me
> I pulled out my private New York
> It fitted in just like a cork
> I bet you ten quid she'll be having a kid
> In the shade of the old apple tree.

While John was passing on these pearls to Pete, probably thinking they were awfully naughty and original, several thousand other small boys were doing much the same. Probably girls as well. I can remember variations of these lines going round my primary school in Carlisle. Were they adapted from the Music Hall, or handed down verbally, as Uncle George had done, from one generation to another?

It inspired John to write his own dirty poems, illustrated with his own crude drawings, which he let Pete and others see, hoping they would crease themselves. "Squeaking" was how John described Pete's paroxisms of laughter. Pete could be so convulsed that he would not only wet himself but be lying on the floor, clutching his stomach in agony, letting out little high-pitched, breathless squeaks. "Let's hear you squeak then Pete," John would say.

When they were fighting each other, as opposed to laughing with each other, and Pete was getting upset, John's pet phrase was "Getting the egg then, Pete?" Just to taunt him further. Pete today can't remember where the phrase came from.

Pete also passed for Quarry Bank High School. So in 1952 they embarked on their secondary education together. Their juvenile japes and jokes now had a chance to go up a few notches, be a bit more serious, be better organised, but of course be just as jolly good fun.

★   ★   ★

Rod Davis, compared with John and Pete, was always considered a bit of a swot, good at school, keen to do the right thing, conform, be polite. He too wore specs but unlike John, he kept them on. The better to see of course, the better to fit in. His eyesight was even worse than John's and at school he used opera glasses to read the blackboard.

Rodney Verso Davis, to give him his full and imposing name, which anyone with Winston in his name should not mock, was born on November 7, 1941, at Sefton General Hospital, Liverpool, the first of three children. His father was a cost clerk at Tate & Lyle's sugar refinery and had been born in Dublin but moved to Gateacre, the next village to Woolton. Rod's mother was a true Wooltonian, having been born and bred in the village.

They lived at 129 King's Drive, Woolton, a semi-detached house which Rod's father had bought new around 1939 at a cost of £650. Their neighbours were much like themselves, the better sort of white-collar office workers. Like Pete, Rod can remember some council houses not far away whose inhabitants they considered, well, a bit rough. He remembers one in particular called Peter Sissons – now not at all rough, in fact rather smooth, having become a BBC star.

Rod Davis's father was one of the first in his street to run a car, which he bought in 1952, a 1946 Standard Eight. He was also a keen amateur photographer. The family managed to have seaside holidays when Rod was young. Not abroad, of course, folk didn't go to funny foreign places in the Fifties.

"We were in a boarding house in Southport on VJ day in 1945, when I was about four years old. And I did a terrible thing. I leaned up and took hold of an egg on a shelf. I'd never seen or touched an egg before. All I'd known was dried eggs. So I just grabbed it. Of course it broke and the egg all trickled down my arm. It was the egg for our family for the whole weekend, perhaps for everyone in the boarding house. So I didn't half get it."

Being born in 1940 or 1941 meant you were a war baby, but too young really to remember the war itself. I tried them all, for any memories of bombs or sirens, but only one could recall any action. Rod, having a jolly good memory, was pretty near, with his VJ Day memory.

All The Quarrymen grew up in the post-war years which meant air-raid shelters still around at the end of streets, good for playing in, and smaller ones in the backs of gardens or inside houses, good for hiding in. In many ways, post-war life was just as austere, with rationing, very thin and weedy comics, general deprivations. Rod can remember his first Easter egg, and being sick after eating it all at once. I remember playing football in a park when the cry came up and we all stopped playing and rushed off, as if following the Pied Piper, chanting the same words: "The Co-op's Got Bananas."

Rod went to Sunday School every Sunday – the same one as John and Pete, and Ivan and Nigel. Almost every child did in those days, whether their parents were committed churchgoers or not. Traditionally, it got the children out of the house on the father's day of rest, giving him a chance to enjoy his Sunday roast, Family Favourites, The Billy Cotton Band Show on the radio and perhaps the pleasure of his wife in bed in the afternoon, circumstances and moods willing.

I hated my Sunday School. It was run by the Presbyterian Church of Scotland where we were forced to memorise acres from the Bible in order to be awarded something called a Lord Wharton Bible. Which I still have, somewhere. There was a bit of sticking and drawing, singing and little games, which were a bit more fun, but my main memory is of it hanging over me every Sunday. St Peter's C. of E. in Woolton sounds much more fun, judging by all the happy memories, even if you did get your chewing gum confiscated.

"I first went when I was about four," says Rod. "I can remember an awful argument with my mother on my first day. She insisted I wore white socks. This seemed to be the height of humiliation, so I went that first day wearing no socks at all.

"John and Pete were inseparable, even at an early age. And they were the naughty ones. I do remember them being the only ones brave enough to chew gum in Sunday School."

Rod was never a naughty one, always doing what was required by teachers. He was sent to piano lessons from an early age, doing the best he could, despite showing little talent for the piano. He much preferred playing the recorder. But he proved a whiz on the "Clappers" which were bones held between the fingers to provide a noise very like spoons rattling. Spoons would have been simpler, but it was a daft craze which swept primary schools throughout the land. Ah, life was simple then, none of this computer game rubbish.

"My piano teacher was a Miss Mabel Pilkington, one of three sisters who lived at the bottom of Church Road. There was an air of flickering gaslight in her front parlour which was filled with Victorian ornaments. Almost every item had been hand embroidered. It was an atmosphere which didn't actually fire my enthusiasm for learning the piano."

Both his parents played the violin, and had first met when young at the same violin lessons. An uncle in Wales was reputed to have real musical talent. He was said to play the fiddle in a real dance band, if only part time.

Rod went to Springwood Primary School, in Allerton, where he was good at all lessons. Along with six others, he skipped a year, being considered such a promising scholar. Aged ten, he was put in for the Margaret Bryce scholarship. This gave automatic entry for six boys to the Liverpool Institute, generally seen as Liverpool's best grammar school.

"I went to the Institute to sit the exam and decided I didn't want to go anyway. It seemed like a barracks and the food was horrible. I was a very fussy eater in those days. They gave us stew with beetroot for lunch, so that was it. I didn't want to go.

"So I put down Quarry Bank as my first choice, when I came to sit the Eleven Plus."

★ ★ ★

Eric Griffiths, another rather serious boy, or so he usually struck most people, as he tended not to draw attention to himself, was born on October 31, 1940 – the same month as John – in Denbigh, North Wales. Both his parents were of Welsh origin. Quite common, for Liverpool. Traditionally there has been a mixture of Welsh, coming across the border to the nearest Metropolis, and of the Irish, coming across the Irish sea for work.

Eric's father was a male nurse before the War, then got called up into the Fleet Air Arm where he became a sergeant pilot. He was killed in 1941. It happened in a plane somewhere over the North Sea, leaving his wife with two young children, Eric aged one and his older sister Joan, aged two and a half.

When Eric was about three, they moved to live with his grandparents in

Bootle where he went to the local primary school, an excellent school, he says, despite the image of Bootle as one of the most deprived areas on Merseyside.

At the age of ten, they moved to the Woolton area, a semi-detached house in Halewood Drive, where he lived till he was eighteen. His widowed mother bought the house. Eric presumes his father probably left a little bit of money, perhaps an insurance policy, but his mother always worked. She had a good job in the Civil Service, working in an Employment Exchange, now known as the dole office.

What number Halewood Drive did you live at, Eric? I do like to get all the facts.

"I can't remember," replied Eric. This was your teenage home, Eric, where you lived your formative years, surely you can remember the exact address?

"No. As I have gone through life, I have thrown out those things I don't need to remember. Ask Rod. Rod remembers everything."

Hmmm. Let's hope Eric can remember going to Quarry Bank School.

"Oh yes, I can remember passing the Eleven Plus. But it was a near thing. The Woolton primary I was sent to, Belle Vale, was bloody awful academically. In Bootle, about 30 out of 40 each year passed the Eleven Plus. At Belle Vale in my year, I think only two of us passed. I realised fairly quickly it was a poor school in a poor area, surrounded by prefab estates. I don't think it was the quality of the pupils, but the teaching. I'd been about top in my old school but I soon sank to their level."

His big sister Joan, who had already passed the Eleven Plus in Bootle and been at Bootle Grammar School, went to Calder High School, the sister school to Quarry Bank.

It was a bit worrying for Eric, going to Quarry Bank. He'd only been in the area a year, had not gone to the Sunday School, knew very few people and the only other boy from his primary who had passed the Eleven Plus was going to another school.

On September 4, 1952, on his first day at Quarry Bank, Eric found himself in 1R with John Lennon and Pete Shotton. The system was for the first year to be randomly split up, then they went into A, B and C streams.

All Eric can remember about his first days is being chased around the playground, being called newt and having his cap stolen.

★ ★ ★

Len Garry didn't go to Quarry Bank, but his background and birth was much the same as our other heroes. He was born in Liverpool on

January 6, 1942. His father Harry was a printer on the *Liverpool Echo*, not technically a white-collar job, but better in many ways, well paid and secure, thanks to the strength in those days of the print unions. His mother Phyllis had been a hairdresser and still did it occasionally, working from home. Len had one brother, Walter, three years older.

They lived at 77 Lance Lane in Wavertree, a three-bed semi-detached house with a garage. They didn't have a car when Len was growing up, just the garage. His grandmother, on his mother's side, owned a baby shop at 113 Woolton Road. It didn't sell babies. It sold baby clothes, prams, linen and stuff.

Len's earliest memory is of being given a banana and trying to eat it with the skin on. His other early memories include playing marbles, known as ollies in Liverpool, in the playground at school or the gutters at home. With few cars around, the nation's children played in the street. Marbles or football for boys. Skipping for girls. We were happy then.

Len went to Mosspits Lane Primary School where Pete Shotton was in the year ahead, though he doesn't remember him. Len was quite good at cricket and got in the school team and also good at spelling, thanks to the influence of his father, the printer. He went home each day at dinner time, as he lived so near, thus avoiding school dinners, the smell of which, particularly boiled cabbage, used to make him feel sick. He had a delicate stomach as a child and was always very skinny.

His mother was quite musical, could sing and play the piano, and she sent Len to piano lessons. Len went, being easy-going by nature, but he was never keen on practising, of any sort, so soon gave up, though he did master one tune, the Blue Danube. But he liked listening to music. He would often go to the baby shop in Woolton Road, where his grandparents lived above their shop, and listen to records on his grandfather's wind-up gramophone. His favourites were the Ink Spots, Bing Crosby and Frank Sinatra.

Despite being so easy-going, not an obvious student like Rod, or serious like Eric, or quick and sharp like John and Pete, Len passed for the Liverpool Institute, la crème de la city. He was immediately bought a Raleigh Rudge bike by his proud parents.

The Institute was in Mount Street, near the centre of the city, some four miles from Lance Lane. Len decided to go on the 73 bus. He didn't fancy a long bike ride, especially in the winter. The bus was bad enough, with no heating in those days.

Len was quite frightened by the size of the Institute's buildings when he first arrived. "The decor was brown hardwood so it all seemed so dark, creating a sort of miserable and oppressive atmosphere. There were no playing fields, just a concrete slab of pavement with high iron railings separating us from the College of Art next door. The whole place seemed more of a penitentiary than a place of learning."

But there was one boy with whom he quickly became friendly, Ivan Vaughan, a rather studious boy who lived in Woolton.

★  ★  ★

Colin Hanton didn't go to Quarry Bank High School either. Nor any of Liverpool's other grammar schools. In fact, sorry to have to mention it, he went to a secondary modern.

That was the sort of thing, in certain circles, you kept quiet about 50 years ago. I know, because I went to one. From the age of 11, having been shuffled back and forth from Scotland to England twice, I missed sitting the Eleven Plus, so until the age of 16 I was at a secondary school. A good school, of its type, where the top stream got to do 'O' levels. Having passed enough, I then went on to Carlisle Grammar School. Yet even now, all these decades later, I often give the impression I was always a Grammar school cad. It was only when I got to 16, going into the sixth form to rub shoulders with the quality, that I met Woolton type people, the sort who lived in a semi-detached, often with their own garage, if not their own car, but  definitely always with a door bell as well as a knocker.

Colin was the odd one out, grammar school wise. And also in age. He is the oldest of the original Quarrymen – two years older than John. That matters, when you are young.

He was born on December 12, 1938 in Bootle. His father's family had come originally from County Wexford, his mother's from Dublin. He has an older brother, Brian and a younger brother and sister. His father, John, was a fireman in the Bootle Fire Brigade. During the War, Bootle was in the thick of things, being so near Liverpool Docks which the Jerries were trying to raze to the ground.

Being older than the others, Colin has clear memories of going into air-raid shelters to take cover, rather than to play, and of picking up shrapnel after bomb raids.

"My earliest memory is of standing outside with my grandfather, looking up at him, and he seemed to be all lit up because in the background, the whole of Liverpool was on fire."

During one of the dock raids in 1942, his father was in a fire-fighting crew which received a direct hit. Every one of the crew was killed, except

Colin's father. He was blown up in the air, severely injured, and had to spend months in hospital.

"When I visited him, I was fascinated by this cage he had over his leg. It was really to keep the blanket off his wounds, but he told me he had a canary in it – and I believed him."

When he eventually came out, one leg was shorter than the other and he spent the rest of his life wearing special shoes and a calliper.

Being born in 1938, Colin, like me, can also remember the excitement of bananas arriving. Such as it was.

"I was playing in the street one day and this woman came rushing out of her door, skirts flying, shouting, 'There's bananas in the shop!' I turned to the boy I was playing with and said, 'What's a banana?' I just had no idea.

"Later on someone came to our house with a banana and it was split up into little slices, amongst however many was there. It was my brother told me this afterwards. I wasn't there that day for some reason. So I didn't get any.

"When the War finished, we all had street parties and we were promised we'd get ice cream. You had to bring your own bowl and spoon and put it on this long trestle table and leave it there. The ice cream was in a sort of milk churn which two older women were dishing out.

"When we came to collect our bowls, mine wasn't there. Being a silly, shy boy, I said nothing. Just walked away. I then saw two women in a doorway, aged in their twenties I suppose. One of them had my bowl which I recognized. She was saying to her friend, 'I don't know who's bowl this is, I just picked it up.'

"But once again I was too shy to say anything. So that was it. The War was over – and I didn't get either a banana or any ice cream . . ."

At the end of the War, when Colin was about seven, the family moved to a rented house in Woolton. One of their relatives had had it, but was moving back to Bootle, so Colin's father decided to do a swap and take it over.

"It was strange, moving from bomb sites to green fields and trees. We were the townies, who were viewed a bit suspiciously by the local kids. The first day we were there, or maybe it was the second day, after we'd unpacked and had our breakfast, Mum said, 'Right, go out to play and meet your new friends.'

"I went out with my brother Brian and there was a gang of boys playing in the corner of a field with a big white sheet. Brian asked them what they were doing and they said they were trying to make a tent. Brian said, 'Oh we've got a proper tent.' Which we had, a big old-fashioned ridge tent with a pole. So we went back and got it – and things went on OK from then on."

Despite being a Catholic family, and having gone to a RC school in Bootle, his parents decided to send him to the local primary, Springwood School. Colin was only there about a year when his mother was taken ill with tuberculosis, seen as the killer disease of the day.

She went into hospital while Colin and his brothers and sister were sent back to Bootle to stay with their grandmother, returning to their old RC primary school. When Colin was aged nine, his mother died.

Some time afterwards, Colin moved to Woolton, once again, going this time to the St Mary's Catholic primary in the village. He moved back into the same house, at 4 Heyscroft Road, a semi-detached house, no garage, at the opposite side of Woolton village from Menlove Avenue.

Aged eleven, it was time for the Eleven Plus, a big event in the life of the nation's children.

What is it like, Colin, when you failed?

"I didn't fail it. I didn't even sit it. I had no idea what was going on, what it all meant. I just came into school one day and the teacher said you're going to sit the test today to see if you can sit the Eleven Plus. I didn't even pass the test! I failed so miserably they didn't even put me in for the exam."

So, no bike for poor Colin. "Oh, I did have one. It was a B.S.A. – Bits-Stuck-Anywhere bike. Also known as a Bloody Sore Arse . . ."

# THE FIFTIES

QUARRY BANK HIGH SCHOOL FOR BOYS

HARTHILL ROAD. MOSSLEY HILL

LIVERPOOL.18

10th July 1952

TO PARENTS OF NEW BOYS.

Dear Parent,

Your boy has now been allotted a place at this
School and,as has been my practice ever since I came to this School,
I should like the opportunity of meeting you to talk about the work
of the school, particularly as it affects your boy.

As times of holidays vary, I think it would be most
convenient if this talk were given the day before term starts so this
is to notify you to come to Quarry Bank School on WEDNESDAY, the
3rd SEPTEMBER. at 11 o'clock in the morning.

You will know that books and         . exercise books
are issued free when the boy comes but you may want to know certain
questions about school uniform.   The essential article of clothing
is the school cap and this will be on sale at school during the first
few days of term at a cost of  8/-.

Most boys will want to buy the School blazer, ties
and stocking in School colours and we very much hope that you will
try to fit out your boy with these.   These articles may be purchased
from Wareings & Co. Outfitters. Smithdown Road, who are the official
School Outfitters.

I enclose herewith health certificate and admission
forms which I should be glad if you would please fill up and bring
with you or send by your son on the 4th September.

Yours faithfully,

E.R.TAYLOR.

Head Master.

The letter sent to the proud parents of John, Pete, Eric and Rod.

# 2

# Secondary Considerations

Quarry Bank High School was founded in 1922, not as old or as distinguished as the Liverpool Institute, but it has had its fair share of pupils who later did well in life, including two who became Labour Government Ministers, Peter Shore and William Rodgers, a well-known actor, Derek Nimmo, a famous footballer, Steve Coppell, and a distinguished architect, James Sterling. Two years ahead in the school, when John and Pete started, was Jonathan Bailey, later Bishop of Derby.

The first headmaster, R.F. Bailey, was an old Etonian who had been a housemaster at Shrewsbury. He organised it along the lines of a public school with houses and prefects who were allowed to beat younger pupils. By the early Fifties, under the headship of E.R. Taylor, it was still run on very traditional lines. It had been fee paying before the War, though with lots of scholarships, but since the 1944 Education Act, it had become a free, state run grammar school, open to all, if they could pass the entrance exam.

The school's motto was 'Hoc ex metallo virtutem' meaning out of this quarry cometh forth manhood. There was a school song, written by the first headmaster, which all new boys, known as 'newts', had to learn and sing lustily at all school occasions.

Boys had to wear black blazers which had a thin band round the sleeve cuff depicting a stag's head picked out in gold. Rather discreet, really. Caps of course were essential for the younger years. There was a thin piping on the cap depicting the house you were in. Ties were black with gold stripes.

Not a particularly showy uniform, compared with some grammar schools of the period. At Carlisle Grammar School the black blazers had yellow piping all the way round, making it easy to spot a grammar cad about a mile away.

On July 10, 1952, Mr Taylor, the head, wrote to all the new boys [see letter], as he did every year, informing them of various essential things,

19

such as the cap could be bought at school, price eight shillings, while the rest of the uniform was available from Wareings and Co, Outfitters, in Smithdown Road.

The uniform made it clear to all the community that you were definitely not at a secondary modern. You were part of a privileged elite, and lucky to be so. Boys should not waste their time, or the school's time. The school would get them into higher education, or at least on the first rungs of a managerial or professional career. Boys of course had to be motivated, want to succeed and pass exams. Otherwise, well, they would soon fall behind. In school, and in life.

On arriving at Quarry Bank, John, Pete, Eric and Rod were met by masters in gowns, some of whom had strange habits and unusual mannerisms.

Rod, of course, can remember them all and has kindly written out his memories of them. Take it away, Rod.

"Many of them had served in the war and were wonderful characters and storytellers such as 'Fred' Yule, the Maths teacher who had been a bomber navigator and sported a metal leg which creaked so that you could hear him coming for some distance! He was so strong that he once lifted Lennon clean off the ground by his lapels!

"Our form masters during our first year were 'Porky' Burrows (form 1R), an English specialist (acknowledged by actor Derek Nimmo as the man who got him interested in English literature), Cliff Cooke (form 1F), the woodwork teacher and pianist who played as we sang the school song (I was in this class) and 'Oscar' Greaves (form 1B), a kindly old man, also an English specialist, whose life Lennon made very difficult.

"Other notable figures included 'Harry' Dautch, an inspired French teacher who also taught boys to speak Latin rather than simply read and write it; 'Tripe' Galloway, the geography teacher with his personal alternative to the school's 'bad mark' system. (Two bad marks in a week earned you one hour's detention after school.) If a boy misbehaved he would frequently ask him if he wanted a 'Bad Mark or a dirty look'. Invariably the choice was made of a 'dirty look', whereupon 'Tripe' would scowl at you and the class would laugh.

"Then there was 'Dippy' Dawson, the tall, thin maths teacher; 'Fred' Nixon, the old science teacher with the even older motor bike and sidecar; 'Sandy' Morris, the Latin teacher who smoked as he lounged across his desk; 'Boggy' Marsh, the history teacher who advised us all to become window cleaners; 'Eggy' Bacon, another French teacher; Fred

'Clipper' Shears, another history teacher; 'Eric' Oldman a chemist who was also head of Woolton house; 'Jocky' Roberts, the history teacher with the ancient Austin Seven with the yellowed glass windows; Jim Martin, the Scots art teacher with the motorised bicycle ('round the world on half a gallon!'); the eccentric 'Jacky' Simmons the art teacher; 'Daddy' Bryant, the biologist; the diminutive 'Biddy' Paris – maths, 'Arthur' Emmett, the gym teacher; Spanish teachers Pomfret and Dickie Kerr and of course 'Ernie', E.R. Taylor himself, the tall, distinguished grey-haired headmaster figure who swept through the corridors of the school in his academic gown like an avenging angel. Most of the masters wore gowns in my early years and one of them, 'Sandy' Morris, kept a golf ball in one sleeve with which he swatted the inattentive pupil. The school caretaker, Albert 'Yocker' Yoxall was also a figure to reckon with!"

★   ★   ★

John Lennon got into some fights the moment he arrived at Quarry Bank. "I lost the first one – and I lost my nerve when I really got hurt. Not that there was much real fighting. I did a lot of swearing and shouting, then got in a quick punch. If there was real blood, you packed it in.

"I was aggressive because I wanted to be popular. I wanted to be the leader. It seemed more attractive than being one of the toffees. I wanted everybody to do what I told them to do, to laugh at my jokes and let me be the boss."

John got caught by a master with an obscene drawing in his first year and then Mimi found an obscene poem under his pillow. "I said I'd just written it out for another lad who couldn't write very well. I'd written it myself of course, the sort you write to give yourself a hard on. I'd wondered who wrote them, and thought I'd try one myself."

In the first year, he did reasonably, tried reasonably hard. He was in the same class as Pete and together they tried to be as disruptive and inattentive as possible, or, as they thought, to enjoy themselves as much as possible. If Pete had to stand up in class to say something, John would get behind the master's back, doing something stupid, or hold up some obscenity to make him laugh, which of course Pete did, squeaking like a pig.

Even when they were sent to the head or deputy head to be caned, they turned it into a laugh. On their first visit, John crawled out of the head's study on all fours, as if he'd been beaten alive, groaning in agony, much to Pete's consternation who was waiting his turn, not realising the head had two sets of doors.

Their tricks and japes got more serious, better organised, as they went up the school, and as they went up, their grades went down. By the third year they were both in the B stream. John's reports contained remarks like "Hopeless. Rather a clown in class. Shocking report." To which Mimi, in the column for parents' comments, added, "Six of the best."

While Mimi tried her best to make John concentrate on his school work, stop showing off, stop being so silly, worried that he would turn out like his father, Fred, someone came back into his life who encouraged pretty much everything Mimi feared – his mother, Julia. John had known she was alive but had never realised she was living so relatively near, with her new partner and two daughters. From about the age of 13 or 14, John would go and visit Julia when he'd had a row with Mimi, when he should have been at school, or just when he was bored. Julia played silly tricks herself, wearing a pair of knickers over her head or spectacles with no glass in. She was not against John smoking, didn't tell him off the way Mimi did.

By the fourth year, John had dropped to the C and lowest stream. "I was really ashamed this time, being with the thick kids. The B stream wasn't so bad, because the A stream had all the drips. I started cheating in exams as well, but it was no good. I did as badly as ever."

Pete went down with him into the C stream. "I wrecked his life as well," said John.

At the end of his fourth year, by which time John was 20th in the class of 20, one master wrote in his report, "Certainly on the road to failure."

Presumably meaning failure in his GCE 'O' level exams. Though he might have meant failing in life generally.

Ten years later, in 1967, John had no regrets about messing around at school, doing no work, being a pain in class, making life hell for several of the teachers. "I've been proved right. They were wrong and I was right. They're still there, aren't they, so they must be the failures.

"They were all stupid teachers, except one or two. I just wanted a cheap laugh. There was only one master who liked my cartoons. He used to take them home to his digs with him.

"They should give you time to develop, encourage what you're interested in. I was always interested in art and came top for many years, yet no one took any interest."

Naturally enough, John did fail art at GCE. "I was disappointed, but I'd given up by then. All they were interested in was neatness. I was never neat. I used to mix all the colours together. We had one question which said do a picture of 'Travel'. I drew a hunchback, with warts all over him. They obviously didn't dig that."

22

Looking back at his school days generally, most things did still make him smile. "I came out aggressive, but I was never miserable. I was always having a laugh . . ."

★ ★ ★

Pete says it was all fun, his childhood with John, and got better all the time as they moved on from tying string to the doors of old ladies' houses to petty shoplifting. At Quarry Bank, their japes included hiding alarm clocks to go off in lessons, rigging up blackboards to collapse when a master started writing on them, filling bicycle pumps with ink to squirt at people in the playground. Then came some more serious tricks. Such as financial fraud.

This began when by chance they found several thousand school dinner tickets in a sack, ones already used, waiting to be disposed of. They then sold them to other boys for half price, making themselves £5 each a week, a fortune at the time, which they spent on stuffing their faces with sweets and drinks or buying cigarettes.

They continued this scam for some weeks till one day they noticed a master was writing down the serial number of every dinner ticket being handed in. They immediately stopped selling their dodgy tickets, convinced that this was it, they would soon be caught, the police brought in, they'd be sent to prison. They each had a sleepless night, making plans to run away to sea. Fortunately for them, on this occasion they were never caught. One boy, who was apprehended with an illegal dinner ticket, lied his way out of it by saying it was an old ticket, which he'd had at home.

Another, less dangerous, trick occurred in their Religious Education lesson, taken by Mr McDermott. "We quite liked him as he never read our essays properly," says Pete. "However badly you did them, he still gave you a red tick in the margin.

"We had to write about St Paul's journey to Damascus. In John's essay he wrote, 'On the road to Damascus, a burning pie flew out of the window and hit St Paul right between the eyes and when he came to he was blind for ever.' This essay was returned with the usual tick.

"We were talking about him one day when I said, 'What McDermott really wants is a class full of fucking vicars.' John said, 'Why not, why not give it to him.'

"So we went home and got all the Shredded Wheat cartons we could find. We both had masses as we loved them. We then cut out forty cardboard dog collars. Before Mr McDermott's next lessson, we gave one to each person in the class.

23

"Mr McDermott comes in, snaps open his briefcase as usual, pulls out some papers, and starts reading out to us in his boring religious voice. Suddenly, he looks up at the class. His voice freezes, his mouth drops in mid sentence – and then he laughs and laughs and laughs . His enormous frame shakes so much I thought he'd have a seizure.

" 'That was terrific, boys,' " he says. " 'What a prank.' He enjoyed it so much he made us keep on our dog collars for the rest of the lesson."

That story rather puts the staff in a good, tolerant light, but looking back, Pete still shares John's opinion that the staff and the school failed them rather than that they failed the school. He thinks it was all a waste of time. They were being force fed by out of touch masters and a dated system.

"It is true no one encouraged John. He had a passion for English which was ignored. He kept up his poems and little books right through his school life. He'd bring in copies of the *Daily Howl* to amuse the class. Yeah, they were mainly rude or crude but they were also literary, with references to things he liked, such as *Alice In Wonderland* or Edward Lear.

"One story was about a carrot in a potato mine. Another was about Davy Crutch Head which was a skit on Davy Crockett. These stories were interspersed with news flashes, such as a weather report. 'Tomorrow it will be Muggy, followed by Tuggy, Wuggy and Thuggy.' I thought they were dead funny, and clever."

Much of John's school years, and Pete's, once they got to 13 or 14, was devoted to sex and girls. Even earlier, if all Pete's memories are correctly dated. "John was about 11 when he first boasted he could masturbate. We went into the garage of our house in Vale Road and John demonstrated he could do it. I tried, but couldn't manage a climax for several months. When I got going, we used to toss off in the bushes on our way home from school.

"We'd also get the gang together for mutual wanking sessions in the park. John would shout out the name of someone we all fancied, such as Brigitte Bardot. We'd then pummel ourselves to see who came first.

"Once John decided to shout out 'Winston Churchill!' None of us could manage it for laughing.

"John used to come very quickly, but he also had an amazing ability to get an erection again very quickly. I once challenged him to do it 10 times in a row, promising him he could watch our TV for as long as he liked. He did it nine times. He couldn't manage a tenth."

That reference to TV is interesting. Pete was the first in his street to have a TV. "I was very proud of that. We watched the Coronation on it, so that must have been 1953. It was a 12-inch black and white set."

This had come about because his mother had developed into a business-woman, having taken over a little grocer's shop in Quarry Street. She then acquired a second shop, a wool shop, then a third, a hairdresser's. Pete thinks she never had much ready cash, moving on to the next shop by using the income from the first, but it meant that in his early teenage years, they became relatively affluent. His mother even sat her driving test and bought her own little car, most unusual in the Fifties. Anyway, back to sex.

It was thanks to a school friend, Billy Turner, a member of their gang, that they eventually found a way of getting to grips with real girls. On Saturday afternoons, so Billy told Pete, if you went to the Abbey Cinema near Penny Lane, went up to the back of the balcony where it was very dark, you'd always find two girls sitting together. You could touch them up, he said, in the dark, and they wouldn't complain.

"I didn't believe this at first, but I went with Billy the next week and it was true. Girls didn't put up any resistance, even when you fondled their breasts or put your hand up their knickers. It was amazing. A dream come true. Naturally, you'd come in your pants.

"John didn't believe it either, when I told him, but he came along with me and found it was true. I still can hardly believe it. I suppose the girls were as sex starved as we were."

They finally lost their virginity when they were about 14, so Pete maintains.

"John did it for the first time before me. I can remember when he told me. We were standing at the corner of Menlove Avenue and Vale Road and he said, 'I've had my first screw. It was a hell of a job getting inside. It was like trying to get it into a mouse's ear 'ole. Actually, I'd rather have a wank.'"

"I managed it some time later. I had a fight with this boy over a girl. He was called Murphy. I can still remember what he looked like. Anyway I beat him up and he went off and I got the girl.

"We went into the grounds of Strawberry Fields, the Salvation Army home behind John's house. And I did it. Or at least she did it. She did the leading. She knew what it was all about. I didn't. She lived in Strawberry Fields which was a home for naughty girls. And as I found out, she was very naughty indeed . . ."

According to Pete, John regarded most girls as pure sex objects, with little regard for their feelings or personality. He'd rather be out with the friends in his gang than bother too much or too long with any girl.

"One of his favourite remarks was 'chuck your bird before Chrimble'.

That was his word for Christmas. It meant you wouldn't have to waste money on a prezzie."

*   *   *

Rod's memories of his Quarry Bank days are, not surprisingly, rather different. He enjoyed the work, went along with and approved of most of the systems and traditions. The Houses, for example, he still thinks were a good thing. In the second year, Rod was put in Woolton House – whose house colour was pink – along with Lennon, Shotton and Griffiths. The Houses were based roughly on where you lived and were mixed vertically, old and young. Individual House meetings were held each morning which meant you got to know people ahead of you in the school. It felt to Rod like an extended family.

Rod was also impressed by most of the teachers. He couldn't quite understand the attitudes of certain boys, for example, Lennon and Shotton, who appeared anti school and anti teachers almost from the beginning, for no apparent reason, as far as he could see. Looking back, Rod thinks on the whole the teachers were exceptionally well qualified. "Many were real characters who had served in the war and had a wider perspective than teachers today."

All the same, he was a friend of John's, had been since their Sunday School days. He too remembers John passing round his little caricatures of Quarry Bank masters, finding most of them very funny, though some of them rather cruel, not to say obscene.

Rod was in short trousers for a long time, much to his embarrassment. "One of the problems with shorts was that you froze in winter and your thighs got chaffed." Being weedy and wearing specs, and being a bit of a swot, he did suffer some bullying. "I was used to it, I suppose. I'd had it from the local roughs down our road, so Quarry Bank was no worse. I got picked on there as well. I bear no grudges. Perhaps it was worse than I now admit. Memory can be selective."

One of Rod's escapes was to go off on his bike. Every boy had a bike, or wanted a bike, in those days. It was common to get one on passing the Eleven Plus, as Len Garry did. John had a green Raleigh Lenton Sports – which was exactly the same as the one I had. I'd bought it myself on the never never, paying it up out of my wages delivering newspapers. Bikes were not just a form of transport, to get you to school, but enabled you to go round in a gang, all on bikes together, or go off on your own, as a form of escape, into the country, away from parents and home. You didn't look sad or pathetic or lonely, a Billy-No-Mates, not if you were out on your bike.

It was also a form of status, to have the best, latest, fastest, most sporting or fashionable bike. No one wanted a boring, sit up and beg old Hercules. We wanted drop handle bars, narrow seats, derailleur gears, thin alloy wheels and, especially, a plastic drinking bottle in a cage. A Raleigh Lenton was quite smart, but the most desirable was a Claud Butler. Eric Griffiths had one of those. Rod had something called a J.F. Wilson lightweight which he got on his fourteenth birthday, second-hand. He still has it today.

Apart from being good at all lessons, Rod was a reasonable swimmer, and became captain of the Woolton House swimming team. The Swimming Gala, like the School Sports and Speech Day, were big events in the school year.

"Lennon was never known for any interest in anything sporting, but I did once manage, as house swimming captain, to get him to join the relay team. I can't remember if we won or not. Probably not." Rod, I thought you remembered everything.

Although friendly enough with Lennon and Shotton, Rod did not have much luck with girls. He was mainly at home, doing his homework, though he did do some aeroplane spotting. He went into 2A and stayed in the A stream from then on. At fourteen, along with a select handful, he jumped a year, sitting four 'O' levels while still in the fourth year. He passed them all and began thinking about what 'A' levels he might do in the Sixth form.

He had an interest in foreign languages which had begun quite young, on first reading the back of a bottle of HP Sauce. "I can clearly remember 'Cette sauce de haute qualité est un mélange d'epices orentientales.' I didn't know what it was, what it meant, so I asked my dad. He said it's French, son, the language which French people speak.

"I don't think I realised till then that other countries spoke different languages. That incident really did first spark my interest. Then at Quarry Bank, we did have some good language teachers. In September 1956, we got a new headmaster, William E Pobjoy, known behind his back as Bill. He'd got a double starred first from Cambridge in French and German. He encouraged me to think of studying modern languages.

"I know John always rubbished the school and his education. Pete still does the same, always has done, yet he is an articulate bloke.

"I learned only recently that at primary school, Pete had also been put in for the Margaret Bryce scholarship. He didn't get it either. But it shows he must have been good enough or interested enough in school at that time. Something must have come along and robbed him of his interest. John, I suppose.

"But it still rather upsets me when people like Pete says his education at Quarry Bank was rubbish. I still think it was a fine school."

★ ★ ★

Eric, on arrival at Quarry Bank, may have appeared as serious a little boy as Rod, one who might make a good scholar, but he says that underneath he was just like most of them, up for any mischief that was going, joining in when others got unruly.

"I was in John's class in the first year and we were all as bad as each other, all fairly disruptive, making life hell for a couple of teachers. One called Burnett was close to a breakdown. And there was one we called Oscar. We gave him a hard time as well."

After the death of his Uncle George, John was being brought up in what we'd now call a one-parent family, in the care of the redoubtable Mimi. Eric had a similar domestic background, but in his case his widowed mother went back to work when Eric was quite young. He was therefore a latchkey kid, with more freedom in some ways but also more responsibilities.

"I had to do the garden which I hated. It was a new house when we moved in and I had to dig it all up. It was full of clay and bloody hard work." He and his sister Joan were brought up to help in the house, laying the table, doing the dishes.

As Eric went up through the school, he soon realised one big advantage of the latchkey. He could come and go when he liked. If he bunked off school, sagging off as it was called in Liverpool, he could go home and nobody knew. He could also bring friends home, should he want to.

And did he do such things?

"Not till about the fourth year. Till then I was getting good grades. I was good at Latin, and was second in the class when I was in 2A. I was also good at Maths which I did like. But in the third year, well, I started to slide."

Why was that Eric?

"Girls, that was one reason, and the other was John Lennon."

It seems remarkable to me, considering the culture and attitudes of the Fifties in England, that John and Pete went out with girls from the age of fourteen. In the Sixties, perhaps, a time of less repression, at least for a few, but not the grey, conformist boring old Fifties. How and where did they manage it? How did they find willing girls? They were just as scared as any boys. Did they use contraceptives? When I asked one of them, he just muttered something about withdrawing. Oh yeah, at fourteen or fifteen.

John's remark about the mouse's ear would indicate it wasn't quite the full monty, hardly the whole shilling.

Paul McCartney, about to enter our story soon, also cracked it when he was fifteen. "I was about the first in my class. She was older and bigger than me. It was at her house. She was supposed to be baby-sitting while her mum was out. I told everyone at school next day. I was a real squealer."

I clearly led a very sheltered life in Carlisle. At fourteen I was still in short trousers worrying about chapped thighs. I didn't manage it till I was aged twenty, with the female, now my wife. There must have been something in the Liverpool air, or the Liverpool teenage mores, which I missed out on.

Once Eric had girlfriends that was it, he says. From then on he thought more about girls than his school work. In fact everything – girls, clothes, music, the whole teenage jing bang – was preferable to boring old school.

"In school, I was quietly disruptive. I was rarely caught, not like John and Pete. They were once suspended from school, both of them, for some misdemeanour. I'd been with them, but I wasn't caught. I was usually pretty crafty, though I was caned by the head a few times."

Eric joined John and Pete in cheating in the house cross country runs and was with them on the occasion they mistimed it. "We were hiding in someone's garden, waiting for the runners to appear down Harthill Road, red in the face and panting. We waited, but they didn't come, so we thought they must have passed us. We ran back to school – to find we'd won the race. No, we didn't have to turn out for our House. Everyone knew we were useless.

"John and I always got on well. I liked his wit. Yes he could be a bit cruel, but he never was with me. Not that I was aware of. Perhaps we got on because neither of us had the normal family, with a mum and dad at home. Almost everyone did in those days."

One of Eric's personal scams was having two Absence Cards. You were meant to bring your Absent Card to school, after you had been ill or absent, with the date and reasons for your absence, signed by a parent. The teacher would check it, sign it, then it would be taken home again, given to your parents to keep safe. Eric sussed out early on how useful it would be to have two Absence Cards. While still quite new to the school, still solemn and serious looking, he pretended to have lost his card. He was given another – which was the one he used, signed by himself, when he played truant. The first one was kept by his mum, and signed by her, when he was really ill. A teacher never had the two cards together so could not compare the signatures, nor could his mother.

"By the fifth form, I was only at school half the time. I had a regular girlfriend for two years, so I spent a lot of time with her. I suppose the school must have known I was skiving. But by then they didn't care."

Grammar schools cared most for the dutiful and willing, who wanted to learn, do well in exams, bring glory to the school, perhaps get their names carved out on the scholarship board in the school hall. By the fifth year, proven slackers and skivers like John, Pete and Eric were virtually ignored while long-suffering masters waited for them to leave.

Eric was also proving a bit of a pain at home. He thinks he possibly grew up quicker than most teenagers, as John also did, without a dad, without a discipline figure at home.

"I was flexing my muscles at an early age which meant I was a very difficult teenager for my mother. And I was always fighting with my sister. I went to her room one day, to hit her for having done or said something, and as I went in, I banged the door. It locked – and we were both trapped inside for hours and hours till mum came home from work to rescue us. That was one handicap about being a latchkey kid."

★ ★ ★

Over at the Institute, Len and his friend Ivan Vaughan devised a wheeze for getting out of games. "Before gym lessons, Ivan and I would say to the master 'Spasms, Sir, spasms.' I never really knew what this meant, but it frightened the gym master and he would let us off. I think Ivan had picked up the term spasms from his friend Nigel Walley who had asthma."

It was through Ivan and Nigel, who lived in Pete Shotton's road, that Len eventually got to know John Lennon. One day in the long summer holidays of 1955, probably in August, so he thinks, Ivan invited him over to meet John.

Len got on his Raleigh Rudge bike and rode over to Woolton. He ran into Ivan, Nigel, Pete and John who were all standing around on the pavement in Vale Road with their bikes.

"When I was introduced to John, I made some remark about his name being like his bike, his Raleigh Lenton. John said yes, it was made for him."

Ivan told John to show Len his cartoons which he was carrying. Len looked at them, and didn't of course recognise the caricatures of the Quarry Bank masters, but he remembers drawings of people with two or three heads and also the one Pete remembers, the Story of Davy Crutch Head.

They stood around, discussing which pop singers they liked best, which film stars, especially the female film stars, making silly jokes, word plays, looking out for girls. Much like most boys, then and now. Len could sense that John was the leader of this gang but he, Len, seemed to fit in, to be accepted by them all. Len of course fits in most places, being relaxed and amused, never pushy or clever clever.

As part of their gang, he met up with them from then on, at weekends or evenings in the summer at Calderstones Park, where they sat on a grassy bank, looking over the lake, talking, smoking, hoping to spot some girls. Sometimes they went swimming at the baths. They didn't play either football or cricket which surprised Len. He was quite keen on cricket. He decided it was because John could hardly see without his glasses, thus he hated all games and as leader wouldn't let the others play.

Their favourite sport was girls. One day Len and John managed to chat up two girls, Barbara and Miranda, and persuaded them to go into a tunnel in the park with them. Barbara was considered the prettier one and Len, so Len maintains, was the one to get off with her first, not John. That's Len's memory, so who can doubt it? This particular Barbara is one who became John's first regular girlfriend, still remembered by all their gang.

There was one escapade which Len was involved in and is clearly remembered by everyone who was around at the time. While mucking around in the park one day, it came out that Len and another friend, Billy Turner, both pupils at the Institute, had a day off school on the following Wednesday. It was some sort of staff training day. Quarry Bank did not have the day off, much to their disappointment. While moaning about this, John suggested that on their day off, Len and Bill should come over to Quarry Bank and enrol as new boys.

On Wednesday morning, they both cycled over to Quarry Bank – in their Institute school uniform. Which seems a bit silly, if not provocative.

"Our plan was to say that our fathers had just been transferred to Liverpool from abroad," says Len, "and our mothers had bought the wrong uniforms."

They made their way to the art room where a class containing John was about to start with Mr Martin. Len and Billy sat in vacant seats near the door, in case they might have to make a quick run for it.

"Sir," John said when Mr Martin arrived to take the class, "we have two new boys who have only recently arrived in Liverpool."

"I know nothing about it," replied Mr Martin. "I'll have to see the head afterwards. Meanwhile get yourselves some paper. I want you to draw this bowl of fruit."

As they started on their drawings, Len and Billy pulled their Institute scarves out of their school bags and put them on. Green and black scarves, recognised by almost everyone in Liverpool – except apparently Mr Martin. Even John could not believe they were being so daring.

"Are you two boys cold?" asked Mr Martin.

"Yes, sir," said Len. "We've been living abroad, in Australia, and are not used to this climate."

"What is your name boy?"

"Garry," said Len.

"Garry what?" asked Mr Martin, writing it down.

"Garry's my surname, sir."

"Oh, I see."

Len, for some reason, never thought of giving a false name. When asked, Billy also gave his real name.

Suddenly there was a knock at the door and in walked Pete Shotton. He was not a member of this art class but had been unable to resist making an excuse to find out how the jape was going.

"Yes, Shotton. What do you want?" asked Mr Martin.

"I've come to get my pen, sir. I lent it to Lennon this morning, sir."

"Is that correct Lennon? If so, could you hand it over quickly."

"I don't know what you're talking about Shotton," said John. "I haven't seen your pen. Furthermore I strongly object to you coming in and disturbing me working. And I am sure I speak on behalf of Mr Martin as well."

"I must say I agree with Lennon on this occasion," said Mr Martin. "Shotton, you will write out 500 lines saying 'I must not interrupt Mr Martin's Art Class,' and let me have them in the morning."

According to Len, and also Pete, who has an equally clear memory of this incident, both Len and Bill were practically wetting themselves by this stage – at the sight of John keeping a straight face and at Pete's fury. But they settled down and went back to their drawings. Just before the end of the class, each excused themselves to go to the toilets – and ran like hell out of the school.

An enquiry was later held at Quarry Bank, by which time it was all round both schools, but the names had not come out.

"A week later," says Len, "in our morning assembly at the Institute, the headmaster, J.R. Edwards, mentioned in passing about an incident in which Quarry Bank had 'been infiltrated by the enemy.' We were later given a sharp reprimand by the head – but we got knowing smiles from the other teachers. For the rest of that term, we were heroes in the school . . ."

★　★　★

Colin at his school didn't have such japes. They didn't even have a uniform at the Roman Catholic secondary modern school he was sent to – Horrocks Avenue Senior School.

"I don't remember much about it, except all the buildings seemed to be prefabs. There was a teacher I quite liked early on called Mr Roos who was an ex-soldier but quite fair. But in my last year, we had a nun, Sister Gertrude who was very strict. She came into our class one Monday and said, 'Did you all go to church on Sunday?' One boy held his hand up and said no, he'd gone fishing with his dad.

"She walked over to him and went Slap, Slap, Slap, right on his face. She hit him with the flat of her hand first, then the back, at least six times. She then asked if anybody else had not been to church. Naturally we were all shaking, but we all managed to say, 'Oh yes, we went to church yesterday, Sister. . . .'"

Colin often got the cane, but not for anything serious, like those naughty boys Lennon and Shotton over at Quarry Bank. "If you were in the late book three times in a week, you got the cane. I was terrible at getting up in the morning."

At home, there was at last some stability in his family life, after the earlier upheavals of his mother dying and then moving back and forth from Bootle. His father, after many years off work after his wartime injury, which was followed by getting TB, managed to find a job on the counter in the Co-op. He eventually rose to become manager of the Co-op in Smithdown Road. He also got married again, when Colin was about eleven.

"That was a bit hard, getting used to a new mother. I used to call her Aunty Peggy for the first few years, till my father took me aside one day and asked if I'd call her mum. My younger sister Jacqueline, who'd only been three when our real mother died, had always called her mum. So I did. And it was fine. We all got on really well."

He came home from school one day, when he was aged 14, to find a 16-year-old girl in the front room. "She was warming her backside by the fire. This was my Aunty Joan, my stepmother's younger sister. I hadn't met her before. She seemed grown up for her age, and I was very young. She took me out to the pictures that night, which was nice."

Around the same time, while coming back from school on the bus one day, he got talking with a boy who turned out to live not far away in Halewood Drive. This was Eric Griffiths. It didn't matter to Colin that Eric was younger and a grammar school boy.

"I didn't feel any jealousy. I suppose it's my nature, not to be bothered about such things. I used to think people on the other side of Woolton were the upper classes – but that was only because some of them had cars."

Colin left school in the summer of 1955 with a school report which said, 'Colin works well, tries hard, will tackle willingly the labour sent.'

"I knew what it meant – this boy will make a good labourer. That's what they were trying to tell me. But I had no idea what I wanted to do. In those days, though, finding a job was very easy. Not being particularly good academically, I told the school's careers fellow I'd like to be a carpenter. I was certainly better with my hands than my head, let's say.

"He sent me off for an interview with a furniture company called Guy Rogers in Speke. It was a big place, making all different types of furniture. They had a good reputation. High class. They made three-piece suites for Times Furniture.

"I got taken on more or less as a labourer in the French polishing shop. After about six months, working quite well, and quite hard, I was told I'd earned the opportunity to become an apprentice upholsterer. I wasn't quite sure what upholstery involved, but Dad said I must strive to have an apprenticeship. So I went for it. I was accepted and became an apprentice upholsterer on £3 a week which went up to £4 a week. That wasn't bad, for a lad of 16 in the mid Fifties, living at home.

"At work I got to know a lad called Nicky Cuff quite well. He was very small, just four feet high, a dwarf, I suppose you'd say. He had a very good voice. One of George Harrison's brothers worked there at one time, but I never met him."

Colin himself was still quite small. By the age of 18, he was only five foot six. When out drinking, which he did quite soon, and quite a lot, he always took his birth certificate with him.

# 3

## Skiffle Break

And then skiffle arrived. In 1956, it blew across Britain, swept the country like a contagious disease, creating the same symptoms, same reactions amongst the same types of sufferers. Two or three years later, it had gone, almost as suddenly as it had arrived.

They often say after any interesting or revolutionary arrival, that it changed everything. Usually it's a gross exaggeration, or just marginally true, or was true for only a very short time. But a case can be made that skiffle did change things, which remained changed.

Firstly, until skiffle, popular music was made by 'musicians' – people who had real instruments, like the trumpet and clarinet, which cost money, were hard to play, required learning. This put music on a pedestal, performed by experts or the special and gifted whom the ordinary person never met. The stars, as heard singing or playing on the radio or on records, tended to be American, or speak with a mid-Atlantic accent, copying music which had originated in America. America was where all popular music, including jazz, had come from. The main performers, except in jazz, tended to wear shiny suits, to thank the audience sincerely in a very American way, for being a very lovely audience.

Skiffle was primitive music, played on primitive instruments. It encouraged anyone to have a go. No need to have been to music lessons or been taught to play an instrument. Music became democratic, open to all. Which it still is. In this electronic and computer age, you now don't even need to play an instrument. A machine will do it for you.

Secondly, skiffle was part of a more general change in society which was happening around the same time. Almost overnight there appeared clothes, fashions, haircuts, attitudes, language, as well as music which appealed primarily to one section of the public – youth. And lo, teenagers were created. Until then, neither the word nor the concept had existed.

When I was growing up, like countless trillions before me, I expected I would end up pretty much like my father – wearing his clothes, with his haircut, following his styles. That was how it was, since we walked out of the caves. There would come a day, without any intermediary stage, when I would change from being a child into an adult, be grown-up, go out into the world, turn into another one of them.

Around the age of 15 or 16, I did start wearing his coat, his shirts with a detachable collar and a horrible collar stud which just thinking about now makes my Adam's apple ache. Then, suddenly, haircuts and tight trousers came in which were worn only by teenagers, not their fathers. Music could be heard, and played, which was aimed at us, not our parents.

I have told my own children all this, that there was a time when there was no such thing as teenage fashion, teenage music, and they don't believe it. They think that's how it always was. As nature must have intended it. Teenagers surely always had their own culture, till the next set of teenagers came along and said gerrof, what a load of rubbish, this is what you do, wear and say now.

Skiffle faded relatively quickly because rock'n'roll, which came in around the same time, proved the stronger, richer, more exciting, more dynamic form of popular music. Rock'n'roll needed proper instruments, so in a sense it had a traditional base, but many of those who began their musical self-education with skiffle moved on to playing and preferring rock. A minority didn't, of course. Some stuck with skiffle, or forms of skiffle, such as folk music or went back to jazz from whence skiffle in Britain had come.

There were three defining dates for the arrival of rock'n'roll and skiffle. The first was April 12, 1954, when Bill Haley and his Comets produced 'Rock Around The Clock'. It took a year for it to have any effect on Britain, but when it did, as the theme song for the film *Blackboard Jungle*, rock'n'roll hit Britain and cinema seats were being ripped up right across the land.

The next and more important event was the emergence of Elvis Presley in early 1956. By May, his 'Heartbreak Hotel' was top of the charts in 14 different countries. It was inevitable that a figure like Elvis would appear. You just had to look at the fleshy, podgy, middle-aged Bill Haley to realise that this new, exciting, sexy music needed an exciting, sexy singer to go with it.

The defining date for skiffle in Britain was January 1956 when Lonnie Donegan's single, 'Rock Island Line', became a surprise best seller. This had nothing to do with rock, despite its title. Donegan had recorded it for an LP (long-playing record, you can't have forgotten) in July 1954 while playing with Chris Barber's jazz band. Over a year later it was released as a single, got to number one in 1956 and even made it to number eight in the USA, from whence it had originally come.

The word skiffle goes back to the Twenties in the USA when it referred to a form of black music played at parties by plantation workers, or ex-workers, who wanted to make music but had no instruments. Instead they used any handy domestic items, such as jugs, pots, paper and comb, old bones, old washtubs or washboards. American washtubs were made of steel and produced a nice resonant sound when you stretched a bit of string or catgut through the middle of the tub and twanged it. They played songs whose lyrics betrayed their plantation past, such as 'Bring A Little Water Sylvie', or working or travelling on the railroads, such as 'Take This Hammer' and 'Alabammy Bound'.

Lonnie Donegan went on to form his own skiffle group and produced a further fourteen singles. He did national tours, appearing at the Empire Theatre in Liverpool where the fourteen-year-old Paul McCartney queued up outside to get his autograph. Fifteen-year-old John Lennon bought 'Rock Island Line' which he played so often it was practically worn away, then he sold it to a boy at school, Rod Davis. (And Rod, of course, still has it.)

Radio and TV programmes devoted to the new music appeared, such as *Six Five Special* on the BBC, my favourite prog for so many years. I can still hear the strains of 'A White Sport Coat And A Pink Carnation'.

All over the country, in every school, boys started working out ways of playing skiffle, reproducing that new sound. Skiffle competitions were organised to find the best groups of boys. Looking back, I never heard or noticed any girls playing in a skiffle group. Why was that? Because Donegan's group were all male?

By 1957, it was estimated there were 5,000 skiffle groups in Britain. I played the washboard one evening in an ad hoc group who had been at Carlisle Grammar School with me. We did it outside, in the dark, down by the suspension bridge over the River Eden. I can't remember why. Maybe we had nowhere else to go. Or maybe the main object was to sit around drinking beer, with music an optional extra. At Durham, as a student, I held skiffle parties. Still have the tickets somewhere.

So what happened in Liverpool in 1956–57 was totally typical. Those lads in the fifth form at Quarry Bank High School who might have thought they were being unique and enterprising were in fact part of a mass movement, part of the herd instinct.

What happened afterwards, of course, that was a bit more original. But in a way, not completely unexpected. Give a million monkeys a type-writer and one of them is likely to get a few words in the right order.

★ ★ ★

John Lennon never learned to play an instrument. Mimi said that she would have sent him to piano or violin lessons, but he didn't want that. "He couldn't be bothered with anything which involved lessons. He wanted to do everything immediately, not take time learning."

She was not musical herself, and rather looked down upon the sort of slushy, American-style music which shop girls liked. She discouraged him from singing pop songs he picked up from the radio, as sung by Johnnie Ray and Frankie Laine, not that he really liked them very much anyway, but they were what passed for popular mass music, before rock came along.

He did have a mouth organ from an early age, given to him by his Uncle George, which he taught himself to play, after a fashion. On a bus ride from Liverpool to Edinburgh one summer, to stay with relatives, the bus conductor heard his primitive attempts on his very cheap mouth organ and gave him a much better instrument. "It was the first musical encouragement John ever had. That conductor never knew what he'd started," said Mimi.

When skiffle and rock came in, and swept the school, John took a guitar from a boy in his class. He tried to play it, but found he couldn't, so gave it back. He then went to see his mother, Julia, and it was she, he said, who got him his first guitar. It was a second-hand Egmond and cost about £5. Later he persuaded Mimi to buy him one on mail order which had on it "guaranteed not to split".

The actual date of the formation of John's first group is still a matter of debate amongst our leading Beatles Brains. Mark Lewisohn, in his monumental work *The Complete Beatles Chronicle* gives it as March 1957, but, as we shall see, some of those who were there at the time disagree, maintaining this was when they were first beginning to play in public. Before that, they had played at homes or at private parties. The actual formation, therefore, when the idea first came about, was more likely to have been at the end of 1956, when Lonnie was at his height.

The day itself would not have been thought of as remarkable. Just another day, another fad, another idea for John and his gang to get together and do something.

The order in which the first members were recruited is also still a matter of debate. It was so informal, a movable feast, a matter of ebb and flow, people coming and going, that exact line-ups are hard to establish in these early months.

But everyone is agreed that the first recruit, once the idea had come into John's head some time in 1956, was Pete Shotton. Naturally enough, John wanted his best friend to be in, whatever it was he was getting into.

★ ★ ★

Pete's first reaction was to say no, he couldn't play in a group, he wouldn't have a clue.

John said, "Come on, don't be daft, of course you can take part, anyone can. I know, let's make ourselves some instruments together."

To Pete, it did seem like just another *Just William* wheeze, like building a camp, forming a gang, cutting their wrists to draw blood and promise eternal friendship. They'd done that aged 11 in an abandoned garage, but the knife was so blunt that all they drew was a large weal. With imaginary blood trickling down their wrists, they vowed all the same to stick together, for ever, as blood brothers. Then they went home for tea.

Pete thinks now that if he had said no, John would not have gone on to begin the Quarrymen. All rather hypothetical, and pretty unlikely, considering the passion John quickly showed for music. Surely if Pete had said no, John would have started a group with someone else?

"All I'm saying is that at the time, John and I were inseparable. It's inconceivable that either of us would have got involved in something if the other wasn't keen. He was accustomed to being the ringleader, but he feared stepping out on his own. He desperately needed the supportive presence of whoever he felt closest to at the time. It wouldn't have occurred to him to organise a band from a group of strangers."

Pete was persuaded and together they set about making or finding instruments. From the shed in Pete's garden they found a washboard which Pete said he would play, as it seemed the easiest and simplest. With the help of Pete's mother, now a shopkeeper, they acquired an old tea chest which they cleaned up and inside it they stuck a broom handle. This was the British version of the steel washtubs as originally used in the States. String was tied from the top of the broom handle to the side of the tea chest. When twanged, there was a noise, of sorts. And if you moved the broom handle, to increase or lessen the tension of the string, the noise did change slightly and hey presto, you had a home-made double bass.

John asked a boy at school called Bill Smith if he wanted to have a go on the tea chest bass. Pete wasn't so keen, as he and this boy had recently had some arguments. Their first rehearsals took place in the old air-raid shelter in Pete's garden where they struggled to copy Lonnie Donegan's 'Rock Island Line' and 'Cumberland Gap'.

For the first few weeks, messing around, they didn't have a name. Pete thinks it was he who thought of their name, The Quarrymen. They all attended Quarry Bank school and there were still quarries in the Woolton district. A line in their school song, which they had always mocked, seemed quite apt. "Quarrymen, old before our birth."

Bill proved unreliable when it came to rehearsals, so other friends had a go on the tea chest, such as Ivan Vaughan and Nigel Walley. But their main need was someone else who could play the guitar, as John was clearly struggling. The only one they knew at school was Eric Griffiths.

★   ★   ★

So Eric, was this the reason you were asked to join?

"I can't even remember if I had a guitar or not when the idea came up. My memory is that a boy called George had suggested a group to John and me – and that was when we started to learn the guitar together. It would have been natural for me to have been asked to join, as I was part of John's gang.

"All I know is that me and John got our guitars at around the same time – and neither of us could play them.

"I remember John getting his mail order. I don't know anything about Julia paying for an earlier one. I must have got mine from a shop in Liverpool, paying it up on the never never. I had a paper round and I got pocket money. Yeah, I'm sure I paid it up myself.

"We then saw this advert for guitar lessons, in a shop window. It was a bloke over in Hunt's Cross. John and I went to him for two lessons – but then gave up. He was really a classical guitarist. He wanted us to do things like theory and learn music. We could see it would be months if not years before we could play anything. That was no good to us."

Eric had not gone to any music lessons as a child, nor was there any history of music in the family, but like the rest of them, he was excited by the new music, especially when Elvis came along. Eric was also very keen on dancing, not just as a good way of picking up girls but because he really enjoyed it.

"John was useless at dancing. I tried to teach him how to jive, but he could never manage it. He couldn't pull the girl towards him on the beat."

It was Julia, John's mother, who taught John and Eric how to play the guitar, after a fashion. She had a banjo and taught them to play banjo chords on their new guitars.

"We used to skive off school, buy 10 Woodbines and a bag of chips, then go to Julia's house. She always let us in. She wasn't like anyone else's mother. She was young at heart.

"I got on OK with his Aunt Mimi. I think she approved of me. Well she didn't ever turn me away or tell John not to play with me.

"I know it's been said that Mimi wouldn't let him play in the house, and would send him out to the front porch, but I can definitely see myself with John, playing in his house, trying to master the chords. Perhaps Mimi was out that day.

"Mostly we went to my house, as my mother was out all day. My mother quite liked John – which most mothers didn't. She found him quite amusing, even if he was cheeky. A few years later when he was at Art College, he'd come into the Employment Exchange where my mother worked, to collect his dole money, and he'd shout across the counter, very cheekily, 'Hello Mrs Griffiths.'"

The Quarrymen practised in either Pete's air-raid shelter, Eric's house or Julia's for several weeks, off and on, with or without anyone playing the tea chest bass. It was mainly Eric and John trying to put into practice the simple chords which Julia had shown them, trying to copy or teach each other.

They then approached another boy at school, more studious than either of them, who actually had an instrument. To the surprise of many, he agreed to join. Step forward Rod Davis.

★　★　★

Rod, the memory man, can clearly recall where and when he first heard 'Rock Island Line'. He was in St Helens on a day outing with his parents in the family car, visiting the Saturday market. Through the open door of a record store he heard this music.

"It sounded so fresh and energetic, unlike anything I'd ever heard. There was no orchestral backing, it obviously wasn't jazz, but there was a terrific rhythm. Donegan was forcing out the lyrics with a passion and urgency in his nasal whine which was halfway between cockney and deep South."

When Rod got home, he tried to fix up an old ukulele which had been lying around the house since he'd been a kid, but it was unplayable. Then he learned from his Uncle George in Wales, the one who had played part time in a band, that someone was selling a guitar and banjo, both proper instruments, not toys.

Rod for once is not quite sure of the exact day but he persuaded his dad to drive him over to Denbigh to see his uncle. Alas, by the time they got there, the guitar had been sold. Instead he bought the banjo. It cost him

£5, or it may have been £6, but he clearly remembers it had five strings – a fifth was unusual. It ran down a tube through the fingerboard to a fifth peg set in the centre of the headstock. It was made by the Windsor Company, a 'Victor Supremus' model, probably in the Twenties. The fingerboard had only a very thin layer of ebony and very little pearl decoration, but it did come with a proper case. Rod was very proud of this. Kids with cheap guitars usually carried them on their backs.

At school the following Monday, he boasted to Eric about his new acquisition. Eric immediately told him that he and John had formed a skiffle group, with himself and John on guitars, plus Pete Shotton on washboard. Someone with a proper banjo, which had been played professionally, even if Rod couldn't actually play it himself, and had only bought it the day before, would obviously be a worthwhile addition.

Later that week, Rod was invited to join the group for a rehearsal. It was at someone's house, he can't remember whose, but he can remember that John and Eric still couldn't play guitar chords.

"Julia had tuned their guitars like a banjo and taught them banjo chords, despite the fact that a guitar has six strings and a banjo only four principal strings. So they just ignored the fifth and sixth strings of their guitars entirely.

"They both had the same model, but in different colours. John's guitar was brownish while Eric's was more beige. While they rehearsed, Eric shouted out the chord he thought he was playing, hoping I would follow suit, or at least somehow fit in. I began to find I was quite good at busking."

Rod says they had acquired several tea chests by then, all of which they had made themselves, buying the tea chests from Ashe's grocers in Woolton for two shillings and six pence. One of their early versions was covered in an old roll of brown and white wallpaper, left over from when Rod's mother was decorating their front room. They eventually settled on one which they painted black. Rod's dad cut out the shapes of the treble and bass clefs and notes.

They were still practising in the homes of friends, or at Julia's. "At Julia's, we used to stand playing in her bathroom as the acoustics seemed to improve the sound.

"When we practised at Julia's, she'd grab my banjo to show me some new chords."

But Rod, being the studious one, soon bought a proper banjo manual and set about teaching himself some chords, something John and Eric never did, hoping to pick it up as they went along. Rod still has that manual, one of the treasured items from his teenage memorabilia.

"It meant I soon knew more chords than John. And I was venturing right up the neck, but he told me not to play there. I think he thought I was being flash, trying to be better than him.

"He was no great shakes on the guitar, but then none of us were much good. But when we started playing at people's parties, we found that John could hold an audience.

"People at school used to say to me, 'How come a swot like you is in this group with people like John and Pete, the troublemakers?' I suppose it was strange. I didn't have their street cred, or Eric's. Eric was also considered good looking, which I wasn't. But I got on with John. I'd known him since he was seven, so I knew what he was like."

The lack of a regular person on the tea chest bass didn't matter too much, someone could fill in or they did without, but they were aware from the beginning there was one serious omission – a drummer. More and more boys had acquired cheap guitars, as the papers were full of special offers, but you rarely heard of anyone who had drums. They cost quite a lot of money for a start and secondly it wasn't the sort of thing parents wanted their children to learn at home.

They now had three guitars, or three on strings, counting Rod on banjo, so they were beginning to be a bit lopsided.

It was Eric who first said he knew a boy who lived near him who had a full drum kit.

★   ★   ★

And how did Colin come to have a drum kit? Because, unlike the others, all schoolboys, he had been a working man for two years.

Aged 17 in 1956, he had money in his pocket and was able to treat himself to the odd gramophone record when he heard anything he liked the sound of.

They had a big radiogram at home, a cut above a basic record player, which had been bought by Colin's big brother, Brian, but Colin was allowed to play his records on it.

Brian liked Frankie Laine and so did Colin but Colin also took a keen interest in jazz. Colin started buying his own jazz records and in order to hum or beat along to them, he bought himself a pair of drumsticks. While listening to Chris Barber, Ken Colyer and his other faves, he would follow the beat with his own drumsticks, tapping on a table or a chair at home. He became quite a dab hand at playing on the furniture. (In my home, all I played on was the linoleum. V. old joke.)

Colin even took his drumsticks to work, tapping on his bench if he liked any of the tunes being played on the factory floor. "Eventually I asked my parents if it would be all right if I bought a set of drums. They said, 'OK, as long as you're going to pay for them.'

"So one Saturday I went with my Mum to Hessy's in Whitechapel. This was the main music shop in Liverpool, always full of boys looking at guitars.

"I don't know why I'd never fancied a guitar. It was always the drums. In the Benny Goodman band, I always liked Gene Krupa best. I suppose I've always been a noisy bugger.

"On the top shelf, I saw a set of drums which were all sparkly, blue with some gold sparkly stuff, quite an elaborate drum kit. I asked Frank Hessy how much they were. 'Do you want to sit down before I tell you,' he said. The price was £65! Well, I couldn't afford that.

"Instead I bought a Broadway set, all white, which cost £34 19s 6d. I paid a few pounds deposit, there and then, and signed a form to pay ten shillings a week from then on, till I'd paid it off. My Mum had to stand as guarantor.

"I took the drum kit home and started playing. Yes, totally self taught. I didn't even have any manuals. If you've ever heard me play, you'll know I was self taught . . .

"I just put a record on the radiogram, and played along as best I could, just to amuse myself.

"I didn't think of being in a proper band. To be a real musician, you had to have learned to play something properly. For a dance band, say, you had to be able to play the sax, the clarinet or whatever. But of course when skiffle came in, it all changed.

"Until then, when I'd gone to dances, there was a dance band and you did proper dances – waltzes, valeta, quickstep, slow foxtrot. I went to dance lessons at Billy Martin's where thousands of people on Merseyside had learned to dance for generations.

"When skiffle arrived, you not only got a different sort of music, you got a different sort of dancing – jiving.

"I can remember going to dances when it just started. At the back of the hall, people would be doing waltzes, slow foxtrots, or whatever, while at the front, near the stage, people would be jiving. You'd have two groups of people in the same hall, doing different dances. Glen Miller stuff was good – you could either jive to that or do the old-fashioned quickstep."

One day, in the summer of 1956, a sunny Sunday, so Colin remembers it, possibly a Bank Holiday Sunday, there was a knock on his door at 4 Heyscroft Road. There was Eric Griffiths, his friend from down the road. News had travelled fast, at least one street, that Colin Hanton had a full set of drums.

"Eric told me he had got a group together from his school called The Quarrymen and was it true I'd got my own drums. I invited him into the house, set up my drums and played along with a record. He said, 'Great, do you fancy coming over and meeting the lads.'

"I packed up my kit and went round to Eric's house in Halewood Drive. No, I can't remember the number either, but it's near the English Rose pub.

"John and some others were there, probably Pete Shotton. There seemed a lot and I didn't take in their names at the time.

"I played a bit on my drums – and that was it. I was invited to join the group, there and then. Simply because I had a set of drums. It wouldn't have mattered how badly I played."

Colin is confident this happened in the summer or autumn of 1956 – because in December, he had his 18th birthday party, a real drunken affair, which John and other Quarrymen attended.

"I hadn't met John till I joined The Quarrymen. So that proves the group was formed in 1956, not 1957."

Reaching eighteen at the end of 1956 meant something else, apart from going into pubs legally and getting drunk. It meant National Service.

"I was looking forward to it. I thought it would be a good experience. I went for my medical with another upholsterer who was dreading it, didn't want to be in the army. He passed his medical, and went off. I failed. So I wasn't called up. I was bitterly disappointed."

If Colin had gone off for two years in the army, he would not have been able to be a Quarryman. Nor would any of the other Quarrymen, if they had been a few years older. But of course by the time John and the others got to that age, National Service was over. So if National Service had continued longer, would we have had The Beatles?

★   ★   ★

Len is not quite sure of the precise dates or sequence of events which led him into the group. He was the last of the original six to join, but he has worked out that it was in 1956.

"I estimate I joined in late 1956, possibly September, because I know I was fourteen and I didn't turn fifteen till January 1957.

"I didn't actually want to play the tea chest. I really wanted to sing, but John was the singer, so in order to play with them, I had to be content with the tea chest."

Len was asked because he was already in their gang, despite being at another school, and because they were by now fed up not having a regular person on the tea chest. Bill Smith had rarely ever turned up for rehearsals. Ivan Vaughan wasn't keen. Nigel Walley really saw himself as their manager, if and when they ever managed to get paid for playing.

Having acquired Len as their new and, they hoped, regular on the tea chest, they were left with one problem – the tea chest itself. They suspected that when they told Bill Smith he was no longer required, he would say, "Ha ha, stick your skiffle group up your bum, you're not having the tea chest back."

Another problem, according to Pete, was that they didn't actually know Bill's address. So what to do?

At morning break at school on Friday, John and Pete told Bill they were going to have another rehearsal, on Saturday afternoon, and could they have it at Bill's house. Bill said yes, and gave them his address. So that was one problem solved.

At lunch time, John and Pete bunked off school, determined to get to Bill's house and steal the tea chest, before he got home. Bill lived in Childwall, an area they didn't know, and it took them several buses to get there.

When they eventually found the house, John knocked at the front door while Pete hid behind the front wall. If Bill's mother or father had come to the door, he had worked out a story about being sent by Bill to pick up their tea chest. There was no answer. Nobody was in. Having come all that way, they decided the only thing to do was break in. They found a kitchen window slightly ajar and Pete, being very thin, managed to climb through.

While they were searching the house, there was a knock at the front door. They were immediately in a panic, knowing they could be taken for real burglars. So they hid behind a couch. The knocking continued. Before Pete could stop him, John got out from behind the couch and went to answer the front door.

There was a smartly dressed young man there who asked John if his mother or father were at home.

"My mum's dead and my father's in jail," said John.

"I am sorry," said the man.

He explained he was a soft drinks salesman, working on a special promotion, giving out free samples of a new drink. He asked John if he had any brothers or sisters.

"Yeah, three brothers and three sisters. Our Uncle Herbert looks after us all."

The salesman left seven bottles of the new cola, and a questionnaire to fill in, saying he could came back later in the week to collect it.

John and Pete guzzled all the cola, only wishing it had been beer. Then they went back to looking for the tea chest, searching every room, with no luck. In the end, they tried the garage – and there it was.

Coming back on the bus, with the tea chest, they realised they had left seven empty cans in Bill's front room. That did make them laugh. Also the thought of the salesman, returning later in the week to ask Bill's mother if her family had liked the new drink and could he have the questionnaire back . . .

# 4

## Bring On The Quarrymen

When they eventually came out of the air-raid shelters, stepped out of Julia's bathroom, felt they'd learned enough from practising in their back gardens or back bedrooms, The Quarrymen moved on to playing at friends' parties. Not for any money, but if they were lucky, they got free food. Very lucky, and they got a free drink.

This all took place over several months – during the second half of 1956, if we are to believe Colin and Len. For weeks at a time, they wouldn't play, or when they did, they would have rows, fall out, or be lacking enough members to make it worthwhile playing. There were other things going on in their lives, other diversions, not to mention the fact that five of them were still at school, supposedly studying for their GCE 'O' level exams.

John told me that the first proper engagement he could remember was playing "at Rose Street". It was their Empire Day celebrations, he said. "We played from the back of a lorry. We didn't get paid anything."

The first public engagement Rod can remember was earlier than that, at Lee Park Golf Club at Childwall. They got it through Nigel Walley – probably the excuse which allowed him to call himself their manager and eventually have little visiting cards printed, one of which said, "The Quarry Men – Skiffle, Rock 'N' Roll, Country Western – Open for Engagements". Nigel had left school and become an apprentice golf professional at the club.

Rod remembers getting himself in a state about what to wear. The agreed uniform was to be black jeans and white shirts, but Rod's parents did not allow him to wear jeans, black or otherwise. Jeans, like Teddy Boy haircuts, were not approved of by many parents and most teachers.

"I was forced in the end to get a second-hand pair from a friend, Mike Rice, for seven shillings and six pence. They were a cheap pair, with very poor quality fly zips. Just as we were about to go on stage, my flies broke.

Rock 'N' Roll

Skiffle                                    Country Western


*The* *Quarry* *Men*


Open for Engagements

MANAGER
C. NIGEL WALLEY.
LEOSDENE
VALE ROAD.
WOOLTON.
*P.T.O.*                                   LIVERPOOL.

---

Country · Western · Rock 'n' Roll · Skiffle


*The* *Quarry* *Men*


LEOSDENE,
VALE ROAD, WOOLTON,        OPEN FOR ENGAGEMENTS
LIVERPOOL.

---

ROCK 'N' ROLL                              SKIFFLE


*The* *Quarry* *Men*


                                           MANAGER
OPEN FOR ENGAGEMENTS                        GATEACRE 1715

---

I had to play the entire set with my banjo slung low, to hide my embarrassment."

Colin thinks their earliest 'public' performances were at St Peter's Youth Club, the church youth club at Woolton, where John and co had gone to Sunday School. They were members, not invited outsiders, and were basically just messing around, playing in the evenings for no money, just for fun, to amuse their friends.

So he agrees that the golf club was probably their first proper gig, where they had been invited to play.

"I remember Nigel and Pete going outside when we got there. There must have been some sort of putting green because Pete came back saying, 'I beat the great Nigel Walley.'

"As for the evening itself, I can remember people sitting around two sides of a room while the band was in a corner. For some reason, a young lady, probably ten years older than me, insisted on pulling up a chair and sitting right beside me while I played the drums. She kept on grabbing hold of my left arm, so I couldn't play. Then she started asking me questions about drumming. The lads were concentrating hard on getting their own bits right. They just carried on playing without me, trying to ignore what was going on with me and this woman.

"When it came time to go home, this young woman said she would borrow her dad's car and give us a lift home. While she went off to get the car, John told the lads he'd sit in front with her and try to make a move on her. I felt this wasn't right, so when she appeared with the car, and we'd put in all our gear, I jumped in the front seat beside the girl. The lads started shouting, 'John's going in there, get out,' pushing and shoving me. The girl said, 'Everyone stop fighting and shut up.' She drove us into Woolton village and dropped us at the Milk Bar. We then all made our own way home."

There was no fee that night, but they did get a slap-up meal and a hat was taken round later. "I don't think much was put in," says Colin, "but we did get a few bob."

Colin remembers rehearsals at Rod's house and Eric's and also the ones at Julia's, John's mother. "She wasn't like a mum, was she? More like a big sister, a friend.

"We did a gig somewhere round Penny Lane, an annual dance for the Vespa Scooter Club. Something like that. Julia came to watch us and at the end of each song, she clapped loudly. I think she was the only person in the place clapping loudly.

"I met Aunt Mimi as well as I often went to John's house. She was quite a formidable woman, Aunt Mimi, wasn't she? You certainly wouldn't give Mimi any cheek."

Colin arrived at Mimi's one day wearing two rings, a new fad he had just acquired. "One was silver, at least it looked silver, but was probably chrome. It had a big lion's head in the middle. The other was gold coloured in the shape of a snake. It coiled round your finger with stones for its eyes. Mimi spotted them and asked me where I'd got them. I

50

couldn't remember and sort of panicked, I don't know why. I blurted out, 'Lewis's.' 'Well, a bit better than Woolies,' said Mimi.

"Strange, wasn't it, that I had this passion for wearing rings? It seems to go with drummers . . ."

★ ★ ★

Their informal performances at the St Peter's Youth Club became quite popular, with club members turning up specially to hear them, even though there was no microphone. "John was always on at the guy who ran the club to get one, and he always said he would, " says Colin. "One Saturday evening there was going to be quite a crowd there because Geraldine Davies, who lived next door to me, said she was coming with some of her friends from school. Geraldine had a Grundig tape recorder and when we practised at my house in our front room on a Saturday afternoon, she would often come in and record us. We thought it was great, being able to listen to ourselves.

"Anyway, this Saturday evening, we turn up at St Peter's with our stuff to find there was still no microphone. John says to the fellow, 'I can't see any microphone, what's happening?'

" 'I couldn't get one,' said the feller, 'it was too dear.' 'That's it then,' said John, turning to us. 'He promised us and he hasn't delivered.'

"It wasn't a case of the show must go on – it was no mike, no show. So we all packed up and walked out, much to the disappointment of the people who'd come to listen to us.

"I couldn't obviously wander round the village all night with my gear, so I went home with it while the others wandered off somewhere, carrying their guitars. When I got back into the village, I couldn't find them. I went back to the Club, wondering perhaps if they were there. 'John's not here,' I was told. 'And if he comes back, he won't be let in.' "

They also entered various skiffle competitions, which again paid no money. According to Mark Lewisohn, their first recorded public appearance was at one of these skiffle contests – on Sunday, June 9, 1957 at the Empire Theatre, Liverpool in a local preliminary heat for Carroll Levis's TV show. He was very big, in the early days of television, taking his talent spotting show round the country, auditioning hundreds of entertainers of all sorts – from ventriloquists, jugglers, musical saw players to singers. The best eventually appeared on TV. Very cheap to make, but highly popular, though at the time, its success did puzzle me. I went to one of his shows in Carlisle where the winner was a girl who did bird noises. I laughed all the way through, but the audience loved it.

"For the Carroll Levis audition," says Colin, "we had to go to the Empire on the Sunday afternoon. We queued up outside with a lot of people to get in this very small door. Forms were given out which we had to fill in. John filled them in on behalf of The Quarrymen. All the acts not playing sat in the stalls while the ones about to play went backstage to get ready.

"Carroll Levis sat at a small writing desk at the side of the stage. Nicky Cuff, my friend from work, was in one group. He came on late carrying his tea chest bass, dressed in top hat and tails, claiming he'd been sent to the Adelphi Hotel. Carroll Levis immediately stood up and told him to stop. 'No no, you've got a very limited amount of time. If you're a comedian, you've got five minutes to tell jokes. If you're a group, you've got five minutes to play. It's one or the other.' So Nicky was not able to do his full act.

"My memory is that we did get through that heat and on Wednesday there was a proper audience. They used a clapometer to decide who was best. We were dead level with another skiffle group, so we were asked to play again. It was all running late so we didn't get much time, but the other group got three minutes more – and they won. Carroll Levis did say afterwards it had been a bit unfair, so we shouldn't give up."

This would explain why The Quarrymen kept on entering Carroll Levis talent shows, though there is some confusion about the precise dates and number of times. John remembered that they "always seemed to get beaten by a midget".

★　★　★

The engagement which John mentioned as being his earliest memory was actually in Roseberry Street, not Rose Street, and was nothing to do with Empire Day. It was held on June 22, 1957, to celebrate 750 years of Liverpool's Royal Charter from King John. Each street in Liverpool had been encouraged to lay on a street party. But he was right about playing from the back of a lorry, a coal lorry, as can be seen in what is the earliest known photograph of the group. John and Eric are wearing check shirts. Pete appears to be wearing a jacket. On Colin's drums can clearly be seen the words 'Colin Hanton' and 'Quarry Men' – spelled as two words.

This engagement came through a friend of Colin's, Charles Roberts, whose mother had helped to organise it. Colin remembers having quite a lot to drink and by their second set, he was quite drunk.

"But I wasn't too drunk to hear some lads who were watching us putting their heads together, muttering and pointing. There was someone in the crowd I knew, so I beckoned him over to the side of the wagon and asked what was going on. 'Oh, they're planning to get Lennon,' he said.

"When I told John, it was guitars away, drums off and we all made a hasty retreat to my friend's house. They were still hanging around, looking for John. I think in the end they actually called a bobby – and the bobby escorted them to their bus stop. I didn't go home with them. I'd met a young girl and I went off to her house with her . . ."

Roseberry Street won an award given by the *Liverpool Echo* for the best decorated street – and to celebrate, they held another street party at which the Merseysippi Jazz Band performed. The Quarrymen were not invited back.

"I had too much to drink another time," says Colin, "when we were playing at the wedding of a friend of mine. The wedding party was in a club in the Upper Parliament Street area. Because I knew them, and the family, I went off with some of them to the pub and spent most of the evening there. The lads had to keep on playing without me – so Pete played my drums that evening. And broke one of my drumsticks. Afterwards he offered to pay for it. I said, 'It doesn't matter, thanks all the same.'

"The following Saturday, I met up with them at the Milk Bar in Woolton village. We were all chatting and that and Pete started to put his hand in his pocket. I said, 'No, it's all right Pete, no need to pay me.' Out of his pockets he took some visiting cards and started handing them around. I hadn't known they'd got Quarrymen cards printed. 'Do you want some,' asks Pete. He then handed me 20 or 25 of them.

"Fortunately, I've still got one left . . ."

★   ★   ★

Their repertoire, in these early months of 1957, was based on what the main skiffle groups of the time were playing – 'Rock Island Line', 'Cumberland Gap', 'Midnight Special', 'Rail Road Bill', 'Worried Man Blues', 'Bring A Little Water Sylvie', 'Freight Train', 'Putting On The Style', 'Don't You Rock Me Daddy-O' and 'Maggie May'.

One problem was getting the correct words. As schoolboys, they had little money and could not afford to buy many records. What John did was guess any missing words, or create his own. For the two lines of 'Putting On The Style' which should have been "But it's only our old preacher, boys,/ Putting on his style" John always sang "But it's only Mr Pryce-Jones,/ Putting on his style."

The Rev. Morris Pryce-Jones was the Vicar of St Peter's, where they had all attended Sunday School, so everyone from Woolton enjoyed the reference.

"There was no question that John was the leader," says Rod. "It was his group. Me and Eric did try singing, but we weren't much good. Len was quite good. John wasn't bad, but he wasn't really seen as either a good singer or a good musician.

"In school, what he was known for was his cartoons, not his music. There was evidence that he had talent as a wit. There wasn't much evidence of him having great musical talent. In fact if I'd been asked at the time if John had obvious musical talent, I would have had to have said no.

"But you didn't think in those terms, not when you're a teenager. You don't look ahead, think how people might turn out, what they might do in life. I didn't think that about John or any other people – or about myself. I just enjoyed the ride, never looking ahead."

John at the age of eight in 1948 with his mother Julia. (*Hunter Davies Collection*)

Eric Griffiths, in 1948, aged eight.

Len Garry, aged 9 in 1951.

Pete Shotton as a schoolboy and with his mother, Bessie.

Rod as schoolboy.

Colin as schoolboy.

John and Pete in the 1957 Quarry Bank school photo. (*Courtesy Bernard Davis*)

Pete (left) fooling around with Bill Turner, John and Len.

Rod standing, with specs, and Eric, sitting, at the Quarry Bank School Fete, 1955.

The famous photograph of John leading The Quarrymen at the St.Peter's Church Fete, Woolton on July 6, 1957, taken by Geoff Rhind. Left to right: Eric, Colin, Rod, John, Pete and Len. A few hours after this photograph was taken, John met Paul McCartney for the first time.

The Quarrymen perform from the back on a flat bed truck in Roseberry Street, Liverpool, on June 22, 1957. The top picture is published here for the first time. Colin is on drums, Eric is wearing the black and white check shirt, John is singing, Pete is on washboard and Len and Colin stand at the back. (*Charles Roberts*)

By late 1957 John and Paul were wearing white jackets to distinguish themselves as co-leaders of The Quarrymen. Here John is singing, and Eric – a non-jacket wearer – concentrates on his guitar.
(*Hunter Davies Collection*)

The Quarrymen on November 23, 1957 at the New Clubmoor Hall; left to right: Colin on drums, Paul McCartney on guitar, Len on tea-chest bass, John on guitar and Eric on guitar. By this time Pete and Rod had left the group.
(*Courtesy Colin Hanton*)

Colin, aged 20.                                    Eric, aged 20.

John at home after the Beatles' 1963 Christmas show, with, variously, his wife, Cynthia, and his mother-in-law, Lillian Powell; Pete and Beth Shotton, and Nigel and Pat Whalley. *(Pete Shotton Collection)*

Rod aged 18, with guitar, posing in front of a bull fight poster, about to go to Cambridge.

# 5

## Hello Paul, Bye Bye Pete

The programme for the Garden Fete at St Peter's Church, Woolton, on Saturday, July 6, 1957, announced that The Quarry Men Skiffle Group were going to play – not just once, but twice. At 4.15 in the afternoon on the church field during a break between a performance by the real musical attraction of the afternoon, The Band of the Cheshire Yeomanry, and then later, at 5.45, after a display by the City of Liverpool Police Dogs, by kind permission of the Chief Constable and the Watch Committee.

The Quarrymen had also been invited to play at the evening dance in the church hall, tickets two shillings, refreshments at moderate prices, in intervals between the main musicians of the evening, The George Edwards Band.

It's quite a detailed programme, listing the route of the procession, the crowning of the Rose Queen, the different classes and times for the Fancy Dress Parade.

But nowhere does it state, and how could it, that this was the day, this was the event, at which Paul McCartney would first meet John Lennon, a fact which is now known to every Beatles Brain throughout the big wide world.

I have to admit, with a shamed face, that in my so-called authorised biography of 1968, I gave the date of this momentous event as June 15, 1956. A whole year and three weeks out. Shows the quality of my research, though I did get that date from The Beatles themselves, and they read the final manuscript.

A whole book has recently been written about this one day, going through it, minute by minute, by an American writer, Jim O'Donnell. (*The Day John Met Paul*, published by Penguin Books 1994 – later as an audio tape by Scorpion Publications, read by the one and only Rod Davis.)

Some of the descriptions and sequences in it are highly colourful, and I suspect verging by now on the mythical, as it is hard to get those who

# Woolton Parish Church

# Garden Fete

### and

## Crowning of Rose Queen

## Saturday, July 6th, 1957

To be opened at 3p.m. by Dr. Thelwall Jones

### PROCESSION AT 2p.m.

LIVERPOOL POLICE DOGS DISPLAY
FANCY DRESS PARADE
SIDESHOWS      REFRESHMENTS
BAND OF THE CHESHIRE YEOMANRY
THE QUARRY MEN SKIFFLE GROUP

ADULTS 6d., CHILDREN 3d.      OR BY PROGRAMME

# GRAND DANCE

at 8p.m. in the Church Hall

## GEORGE EDWARDS' BAND
## THE QUARRY MEN SKIFFLE GROUP

Tickets 2/-

were there to agree on what precisely happened. Paul for example remembers John as "a beery old man breathing down my neck". John at the time was aged 16¾, so must have seemed quite old. Paul had had his fifteenth birthday just three weeks earlier.

John himself said he was drunk that day and remembered Mimi complaining. "She said I'd done it at last. I was now a real Teddy Boy. I seemed to disgust everybody that day, not just Mimi."

Yet Pete and Len have no memory of John being drunk that day. They say the time they do remember him being drunk was at Roseberry Street. So it goes. So much for memory.

---

## PROGRAMME

| STALLS | — | SIDESHOWS | —— | ICE CREAM | —— | LEMONADE |

*Teas and Refreshments in large Marquee situated behind the hut.*

2-00 p.m. PROCESSION leaves Church Road, via Allerton Road, Kings Drive, Hunt's Cross Avenue; returning to the Church Field.
Led by the Band of the Cheshire Yeomanry.
Street Collection by the Youth Club during the procession.

3-00 p.m. CROWNING OF THE ROSE QUEEN (Miss Sally Wright) by Mrs. THELWALL JONES.

3-10 p.m. FANCY DRESS PARADE.
Class 1. Under 7 years.
Class 2. 7 to 12 years.
Class 3. Over 12 years.
Entrants to report to Miss P. Fuller at the Church Hall before the procession.

3-30 p.m. MUSICAL SELECTIONS by the Band of the
to Cheshire (Earl of Chester) Yeomanry. Band-
5-00 p.m. master: H. Abraham.
(By permission of Lt.-Col. G. C. V. Churton, M.C., M.B.E.).

4-15 p.m. THE QUARRY MEN SKIFFLE GROUP.

5-15 p.m. DISPLAY by the City of Liverpool Police Dogs.
By kind permission of the Chief Constable and Watch Committee.

5-45 p.m. THE QUARRY MEN SKIFFLE GROUP

*8-0 p.m.* **GRAND DANCE in the CHURCH HALL**

GEORGE EDWARDS BAND also *The Quarry Men Skiffle Group*

*TICKETS 2/-*

REFRESHMENTS AT MODERATE PRICES.

---

★   ★   ★

It was thanks to Pete's mother that they got the engagement. She had overheard one of the customers in her shop, who turned out to be the church hall caretaker, talking about the church fete coming up. She offered the services of her son's group. After all, were they not local, had they not been keen attenders at the Sunday School.

The Quarrymen assembled at two o'clock in time to take part in the

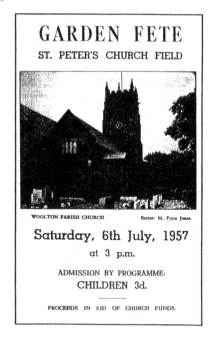

Opening Procession, playing from the back of a lorry. "I felt a complete prat," says Eric. "It was hopeless, trying to play while we were moving." So he gave up and just sat there. John didn't like the lorry either, telling Len it was a waste of time, but he did manage to perch on the edge and kept playing his guitar and singing till the procession was over.

It was at their afternoon session, in the field, that Ivan Vaughan brought along Paul McCartney, his school friend, to see the skiffle group he had been boasting about. Paul stood and watched them play, noting that John was making up many of the words, and not managing all the right chords.

"I noticed Paul while we were playing," says Eric. "He was standing with Ivan. He looked a very fresh-faced kid. I can't remember him carrying a guitar."

Later, while they were rehearsing in the hall, before the evening dance, Ivan brought along Paul and this time properly introduced him to John and the others. 'Properly' probably meant a few grunts.

Paul took John's guitar, retuned it from banjo chords, and demonstrated how to play 'Twenty Flight Rock'. Very smart. This was Paul's party piece. John was most impressed, but said nothing much at the time.

Colin's memory is of several people coming into the hall while they were getting ready. "I was playing my drums, but people would wander in with a bugle or a trumpet and play a bit on their own. We were all just messing around.

"While we were messing around, two lads in long coats arrived. They talked to John for some time. I wasn't aware at the time that it was Paul, and I didn't hear him play the guitar, but he might have done. I was playing my drums, wasn't I? I've read somewhere since that he turned up in a white jacket, but that wasn't true. He had a long coat that day – if of course that was Paul."

Rod has no memory either of Paul demonstrating 'Twenty Flight Rock' at the Fete. "Perhaps I paid a visit to the toilet and missed the greatest moment in rock'n'roll history . . ."

"Paul could obviously play the guitar," so John remembered. "I half thought to myself, he's as good as me. I'd been kingpin up till then. Now I thought if I take him on, what will happen. It went through my head that I'd have to keep him in line, if I let him join. But he was good, so he was worth having. He also looked like Elvis. I dug him."

About a week later, Paul went to visit Ivan Vaughan. On the way back, he happened to bump into Pete.

Pete stopped him and asked him if he wanted to join their group. Paul said yes, and cycled home for tea. So that was it. Paul became a Quarryman.

★　★　★

Not long afterwards, Eric went with John to Paul's house at Forthlin Road where Eric noted they had a piano in the front room. Paul tinkled a few notes on it, even more impressive. He then played his party piece again, 'Twenty Flight Rock'.

This was the first time Eric heard Paul play it. He has no memory of him playing it at the Woolton Fete – but then he thinks he might have gone home in the afternoon for his tea and missed the little rehearsal in the church hall.

On their visits to Paul's house, while Paul's dad was out, Eric says that straight away Paul and John started writing their own little songs. They even completed one, but he can't remember what it was.

"Paul was very good. We could all see that. He was precocious in many ways. Not just in music but in relating to people, getting on with them, being charming, trying to draw people towards him as his friend.

"Some time later we were all walking down Halewood Drive, to my house to do some practising. I was walking ahead with John. The others were behind. John suddenly said to me, 'Let's split the group, and you and me will start again.' We could hear Paul behind us, chatting to Pete,

59

as if he was Pete's best friend. John knew we were all his pals – but now Paul was trying to get in on us. Not to split us up, just make friends with us all. I'm sure that was all it was, but to John, it looked as if Paul was trying to take over, dominate the group. I suppose he was worried it could disrupt the balance, upset the group dynamics, as we might say today.

"I said to him, 'Paul's so good. He'll contribute a lot to the group. We need him with us.' John said nothing. But after that, the subject was never mentioned again. I like to think that was my greatest contribution to the history of The Beatles – not letting John chuck Paul out of The Quarrymen . . ."

★ ★ ★

Paul couldn't make their next engagement, even though he had been officially asked to join. He had a previous engagement which he couldn't miss, having paid his money in advance. He was off to Scout Camp with his brother, Michael. Sort of puts it all in context. These were just school kids, playing at being pop stars.

The gig he missed was on Wednesday, August 7, 1957, at the Cavern Club in Mathew Street, their first advertised appearance at a club that had been open only six months. It was primarily a jazz club but the popularity of skiffle meant that the odd skiffle group – including The Quarrymen – had been given a chance to perform in the intervals. The booking had come about through the father of the owner of the Cavern who happened to play golf at Lee Park. Another triumph for manager Nigel.

They started their set with some standard, fairly acceptable skiffle tunes, but having done so, John broke into Elvis Presley's 'Hound Dog' and 'Blue Suede Shoes'. Rod Davis on banjo was not so keen on this, as he much preferred the group to stick to traditional skiffle fare. He also didn't want to upset the audience and perhaps get beaten up. The owner of the club sent a note to them on stage which read, "Cut out the bloody rock."

Similar things had happened before. Eric remembers playing at the Grafton Ballroom in a skiffle competition – not for money, just for a chance to get up on a stage. "We played 'All Shook Up' that night and we got booed. We were only supposed to play skiffle."

That Cavern appearance had been in the middle of the long school summer hols, hence Paul being away with the Scouts. John himself went away for a short holiday with Eric in Wales.

They spent five days staying with Eric's grandparents at their cottage in the village of Bodfari near Denbigh.

John and Eric each took their guitars with them and played in the outside washhouse of the cottage. It had a stone floor and they liked the echo it created. When not mucking around on their guitars, they went out looking for girls, but didn't have much success. In the village where they were staying they could find only two girls. One looked pretty decent, but the other was awful, so they both thought. They couldn't agree between them who would have to go for the awful one, so in the end they made an approach for neither. Instead they went to Rhyl, where they spotted many more fanciable girls – but not one of them took the slightest bit of interest in either Eric or John.

Back in the village, when not strumming on their guitars, they spent their time fishing. A much healthier pastime for growing boys, as Baden Powell and all Boy Scouts of the time would have agreed.

There was a stone bridge over the stream where they did most of their fishing. John decided he would carve his name on the bridge, taking hours over it, till he had managed to create 'John W Lennon' in stone. Eric noted at the time how he had avoided giving away his middle name.

"About three or four years later, I went to visit my granddad again. While I was there, I went to look at the bridge, to see if John's name was still there. Not because he was just becoming well known, but out of personal interest. It was gone. Everything. The whole bridge had been demolished."

Eric, being the so-called handsome one, according to Rod, and John the aggressive leader, according to himself, usually had most luck when it came to girls. What Eric remembers about their Roseberry Street performance was not John getting drunk, or being chased by toughs, or having to hide in someone's house, but what happened afterwards.

"We had managed to pick up two girls, and we took them with us into the house. We sat there, in the woman's front room. I was hoping to get my wicked way with one of them, but she turned to me and said, 'I'm not doing anything when Four Eyes is watching us.' She meant Rod. He didn't wear his specs when performing, but he'd put them on to have a better look at the girls we'd picked up.

"John never wore his specs – which made him stare very hard. It gave the wrong impression, got him into a lot of trouble. People would think he was deliberately trying to look hard – which was another reason Teddy Boys wanted to fight him."

★   ★   ★

Paul's first known public appearance with The Quarrymen was in October, by which time John had left Quarry Bank School. In September he started at Liverpool College of Art, despite having failed his GCE art exam. Mr Pobjoy, the new headmaster, had set up an interview for him at the Art College and much to everyone's surprise, he had been accepted. It meant John had an ever freer life to devote himself to The Quarrymen, while Mimi could comfort herself by saying, "Yes, he's now a student, doing quite well, actually."

Paul's debut was on October 18 at the New Clubmoor Hall, a Conservative Club in Norris Green. He announced to the others that he would be appearing in a white sports coat. He already had one, like many teenage boys of the time, copying the hit song. According to Eric, John was worried by this, that it might look on stage as if Paul was the leader, so John managed to acquire a similar coat. The others wore white shirts and bootlace ties, as can be seen in the photograph.

What can't be seen in the photo was that Len was wearing two pairs of trousers. He had become self-conscious about being so thin, and having such weedy legs, so he thought two pairs would make him look more manly. Colin that night had to have a Guinness and cider before he went on stage, just to give himself confidence.

There were about 150 in the audience, according to Len's memory, and they were allowed to get away with quite a few rock numbers. "For my next trick," so John announced, "I'll just have to put on my Elvis wig . . ." Then he went into his version of 'All Shook Up'. Such jokes, especially early in a performance, were unusual, so Len says, but it seemed to go down well.

Paul had several guitar solos, which really meant numbers only he could perform, but on the night he was apparently rather nervous, making a bit of a hash of his 'Guitar Boogie'.

"He's our new boy," so John announced. "He'll be all right, given time."

The promoter of the event, who organised dances, skiffle and rock nights in various parts of Liverpool, and was therefore worth impressing, wrote in pencil on their visiting card 'Good and Bad'.

Paul had clearly suffered first-night nerves, but in private, practising at his house or other people's homes, he had had an immediate impact on the group. John and Eric decided they'd better play the guitar properly, using guitar chords, not the banjo chords as taught by Julia.

Secondly, the group now contained three guitarists. They were becoming a bit unbalanced. Would someone have to go?

★   ★   ★

Over the next four months, after Paul's debut, they got only occasional engagements, some of them at unlikely and unusual venues. On November 16, 1957, they played at Stanley Abattoir Social Club in front of the slaughtermen, porters, wives and girlfriends. They were considered to have been 'cacophonous' and were not rebooked.

Another performance was at the Morgue Skiffle Cellar in Broad Green. This was a new club and several skiffle and embryo rock groups had been invited to play on the opening night. About 100 people turned up to the cellar of a large Victorian house which had only one electric light bulb and no facilities at all. A month later, the police intervened and the club was closed for good.

But they did get some return bookings at the Wilson Hall in Garston, a venue noted for its rough crowd of Teddy Boys. All The Quarrymen remember being chased afterwards by toughs, mostly they say, intent on beating up John.

"One night at Wilson Hall," says Colin, "a massive Teddy Boy, who'd had too much to drink, climbed up on stage. I thought he was going to thump John but he went up to Paul and eye-balled him, nose to nose. 'I want you to do Little Richard.' Paul certainly wasn't going to argue with this massive drunk, so he announced that our next song would be 'Long Tall Sally'. We hadn't planned to play it, and Paul didn't know all the words, so he just kept repeating the same ones. But he was brilliant at it. And the drunk was happy . . ."

John and Paul were appealing mostly to the girls in their audiences. The local toughs didn't like their girls fancying them, and so tried to sort them out afterwards. That's one theory for the attempts to beat them up. Another is that it was all John's fault, looking hard because he was half blind.

A more likely explanation is that The Quarrymen were seen as snobs from Woolton, a suburb considered more affluent than places like Garston. They were ex-grammar school boys from semi-detached houses, poncing about, trying to be working-class rockers, performing in front of real hard men who were labourers during the day but became genuine Teds at night, wearing the full gear, plus razors and bicycle chains at the ready. John admitted that he wasn't a real Ted, despite his quiff and tight trousers. He would have run a mile, if anyone had ever wanted a real fight.

They were still of course travelling around by bus. Usually it meant several buses to get across Liverpool. This was always particularly hard for Colin with his drums and Len, or whoever was currently in charge of the tea chest bass, having to drag them around. They had to be put in the luggage area, under the bus stairs, which was often full of prams.

One evening after a Wilson Hall performance, they were chased by the Teds all the way to the bus stop. Pete was in charge of the tea chest that night and dropped it in his panic.

"John and I managed to get on the bus, just as it was moving. But at the next stop, these two thugs got on. We were upstairs, crouching at the front, but they found us and started fighting us. At the next stop, John dived downstairs and disappeared. They took off after him, as it was John they wanted to thump. I could see them standing on the pavement, wondering which way John had gone. I thought he'd got off as well – till I discovered he was downstairs, sitting quietly between two old women. The tea chest lay on the pavement for some days, till we eventually collected it."

They were still entering skiffle contests, playing for nothing, but hoping to be spotted, or win some money. Colin remembers a talent contest held at the Locarno Ballroom. "When we got there, a poster announced there was to be a contest for male singers, not just groups. When Paul saw it he turned to John and said, 'Should we have a go at it, you know, on our own?' It was John who said, 'No way. We're not doing anything on our own. We're a group.' I got the impression that Paul would have instantly dropped everyone else, just for him and John to enter this competition on their own.

"We went to another talent contest at the Wilson Hall. When we got there, we found we had to pay to get in, cough up the normal entrance fee for the dance, even though we were there just to compete, not dance. John didn't like the idea of paying, but some of us tried to persuade him. We said it's only two shillings, or whatever, to get in, but if we win, we could end up with £1 each as prize money. We argued that it was a good investment. So anyway John agreed and we paid to go in. We didn't win.

"I think that was when the promoter, Mr McBain, liked us enough to give us some bookings at the Wilson Hall and his other places.

"One night when we turned up, there was a singer there, on her own. I think she was called Pauline. She was the lead singer of, I think, the Darktown Skiffle Group. I think Mr McBain had brought her along on her own in order to persuade us to have her as our lead singer. John and Paul were having none of this, of course. They were our lead singers. Not any girl.

"I once overheard Mr McBain, after we'd done our set, telling Nigel Walley 'I owe you five.' I thought he meant five pounds, which sounded good. It turned out to be five 10-shilling notes. We must only have been four playing in the band that night, plus Nige as manager, as all we got was ten shillings each.

"John and Paul were always complaining that they had to replace their guitar strings. In the days of no mikes, they did tend to bash them hard. I also don't think Paul was ever keen on Nigel getting the same money as him when he didn't play with us.

"We were playing at Paul's house one day, with Paul moaning about money as usual. It didn't worry me, as I was working. I probably spent more on drink when we had a gig than what we actually got paid for playing. Anyway this day I said, 'Look, I'm only here for a bit of fun. If the money means so much to you, you can have my next share and spend it on new strings.'

"Both Paul and John did used to moan a lot about their lack of money."

★   ★   ★

Fourteen-year-old George Harrison came on the scene early in 1958. His own memory is that he first watched The Quarrymen perform at the Wilson Hall and was introduced to them afterwards. George's mother, who became an immediate fan and supporter of the group, said they all first met in a chip shop. Pete says they first met at George's own house, a council house in Speke, taken there by Paul. Mark Lewisohn opts for George's memory of Wilson Hall, which he dates as February 6, 1958.

However Colin is adamant it all took place a few weeks later – and at the Morgue. "I know it's often said that George met us at the Wilson Hall and played 'Raunchy' to us. The band room was very small and right beside the stage. You couldn't make a noise there without being heard on stage. Whenever I tapped the drums a little, I was told to be quiet. The idea of George playing 'Raunchy' or 'Guitar Boogie' to us in that band room is impossible.

"The Morgue was a derelict place, a dump really, which was why it was soon closed, but its band room was well away from the stage. You could make as much noise as you liked. That's where I'm sure George first played his guitar to us."

Any road up, the connection was through Paul and the Institute, where George was a pupil, and whatever the date of the first meeting, George really arrived sideways, insinuating himself into the group.

★   ★   ★

Pete does not recall being jealous of Paul when he first came along. He didn't consider him a rival for John's friendship. He could see he was a different type, more polite, deferential to elders, though this had failed to impress Aunt Mimi. "Despite Paul's charm, Mimi didn't like Paul coming round to see John. She wouldn't let him in, if John was not at home."

It was probably social snobbery, as Paul came from a council house, rather than seeing him as a bad influence.

"But when George came along, who was more musical, I felt more and more out of the gang," says Pete. "George got himself into the group gradually, playing when Eric couldn't make it.

"George hero-worshipped John, but at first John had mixed feelings about being seen with him. We all looked upon George as a naïve little boy, but we all knew he was talented on the guitar.

"Being John's friend, I hadn't wanted to say I was getting fed up, that I wanted to leave. My contribution was totally non-musical. I just went along to make wisecracks or help carry the gear. I never liked going on stage. It gave me the willies."

The ending for Pete, as a musical member of The Quarrymen, came at a wedding reception in Toxteth given by a friend of Colin Hanton's some-time around August 1957. There was lots of free beer and Pete and John proceeded to drink too much – the first time in his life that Pete remembers John being really drunk.

"John and I were on the floor, sitting cross-legged at the end of the party, surrounded by our instruments and empty beer bottles. John was in fine form, making me laugh hysterically at something or other. I plucked up the courage to say I was leaving. I say 'plucked' because I thought he'd be upset. But he'd obviously been struggling to tell me he didn't want me in the group any more. Anyway, he suddenly picked up my washboard and hit me over the head with it. He then turned to me and said, 'Well, that takes care of that problem, doesn't it?'

"So that was it. I was released from The Quarrymen. We then just laughed till the beers rolled down our eyes . . ."

# 6

## Hello Paul And George, Bye Bye Boys

Despite the arrival of Paul and George, there was not an instant increase in bookings for The Quarrymen, nor their popularity, but their playing was improving all the time, as was their level of individual skill, especially once Pete had left. He was still around as a non-playing member, John's mate, though no longer his only best mate, as at the Art College John was forming a close friendship with another student, Stu Sutcliffe. But Pete still went to gigs with them, helped to carry the gear, went drinking with them afterwards.

And Pete was around on that terrible day, July 15, 1958, when John's mother, Julia, was involved in a road accident with an off duty policeman.

"By chance, I went round to Nigel's house later that evening. He opened the door to me and I could see at once something terrible had happened.

"Nigel said he'd called earlier that day on John, but he wasn't in. Julia was just leaving, having been chatting to her sister, Mimi. Nigel walked with her towards her bus stop – then said goodbye and crossed Menlove Avenue. Behind him he heard the screech of brakes and saw that Julia had been thrown in the air by a car. By the time he reached her, she was dead.

"I saw John the next afternoon. I said I was sorry and he said he knew. We didn't really talk about it, but he began drinking very heavily. I found him at the back of the bus once, spreadeagled. He'd been on it for hours, up and down the route from the terminus and back. I carried him off it and took him home.

"He started being even crueller to people. We were in some dive and he started making anti-Semitic remarks about a Jewish pianist called Reuben, till in the end the poor guy was in tears."

For most of 1958, The Quarrymen might as well have disbanded as a performing group. Paid bookings had almost dried up, with no more than five in that whole year, as far as is known, and they returned to playing at friends' parties and weddings – such as the wedding of George's brother,

Harry Harrison in December 1958. George himself appears to have played with other groups during this period, when he could get time off from his school work.

They did manage a paid performance on New Year's Day, 1959, when they played again at Wilson Hall, Garston. It was not a public dance this time but a belated Christmas Party held by Speke Bus Depot's Social Club – the chairman of which was George's father. After this, there was another long lull of some six months without any known public performance.

It says a lot for the determination of John and Paul that during this fallow period they kept the group going, while spending most of their time writing songs together. Apart from Colin, they were all still at school or college and did not have the immediate worry about earning a living.

They should of course, according to their parents or relatives, have been sticking in at school, concentrating on examinations in order to get some decent qualifications.

It wasn't just Aunt Mimi who said that a guitar's all right, but it won't get you a proper job.

★ ★ ★

Rod, the only one with any serious interest in studying, was the next after Pete of the original Quarrymen to leave the group. Nothing dramatic happened. No row, no sacking. In fact he can't even remember when it happened.

"The last gig I can clearly remember was on August 7, 1957, at the Cavern. On the same bill was Ron McKay, The Deltones and The Demon Five Skiffle Group. No, I hadn't remembered their names – I got them from the listing in the *Liverpool Echo*.

"After that, we didn't have many other gigs that year, not that I can recall, and I sort of just drifted away. In essence, I was replaced by Paul. I had met Paul at John's one day when John and I were practising together. I think Paul had come along just to watch us, so I gathered.

"Perhaps I hadn't realised at the time that Paul had taken my place. As the man on the way out, I'd obviously be the last to know.

"But there was no dramatic parting. We just went our different ways."

Academically, they had gone a different way for some time. Rod had moved through the school in the A stream and was now destined for the sixth form.

"I heard all about John and Pete as troublemakers. Some of it was very funny. When I heard about them putting on dog collars, I thought it was brilliant. Buggering about is one thing, and can be very annoying for teachers, but that was inspired tomfoolery. As a teacher, that would have made my day.

"Some boys were scared of John's tongue. He could be very sarcastic, but really, we were all like that. Most boys at school were quick at improvised repartee, getting digs in, getting your own back, that's how you survived.

"At home, my Dad would say to me, 'Are you rude like that to all your friends.' And I was one of the goody goodies . . ."

Rod also had moved on musically. He had not been as keen as the others on the new rock'n'roll, preferring folk or jazz music. "After I left the group, my younger brother Bernie and I sold our electric trains and bought a Spanish guitar."

In the sixth form, Rod then formed a jazz trio with two other boys, a pianist and a drummer. Cool.

"The pianist was brilliant, Gerald Greenwood, and the drummer, Les Brough, was really good. I was on guitar. On to the guitar I sellotaped a carbon microphone to try and produce some amplification. It didn't really work . . ."

★   ★   ★

Len was also still at school when the end came for him. In early August 1958, aged sixteen, he was at home in Lance Lane, sitting in the dining room about to eat his favourite food – a banana. He had just peeled open the banana in his hand when he suddenly fell unconscious to the floor. An ambulance was called and Len was rushed to the Smithdown Road Hospital.

"I must have been unconscious for quite a few days, in some sort of coma. All I can remember is waking up and asking for a cigarette.

"I was diagnosed as suffering from tubercular meningitis. They put me in an isolation cubicle and said I was very fortunate to be alive, with all my faculties intact. Apparently it was a killer disease – and if it didn't kill you, it left some people mentally retarded, blind or suffering from other things.

"No idea what caused it, but I was told you could get it from breathing in infected droplets in unventilated, overcrowded conditions. So it could have been playing in places like the Cavern, or other crowded, smoky conditions . . ."

Len was later transferred to the Fazakerley Hospital. As the months went on, and he slowly got some strength back, he was eventually allowed to have visitors. Most of his class from the Institute came to see him, including John Duff Lowe who occasionally played the piano with The Quarrymen and Neil Aspinall, later The Beatles' roadie.

John and Paul also came to see him. "I could see a close bond had formed between them while I'd been ill. They came to see me once out of hours, not at the proper visiting time, and had to escape through a French window into the garden when the nurse arrived. They then stood outside making silly faces at me as the nurse gave me various tests.

"George came to see me on his own. He was now a proper member of the group, but I didn't really know him well. He was at my school, but a year younger. I really appreciated his visit as he seemed so understanding and caring."

Len was in hospital for seven months in all, not emerging till the spring of 1959, aged seventeen. Life and The Quarrymen had moved on by then.

\*   \*   \*

When George came along, Eric too was aware how young he was, which was a bit embarrassing in normal street life, hanging around with a kid so much younger, but it was never a problem in the group itself. They all knew it was George's ability that mattered, not his age.

But it meant that there were now four guitarists in the group – John, Paul, George and Eric. One had to go – and it was obvious which one.

"I got a phone call one day from Nigel," says Eric. "He made it clear that I either had to change to the bass guitar, or leave the group. John had already asked me about playing the bass guitar.

"I was pretty angry, at the time of the phone call. I said I wanted to speak to John himself, but Nigel said he wasn't there. I didn't quite believe that.

"I suppose my slight feeling of anger was because I thought I'd contributed quite a bit the group. I had worked with John from the very beginning, when we were learning the guitar together. We helped each other with the chords, worked together on which songs we were going to play, how we would play them.

"John was better than me on the guitar, but not much. He wasn't as good as either Paul or George. But I always got on with John. I never had arguments with him. And I never saw him as 'trouble'. I skived off school far more than John. Perhaps he took things a step further, but only in things like clothes. He always had tighter jeans than the rest of us. That was about the level of it.

"Anyway, when I thought about it, I decided not to bother arguing with them. I wasn't going to buy a bass guitar as it would cost me too much money. Money I couldn't see myself ever getting back. I wasn't confident enough that The Quarrymen would do any better and get better gigs. I had no thoughts at all that their music might blossom. I couldn't see a return on my expenditure, if I lashed out on a new guitar. So, I just left. That was it.

"I soon got over any anger. George had replaced me in the group. It didn't bother me, really. Life moved on . . ."

★ ★ ★

Colin remembers Eric going – but tried to keep out of it. Eric was his friend and neighbour, the one who had introduced him to the group. All the same, he was only the drummer. What do drummers know?

"It was a Saturday afternoon and I was just leaving my house when I saw Nigel riding down our street, pedalling furiously on his drop handlebar bike. He was still our manager and had been to a big meeting with John and Paul. He said they wanted George in and Eric out. He'd been sent to get my feelings. I said, 'Look, I'm just the drummer, John and Paul are running the group. Whatever they want to do, they can just go ahead and do it.' "

And they did. With Eric removed, that left Colin as the last of our original Quarrymen. Apart of course from John.

Drummers are hard to find and harder to replace. So Colin continued playing with them well into 1959, but he is not quite sure of precise dates and venues. He does, though, remember a Cavern appearance not long after George had joined the group.

"In *The Beatles Anthology*, George talked about playing in the Cavern as a Beatle and being given a note to stop playing rock'n'roll. This was definitely during The Quarrymen days, not The Beatles. George has certainly more to remember than me, but I was definitely there the night that note was sent up.

"I remember another night at the Cavern, probably the last night Pete was with us, scratching away on his washboard. We were doing an Elvis number, 'All Shook Up'. It has a long dramatic pause, then it starts again with a smash of the drumsticks on the snare drum. John was right at the front of the stage. It was hard to see him and none of us came in quite in synch – but Pete rounded on me and said it was my fault.

"Well, a washboard player wasn't going to tell a drummer what to do, was he? Pete then told me to stop playing, so I put down my drumsticks, stood up and tried to grab his throat. As we were standing there fighting, John and Paul sang louder and louder, hoping to drown our noise. Later in the band room, they asked what the hell it was all about. They couldn't actually see we were arguing with each other. I suppose it must have been quite hilarious for the audience, but not for me at the time.

"After Pete stopped playing, he still came to the Cavern to watch us, along with Nigel. They'd come backstage afterwards, tell us how it had gone, how the audience had reacted.

"The Cavern had three arches, so it was like three tunnels, the centre one being the largest. It was filled with chairs for people to sit down and watch when they had jazz bands. This evening we went on stage and did all rock'n'roll for a change, no skiffle at all.

"It was very dark, as it always was, hard to see the audience properly, but I realised the audience was getting up from their seats and leaving. John, who could see very little anyway, turned to me between numbers and said, 'What the fuck's going on, why are they all leaving?' But he carried on and we finished our set. By this time the whole centre was empty and John was convinced they'd all walked out on us.

"When Pete and Nige burst into the band room, Pete said, 'That was the most fantastic show I've seen.' John said, 'What do you mean, they all left.' Pete said, 'No they didn't – they all went into the two side bits and were all jiving like mad.'

"I think that might have been the night they took out the seats in the Cavern. From then on, it was all rock'n'rollers."

Another time in the Cavern, Colin had a row with Nigel. "He'd been telling me off for some time that I was playing too loud. He said I should use brushes, not drumsticks. It's true that the acoustics in the Cavern weren't very good and the guitars weren't of course electric. Sometimes they were hard to hear.

"This evening, I'd just got on stage when Nigel jumped up beside me and took my drumsticks away – leaving me with just my brushes. I wasn't having any of that. I just sat there with my arms folded and went on strike. When I didn't start the first number, John turned round to find out what was wrong. He then shouted at Nige, 'Give them back.' So he was forced to. I then carried on playing, as per normal."

Colin was with them when they made their first attempt at getting on TV, and so was Eric, going for an audition to the ABC TV studios in Didsbury, Manchester.

"We hadn't realised how expensive it was, just to get there," says Colin. "We had to get the bus into Liverpool, the train to Manchester, then when we got there, we hadn't realised we had to get another bus out to Didsbury."

They didn't get through the audition, then on the way home, Paul found he had run out of money. "We were on the top of the bus and Paul was moaning loudly that he couldn't pay, and that he now wouldn't be able to get himself home. Some guy on the bus had obviously overheard him moaning. As he got off, he shoved two shillings into Paul's hand. I can still hear Paul looking at it and shouting, 'He's given me money! He's given me money.' Paul ran after the bloke who by now had got off the bus. He shouted after him, 'Thanks mate, I love you.' Now you didn't often hear a bloke in those days shouting, 'I love you' to another bloke. I wonder if later he ever knew who he had given the money to . . ."

They might have failed to get on TV but sometime in mid-1958, The Quarrymen did cut their first disc. Not in a recording studio but in the back room of someone's house in Kensington, Liverpool, where a man named Percy Phillips charged amateurs a small fee to record their sounds.

With John, Paul, George and Colin that day was John Duff Lowe, who sometimes played the piano with them. He was in the same year at the Institute as Paul and Len.

In February, 1953, aged ten, he and Paul had auditioned for the Liverpool Cathedral Choir – and both failed. Duff tried again in the October and got in. "I've worked out that if Paul had got in the Cathedral choir, he could not have met John on July 6, 1957. He would have been singing in the Cathedral choir that day."

During 1958, Paul occasionally asked him to play with The Quarrymen, as he was a good pianist. "I like to think I played with them in their rock'n'roll years, not their skiffle years."

The recording session was organised by Paul and John, says Colin. "They told us it would cost 17/6d, which meant 3/6d each. We thought that would get us a tape recording, plus a disc, but when we got there, Mr Phillips said, 'No, to have a tape and a disc, that would be £1.'

" 'We're not paying a pound,' said John and Paul. None of us could manage the extra 2/6d needed, so we said, 'OK then, we'll just have it direct on to a disc.' Which is what we did. So there never was a tape recording made.

"It must have been a cold day, perhaps late in the year, because I remember wearing a scarf. And why I remember that is because when Mr Phillips did his sound check, he said I was far too loud. He moved me to the furthest part of the room, but I was still too loud. So I took my scarf off and put it over the snare drum to muffle it."

They played two numbers – Buddy Holly's 'That'll Be The Day' and an original composition by "McCartney & Harrison" called 'In Spite Of All

The Danger'. Only one copy of the disc was made and they each took it in turns to have it, playing it to their families and friends.

When it was Colin's turn, after he had played it several times, he let a friend have it who worked at Littlewoods, the pools firm. "They played music while you worked, in their factory place, and our record was played quite a few times. So probably quite a few thousand people heard it."

Colin can't remember what then happened to the record, even though it was the only copy. In fact, he forgot all about it for many years.

When I talked to The Beatles at length in the mid-Sixties, going over their Quarrymen days, none of them mentioned this disc. Not even George, who at this early stage in his career had apparently been involved in composing 'In Spite Of All The Danger', which he didn't return to until many years later.

★   ★   ★

Colin was never sacked from The Quarrymen, unlike Eric, nor did he just fade away like Rod. There might have been some criticism at times about his loud playing, from Paul as well as Nigel, but that was not the cause of his departure. It was only ever in the Cavern, so he says, with its dodgy sound, that his drums might have been a trifle loud.

"I can remember my last gig very clearly. It was in a very nice club, very professional, in Norris Green. There was going to be a theatre manager coming to watch us who might book us to play in the intervals at his shows.

"This club had a proper stage, proper curtains. You didn't just climb up on it. You entered from the side. Very professional. The dressing rooms were clean with pictures round the walls of people who had played there, like Ken Dodd.

"At half-time, when we'd finished our first five songs, the curtain was supposed to close, but the guy pulling them couldn't manage it. They'd got stuck. So John ad-libbed, and was very funny, and we did a sixth song. We went down really well and the audience loved it.

"When we came off, the bloke in charge said, 'Very good lads, there's a pint for you at the bar.' Well, that was the worst thing he could have said to us. In those days, we didn't stop at one pint, did we? And not when it was free. Well I didn't. But I wasn't the only one who got drunk that evening. We all did – except George. His mum and dad were in the audience so he was being careful.

"The second half was a right disaster. We were so pissed, John and Paul got the giggles and started taking the mickey out of George who was sober and trying hard to play properly.

"Afterwards, the guy in charge came to our dressing room and said, 'You've really blown it now lads, but I'll still ask the theatre manager to come and see you.'

"This manager figure comes into our dressing room with rouge on his cheeks, all made-up. No, he wasn't gay. He'd been appearing on stage at his place, but the sight of him cracked John and Paul up. They were pissing themselves even more, laughing in his face, then they started mocking him. I was getting a bit cheesed off by now, with John and Paul, the way they were behaving.

"On the bus home, Paul started making silly noises. It sounded to me as if he was imitating deaf and dumb people, doing the noise they make when they try to talk. John was doing much the same as well. This annoyed me because I had a couple of deaf and dumb friends.

"In the end I rounded on Paul, told him to stop it, and we got into a huge argument. We were all still pretty drunk of course, so that didn't help. It wasn't quite a fist fight. Just a lot of shouting and arguing.

"But I suppose I had begun to feel fed up with them by then, by their attitude, the things they were doing and saying.

"I got so pissed off by how they were behaving, that in the end I just stood up, even though it wasn't my stop. I collected my drums, left the bus – and left them.

"So that was it, basically. I never contacted them again. They never contacted me. That was it . . ."

# THE SIXTIES

## MULTIPLE CHOICE

Before we go any further, and our heroes each step out into the world at large, try and guess what happened to them. We all know what became of John, but what about the other five original Quarrymen? From what you have gleaned about their lives, talents and personalities so far, take a shot at answering the following questions by ticking one or more box.

|  | John | Pete | Rod | Eric | Len | Colin |
|---|---|---|---|---|---|---|
| 1. Apart from John, who else became a multimillionaire? | | | | | | |
| 2. Who went on to manage a boutique? | | | | | | |
| 3. John had two sons – who had three? | | | | | | |
| 4. Who emigrated to New Zealand? | | | | | | |
| 5. Today, which two live in Liverpool? | | | | | | |
| 6. Who formed a small chain of dry-cleaners? | | | | | | |
| 7. Who is the only one today doing the same job he first had? | | | | | | |
| 8. Apart from John, who kept on playing? | | | | | | |
| 9. Who is now mad on windsurfing? | | | | | | |
| 10. Who became a senior civil servant? | | | | | | |

Answers: Sorry, you'll have to read on.
But if you liked it so far, hurry hurry . . .

# 7

## What Pete Did Next

What happened when Colin left was that the others went on to become successful as The Beatles, but not at once, not by a long way. There were many ups and downs, downers and uppers, times when they could easily have packed up, gone their separate ways. They'd had three years from 1956 to 1959 as struggling, amateur, part-time, messing about Quarrymen. There were another three long years to go during which they were still struggling, still ill paid, still liable to splinter, before eventually, oh that wondrous day in 1962, when they produced their real first record.

Along the way, things did repeat themselves, there were arguments with each other, people not turning up, problems finding a drummer. And when they did find one, they went on to drop him, just as unceremoniously as they had dropped Eric, getting someone else to tell him the bad news.

The final drummer, the one they eventually ended up with, was a bit like Colin – small, a non-grammar school boy, cheerful, very fond of rings.

But when Colin packed it in, they were drummer-less, then in August 1959, they had a bit of luck – the Casbah Club opened. It provided them with regular bookings and also their next drummer, Pete Best, whose mother owned the Casbah.

At the end of 1959, they tried and failed yet again to crack Carroll Levis, this time calling themselves Johnny & The Moondogs. Skiffle had finally faded by then so any group with skiffle in their name or in their baggage tried to re-invent themselves. The Gerry Marsden Skiffle Group became Gerry & The Pacemakers.

In May 1960, now calling themselves The Silver Beatles, and joined by John's new best friend Stu Sutcliffe on guitar, which he could hardly play, they got their first tour, eight days in Scotland, backing a singer called Johnny Gentle. As tours went, this was a crap tour, in lousy digs, poor halls, driving hundreds of miles in a rackety van.

Later that year, they made their first visit to Hamburg, organised by their new manager Allan Williams, a step up from Nigel in that he was a

79

professional club man, trying to make a living out of all those competing Merseyside groups, but not with any huge success.

In Hamburg, which they visited three times, the conditions were just as scruffy, just as crummy as Scotland, but at least they were working, doing very long hours, which enabled them to find themselves, acquire their own sound, their own way of making a show, so that when they returned to Liverpool, they had grown better, more professional.

Then into their lives came Brian Epstein, a well-bred public school boy who had gone to RADA but was now back in the family business, running a record store in Liverpool called NEMS. He heard about The Beatles, and that they had produced a record in Hamburg, still as a backing group. He went to the Cavern one day to investigate, hoping he might sell a few of their records in his shop.

In December 1961, it was agreed he would become their manager. But still the struggles went on, trying to get them TV appearances, trying to get them a record deal, trying to make them a bit smarter and more employable. Brian didn't think smoking and fighting on stage was quite the right thing to do. He also tried to make them turn up on time and wear better suits. Meanwhile they trailed round Merseyside, playing much bigger halls, with much bigger audiences than their Quarrymen days, but still very much a local group, one of several dozen trying to break through nationally.

They wondered and worried if it would ever happen for them. Paul, being one of nature's charmers, wrote charming letters to the local papers, mostly full of lies about their careers, hoping for publicity. John, the cheerleader, used to lead a cheer amongst themselves which began with "Where are we going John?" To which they would all reply "To the Toppermost of the Poppermost."

In August 1962, Ringo Starr, who had played in Hamburg with another group, agreed to join the Beatles and Pete Best was given the sack.

In September 1962, George Martin agreed to produce their first record, 'Love Me Do', for EMI's Parlophone label. By December, it had risen to the heights of number 17 in the charts – and didn't rise any further. By that time, they had recorded a second single, 'Please Please Me', which was released in January 1963.

In February 1963, they set off on a national tour, much better organised this time, in main cities, in top venues, but very much as a supporting, down-the-bill act. The star was Britain's new young singing sensation, Helen Shapiro.

It was during the tour, it all changed. 'Please Please Me' got to number one in April 1963. Suddenly they found that fans, mainly young female fans, were coming to the shows especially to see them. In Glasgow, so John remembered, their appearance was received by screams for the first time. After that, the screaming never seemed to stop.

They did another tour in 1963, produced three more records, including 'She Loves You' and 'I Want To Hold Your Hand', which also got to number one. By the end of 1963, Beatlemania had hit Britain.

But you know all that, especially if you are any sort of Beatles Brain. What of the other five young men who used to be called Quarrymen?

★   ★   ★

What Pete did next could scarcely have been predicted, not when you consider that his childhood and youth with John had been spent petty thieving, being anti-authority and non-conforming.

He didn't have a lot of choice, when it came to careers. He took five 'O' levels and – like John – failed them all. In English, he just mucked around. He did an essay on Brendan Behan in which he made up a sister called Les Behan. Her lesbian sister, gerrit. Just a silly sniggery, Lennon-type joke.

After that, he couldn't go back to school and enter the sixth form without any 'O' levels, so what was he going to do? Answer – he joined the police. Pete, how could you? Even now, he finds it hard to explain.

"I think without knowing it, my mother might have put the idea into my mind. She was very law abiding, very status conscious and she always liked people in uniform. My dad had been in the merchant navy. My older brother Ernie was already in the navy.

"Nigel Walley's father was in the police, and became a Superintendent. I had always looked up to him, so that must have been an influence.

"But it was my mother who got me this brochure about being a police cadet. I suppose she suggested it, but I have to admit I fancied it. When I looked at the photos of the cadets, they all seemed to be playing snooker, swimming, boxing. I thought this looks good. I imagined being a police cadet would just be an extension of school and be a good laugh.

"You've also got to realise that the image of the police in the mid-Fifties was different from today. Everyone looked up to them."

So at 16, in 1957, Pete joined the Liverpool Police College, situated just behind Paul McCartney's house in Forthlin Road. He quite enjoyed his next two years as a cadet. There was a lot of sport and quite a few laughs. It was respectable and acceptable, quite hard to get into, with a proper career structure.

He still kept in touch with John, with The Quarrymen and his other boyhood friends. As Colin recalled, Pete stood in the audience at the Cavern, passed on comments, helped carry the gear. At the Wilson Hall, he too was threatened by the Teds, along with John.

"We had a Sergeant at the College, Sergeant John Edwards, a good bloke, for whom I had great respect. He took me aside one day and said they'd had reports that I'd been seen mixing with undesirable long-haired louts at some den called the Cavern. I had to stop going there. I didn't, of course. I just made sure I wasn't seen.

"Funnily enough, I met that same Sergeant in Liverpool last year, 40 years later. Guess what he's doing now? He's a Beatles guide . . ."

In 1959, Pete graduated from the police college and passed out, aged almost 19, as a fully fledged policeman. The ceremony took place in the grounds of the police college, backing on to Paul's house. As Pete was marching with the other graduates, he could see Paul, John and George on the roof of Paul's back washhouse, doing a pretend march with buckets and mops. "I managed, if only just, to keep a straight face and keep in step."

Pete eventually got his own beat, in Garston, not far from the infamous Wilson Hall, the haunt of Teds and toughs.

"I was given a wooden stick, a whistle and sent off to patrol. I had to go under this bridge, at the end of which you were right into about the roughest area of Liverpool. I was shit scared. I wasn't beaten up, but it was a near thing.

"I began to think, What am I doing? I'm not enjoying this. So after nine months, I resigned from the police.

"I think quite a few of those who'd been cadets left as well. That's why they don't have police cadets any more. Too many joined for the wrong reasons when they were too young, as I did, then packed it in."

So Pete was left wondering again what to do with his life. One of the places he'd been hanging around with John and the other Quarrymen and old school friends like Billy Turner, was the Old Dutch Cafe in Smithdown Lane. It was owned by a Dutchman, who'd put up a windmill symbol outside, still there to this day, who was looking for someone to help run it. In 1960, Pete went in as a so-called partner, though without putting up any money. His salary was £15 a week.

"I realised I preferred being free and independent, not part of a big organisation like the police. So it suited me. I quite enjoyed it."

He got to know Stu Sutcliffe, John's new friend at Art College, and could see in him reflections of himself.

"I don't think Stu was any more musical than I was, but he was a brilliant artist. John always needed someone as his best friend – and he usually got them to do what he wanted, to participate in the things he was doing.

"John did ask me to come and visit them in Hamburg. I can't remember which trip it was, but I was quite flattered to be asked. John said I'd love Hamburg. They had everything there anyone could possibly want, at any time of day or night.

"But I couldn't go, could I? I couldn't leave my job in the cafe. And anyway I didn't have the money . . ."

But there were some pluses in being John's friend, when after their Hamburg success they came back to Liverpool.

"The girls at the Cavern tended to come in pairs. When John spotted one he liked, he'd say to me, 'What do you think of her?' If I didn't like the look of her mate, I'd say, 'Hey, what about that pair over there?' So I got my choice as well.

"Often these girls lived together, in some bedsit, so we'd go back to their place and screw them, often in the same double bed. No, nothing kinky. No foursomes and stuff. Just me and my girl on one side of the bed and John screwing his on the other side, trying to pretend the other wasn't there.

"We got friendly with a couple of strippers, so-called models at one of Liverpool's first unofficial topless nightclubs. They were fantastic, knew every sexual trick. Trouble was the first time they took us back to their place I couldn't get it up. She told me not to worry, one of The Beatles hadn't managed it either. I'm not saying which one . . ."

Pete first met Brian Epstein at the Blue Angel, a nightclub where most of the Merseyside groups hung out after they had been playing. Pete had gone there with John. After John had gone off with some girl, Brian made a pass at Pete, according to Pete.

"Brian asked me to step outside to his car, which was a Mark 10 Jaguar. I thought he just wanted to talk to me in private about John. He said John had told him so much about me and he wanted to know me better. Would I come back to his apartment with him? I told him it wasn't my scene. He wasn't embarrassed or upset. We went back inside and had a few drinks. As far as I was concerned, Brian was a perfect gentleman. I always liked him.

"When Brian first came along, and started to clean up their image, John did not object. Nobody could ever make John do anything he didn't want to do – but he wanted success so much that he was more than willing to agree to the little suits Brian got them into, whatever John might have said later."

Despite being so close to John, Pete didn't know about John's marriage to Cynthia (on August 23, 1962) till a few weeks after it had happened. "It was Cyn being pregnant that made them get married, but Brian wanted it all kept secret. He thought the fans would be upset.

"I was going steady myself, with Beth, and we'd already decided to get married, so this day I asked John if he was ever going to get married. He said he already was. But he clearly didn't see it as a very important thing. 'Walking about married,' he later said to me, 'is like walking about with odd socks on or your flies open.'"

In April 1963, just after the birth of Julian, John went off on holiday with Brian to Spain, leaving Cyn with the new baby.

On his return, Pete went round to see him one day when he was at Mimi's. He asked John what it had been like with Brian, nudge nudge, know what I mean John.

"Not you as well Pete," replied John. "They're all fucking on at me about it . . ."

Then to Pete's surprise, John confessed that something had happened. Brian had kept on at John so much that one evening John had dropped his trousers. "Oh for Christ's sake, Brian," said John, "just stick it up me fucking arse then."

"Brian explained that was not what he liked. All he wanted to do was touch John. So John let him toss him off.

"John said Brian was just a sad bastard who'd been having a hard time. There were stories in Liverpool about him trying to touch up sailors and as a result getting himself beaten up or robbed. John felt sorry for him. He felt no harm had been done. The poor bastard couldn't help the way he was.

"I told him I agreed. I couldn't see the harm either. What's a fucking wank between friends. We'd done similar things with each other enough times when we were younger . . ."

But the rumours got round Liverpool and people began making jokes about John being a homo. It ended in blows at Paul McCartney's 21st birthday party, on June 18, 1963, to which most of the Mersey groups had been invited. John got drunk and took exception to being asked about his 'Spanish honeymoon' by Bob Wooler, a Liverpool DJ. John then picked up something and hit him with it. Pete thinks it might have been a shovel, something pretty heavy anyway. An ambulance was called. People were trying to thump John for what he'd done, calling him a bastard.

"I tried to protect him and eventually got him away. He was still pretty drunk. On the way home, he suggested that we should swap wives. I'd just got married to Beth whom John and I had both known for some time. I thought it was a joke, but he said, 'No, let's try it, swap wives for the night.' I said, 'Fuck off.'

"John was in a bad way that night. But then so was Bob Wooler. He was injured for weeks. Eventually John and Brian apologised for what he'd done. Brian I think paid £200 damages – and the matter was forgotten."

# 8

## What Rod, Eric, Len And Colin Did Next

Rod stayed on at school, after all the others had left, hoping to get into Cambridge, which was what Mr Pobjoy was encouraging him to do. In 1959, he sat his 'A' levels and also the Cambridge entrance. He got a place at Cambridge, but not until 1960, which meant he had a spare year. He could have gone to Liverpool University in October 1959, as they would have taken him, there and then, but he decided to go back to school for another term. He was made Head Boy, re-sat the Cambridge entrance and this time got a scholarship, worth £60 a year, an honour for him and of course for Quarry Bank. Mr Pobjoy was most pleased. Rod was going to do Foreign Languages at Cambridge, just as he had done.

Rod went up to Trinity College, one of the big, rich, imposing colleges. There he met old Etonians and other public school boys, types he'd never come across before. He says he didn't feel prejudiced against, despite his strong Liverpool accent. "There were quite a few other Northern grammar school oiks. We'd make a point of eating black pudding, just to annoy other people."

Rod threw himself into the University's jazz and folk circles, where, of course, accents and social background are irrelevant. "At a bonfire party, I met Pete Clarke, clad in a studded motorcycling jacket and clutching his electric guitar. He was an old Etonian, but had lived some of his formative years in Columbus, Ohio, and was a fanatical country fan. Other great friends were Chris Rowly and John Morgen who were very keen on English folk music.

"We were a rather traditional lot in the folk society. I seem to remember Richard Stilgoe being thrown out of it for singing too much of his own material."

Rod also turned out for several jazz bands where he played his banjo. He learned the fiddle and the mandolin, playing with various friends. By now he had moved away from rock'n'roll which the nation's youth in general, inside and outside Cambridge, had become passionate about.

Instead Rod's main musical interest centred on American bluegrass music.

"I was introduced to bluegrass by a Trinity friend, Dick Quinnell, who played me a Flatt and Scruggs LP. I was hooked by the driving, exciting music, the sort of feeling I had first sensed behind skiffle. But skiffle was more rudimentary and basic. With bluegrass, there was some brilliant musicianship, inventive solo playing, smooth harmonies."

Rod also did the usual things, like punting and looking for girls, at which he wasn't very successful.

"Cambridge was desperately short of females. The ratio at the time was about one girl to ten blokes. No, I didn't do at all well. I never got lucky."

He enjoyed his French and Spanish studies, especially the linguistics side, but his most fun at Cambridge was playing music, in whatever form.

He still has a programme for a Footlights Smoking Concert, dated March 15, 1962, in which he played in a jazz group, accompanying various other performers. Alas, his own name is not listed, but it includes several who later became famous, including John Cleese, Bill Oddie, Tim Brooke-Taylor and Richard Stilgoe.

But while at Cambridge, Rod did manage to achieve something The Beatles had not then achieved. For Rag Day in November 1961, some Cambridge students had the idea of getting together a jazz band featuring as singer Herb Elliot, the Australian runner who had won the Gold medal for the mile at the Rome Olympics. He was then a student at Jesus. Rod was invited to join on banjo.

The band was called the Trad Grads and did well enough to be invited to the Decca recording studios in London to make a record. This was the company which famously turned down The Beatles, before EMI accepted them. Their record sold reasonably well, was played on Radio Luxembourg, and led to them making a live appearance with Cliff Mitchelmore on the BBC TV *Tonight* programme. Everyone, in the early Sixties, watched *Tonight*. Back home in Liverpool, Rod's dad not only watched it, glowing with pride, but got his camera out and took photographs of the screen. No videos, in those days. Rod, of course, still has the photos, being a keen collector of memorabilia.

In 1962, Rod was home in Liverpool for the Easter vacation when by chance he bumped in to John Lennon while walking past Owen Owen's department store in Clayton Square.

"I hadn't seen John for some time, but I'd heard from other friends in Liverpool that they'd been doing well in Hamburg and were about to make a record.

"I boasted to John that I'd beaten him to it – with our Trad Grads

record on Decca. In fact The Beatles had already recorded 'My Bonnie' in Hamburg, but I didn't know that at the time.

"But John must have been quite impressed by my boast because apparently he asked me if I could play the drums – and if so, could I come to Hamburg and play with them.

"I say 'apparently' because I'd actually forgotten his offer. It was some years later when my sister reminded me. She was just 12 at the time but had a clear memory of me coming home from that chat with John and telling my mother about the Hamburg offer. She remembers my mother saying it was the last thing I was going to do. I had to finish my degree. I wasn't going to Hamburg with 'that Lennon'. That's how every parent always referred to him.

"So, for a second time, I blew my chance of becoming a Beatle . . ."

Rod graduated from Cambridge in 1963 with a 2.2, a modest degree, but he had spent a lot of time music making.

He then didn't know what to do, in life, the universe, and all that, like so many bright young arts graduates, then and now. They fly successfully through our educational system, then emerge, blinking into the light, while the less clever, less intelligent, who might well have failed all exams, often have a passion which becomes a motivation in itself, even if all they want to do is reach The Toppermost of the Poppermost.

"I'd been good at jumping through hoops which other people had set for me. Now I had to set my own goals. And I couldn't think of any . . ."

★   ★   ★

Eric sat seven 'O' levels but managed to get only three, History, Maths and English Lit. Not enough to have much chance in the sixth form and anyway he wanted to leave and start work. The school, so he says, had given up on him. His mother, still a widow, would also appreciate any money he might bring in.

Aged 16, just about to be 17, he got a job as an apprentice engineer at Napiers on £3 a week. For the first few weeks, all he seemed to do was file down a metal cube, hour after hour, which bored him stiff. Once a week he went on day release to a local college, and hated it.

Most depressing of all was a kindly neighbour who took him to work each morning on the back of his motorbike. "I can still see him, going through his morning routine, putting his gloves and helmet on, as he had done for years and years. I thought that will be me soon, condemned to a life of drudgery. And what for? Just to operate some boring machine."

Eric managed to survive five months at Napiers, then he did what many fed up and frustrated Liverpool youths have done over the centuries. He went off to sea.

"My uncle was in the navy, and I suppose that inspired me. I think my mother was also pleased to get rid of me. I was still a pain at home, arguing with my sister all the time."

Eric sat some tests and was accepted as an officer cadet in the Merchant Navy. In January, 1958, he reported for duty at Liverpool docks to join the MV *Debrett*, one of the ships in the Lamport and Holt line. "I felt quite jaunty, setting off, till I arrived at the dockside and saw this huge ship towering over me. It made me feel so small and insignificant."

They set sail for Buenos Aires. Once they hit the tropics, all he seemed to do all day was change his clothes, getting in and out of his whites and into his boiler suit. As a cadet, he had to do his bit of deck scraping. But as an officer in the making, he had to dress up for meals.

His second boat was the *Devis* and this too went on a journey of some months round the globe. He and some other cadets used to amuse themselves while in port by altering the letters of the ship's name. They did it on the side of the boat away from the quay, so no one getting on, such as the captain, would see it. With a paintbrush, they changed the D in Devis into a P and the V into an N. The work of minutes, but oh what fun.

Eric did five trips on the *Devis*, under a captain known as Black McNeil from Barra. In Recife, he and the other cadets used to wander round the bars and dives in the harbour. "There were lots of prostitutes. The Yanks would have to pay, but we the British sailors, we could have it for nothing . . ."

Oh really? Hard to believe, or was it male teenage fantasy?

"No. Honestly. I remember a prostitute pulling out a knife, the first time I'd seen a woman with a knife. She was fighting over me with another woman. I didn't, of course, go with any of them. One of my friends did and caught a dose. By that time I was a senior cadet and got blamed for not having stopped him."

In January 1963, he was on board an oil tanker, the *Esso Bristol*, heading for the Persian Gulf, when on the BBC World Service he heard the strains of a song called 'Please Please Me' which, to his total amazement, had become number one.

"I was in my cabin, with two younger cadets. I'd become Third Mate by then. I was staggered when I heard the news. I told the cadets that I knew them, that I knew these Beatles. They didn't believe me. The Beatles were not, of course, very famous at the time, but they still thought I was making it up, that I knew anyone in a pop group.

"I had only vaguely heard what had been happening since I left. I'd last seen John and Paul the previous year, some time in 1962. I was home on leave and met them in Liverpool, in the street, in Church Street. John told me they had signed for EMI and 'Love Me Do' was about to come out.

"On another leave, John had come round to my house one afternoon. He often used to, because he knew I'd have bought records from the USA which hadn't been released here yet, things by Buddy Holly or Chuck Berry. On this day he asked if I had anything to drink. My mother had got married again, just after I'd left home to go to sea, and I'd bought my step-father a bottle of brandy as a present. I'd already given it to him, so it was his, but I couldn't think of what else to give John to drink. I went and found it. Me and John spent the afternoon playing records and we got

90

through the whole bottle. No, I don't think we got drunk. It was probably very cheap Spanish brandy.

"I knew John and the others had been to Hamburg by then, but he never talked about it and frankly, I wasn't really interested. I wasn't all that keen on the sort of music they were now playing. I never looked upon myself as a Beatles' fan. They were just blokes I'd happened to know earlier in my life . . ."

★   ★   ★

Len, the one who nearly died with meningitis, was in hospital from August 1958 till April 1959. During one of the visits from his old chums, he learned they were thinking of changing their name.

"John and Paul said they were going to be called Johnny & The Moondogs. Then they became The Silver Beatles – not Beetles but Beatles. I couldn't understand the spelling at first, then I thought it was pretty clever. Everyone was going on about 'Beat' music. They also said they'd done a demo disc of 'That'll Be The Day' and hoped to get a London recording contract. They seemed to think they were going places."

When Len came out of hospital, it was not clear where he was going. The other Quarrymen had moved on considerably in seven months and no mention was made of him returning to play with them. Home-made tea chests were now old hat, or at least old skiffle.

Len came home to 77 Lance Lane where he immediately noticed how small all the rooms were, after all those months lying in massive hospital wards.

He had missed a lot of schooling, including his exams, so decided to go to night school and get some 'O' levels, prepare himself to start some sort of job.

He still went to see Paul, riding over to Forthlin Road on his Raleigh Rudge bike, or hung around Menlove Avenue with Ivan and John, but didn't feel as involved as he had been in the old days. They were now playing at places he didn't know about, such as the Casbah.

In 1960, aged 18, Len became articled to a firm of architects in Liverpool at a salary of two guineas a week. As an old boy of the Institute, it was normal to aspire to a professional career or at least white-collar management, but he thinks it was his dad who fixed it up for him, perhaps through some contact in the Masons. In those days, you could become a qualified architect, or solicitor, without the need for a university degree, training on the job during the day then slogging away at night school or other courses in order to take the appropriate exams.

"Architecture seemed sort of charismatic, compared with being a solicitor. I'd quite enjoyed drawing things like arches and buildings when I was at school. But, really, deep down, I wasn't bothered what I did." Len, of course, was always the cool, laid-back, unruffled Quarryman.

The office was in the centre of Liverpool so in his lunch hour Len used to join the queue in Mathew Street to get into the Cavern to watch The Beatles. Everyone then alive in Liverpool later boasted they went to the Cavern at lunchtime, which must have meant crowds of hundreds of thousands.

As an old chum and fellow performer, Len could have gone backstage, talked to them as Pete did, but he felt embarrassed in his suit and tie.

"I was on the road to a career, which the world seemed to think I should go down. That was what one did. But it was a bit depressing, seeing them enjoy themselves so much. I wasn't, really. I felt music was in my blood, but I wasn't doing anything about it."

During 1962, Len bumped into them twice. On the first occasion he happened to be down at the Pier Head when the *Royal Iris*, a ferry boat which did dance cruises along the Mersey, was just docking. Out of the boat stepped John, Paul, George and Ringo. They'd been playing on the boat, as they did several times. John introduced Len to Ringo, whom he'd never met. He asked Len how archy-tecture was getting on. Then they all went off. That was the last time Len ever saw John.

The other occasion was in Smithdown Road when he was riding on his Raleigh bike. He heard someone shouting his name behind him, running to catch up.

"It was Paul. He was wearing orange shoes which I complimented him on. That pleased him. He boasted they'd just got an invitation to appear on Granada TV. I wanted to say 'all right for some, enjoying what you're doing and getting paid for it.' But I didn't. I just wished him the best of luck, as you do.

"And that was it. I never saw Paul again either. Not in the flesh.

"When I did start seeing them all again, it was on television. . . ."

★ ★ ★

When Colin left The Quarrymen, he hung up his drumsticks, or whatever it is that drummers do when they retire. Find a bungalow, perhaps, and call it Dundrummin. In Colin's case, he put his drums on top of the wardrobe. And there they remained. He made no effort to join another group and no one invited him.

"I was never a great drummer and by that time I'd had enough."

He also had other things he wanted to do, such as going out drinking with his mates on Saturday nights without having to worry about being sober enough to clamber onto some stage and bash his drums.

"I did go out with a lot of mad lads for a while. Nothing I'm particularly proud of today. I got in a few fights, just the normal skirmishes really, which you get into at that age."

He also went out with quite a few girls, nothing serious for some time, till it dawned on him that the girl he fancied most was on his home patch – his own 'Aunty' Joan, the younger sister of his stepmother, Peggy.

"It slowly moved on from Joan taking me to the pictures to me taking her. It was Joan who taught me to jive, dancing to rock music in our front room."

Joan worked in the Co-op, an assistant on the counter in one of those shops where they sent the cash whizzing across the ceiling on a little chain to some cashier, hidden in a far corner. As a kid, I loved going into the Co-op, and into Liptons, just to watch and listen while the little cages rattled backwards and forwards. Come on, Colin, that's what really attracted you to Joan, a chance to pull her chain.

"Yeah, I did love watching it. I was always waiting for one of them to crash, so I could rush and pick up the money . . ."

Having a steady girlfriend meant going to the Grafton with Joan on a Saturday night rather than out drinking with his mates. "The Grafton was very select. They didn't let in any single blokes, just couples, so there was never any trouble."

At work, Colin settled down to a steady career at Guy Rogers, furniture makers. He finished his five-year apprenticeship as an upholsterer in 1960 and was kept on. Not all apprentices were. I remember when my younger brother finished his apprenticeship as an electrician, he was immediately paid off and they took on a new fifteen-year-old at a piddling wage.

"All the apprentices in my year were kept on. We were lucky, but there was a lot of work around. The firm was doing well. And I enjoyed it. No complaints. There is a certain satisfaction in upholstery, in making or repairing a suite or a chair. Mind you, I'm the sort of person who would have been content doing almost any job. It just happened to be upholstery."

In 1960, he was earning around £6 a week, including bonuses. He got paid eight shillings for every chair completed. He was meant to do three in a day, which came to 24 shillings. Any more, and you got a small extra bonus.

"For years and years I used to come home with blue teeth."

Working on blue plastic furniture for G Plan, eating blue sweets, sucking your marking pen?

"No, tacks. In those days, chairs and sofas were made out of wood, horsehair and coconut matting. You nailed everything with tacks. The minute you started work in the morning, you filled your mouth with tacks. That's how you carried on, all day long. When I came home, my mouth had turned blue. I used to have to brush my teeth as soon as I got through the front door before I sat down for me tea."

In that first year after leaving the Quarrymen, he had no contact with them, did not move in circles they moved in, knew nobody at the Liverpool College of Art, but he did by chance meet John a couple of times in the period when he was going out drinking with his mates on those Saturday evenings.

"It was on the last bus home to Woolton from town, the Number 5. John had been saying goodnight to that girl he eventually married, his first wife. Cynthia, was it? We didn't talk much, just said hello and that. I was probably slumped, having drunk too much. But I do remember him telling me they'd got a new drummer called Pete. It must have been Pete Best, I suppose. And that was the last time I ever spoke to John, or any of them.

"I never knew about the Casbah or even heard they'd been to Hamburg. That was a surprise to me, when I learned later on.

"But the biggest surprise was one day in 1962 when I came home from work. I'd cleaned my teeth and was waiting for my tea while watching the telly. It was always on in them days, usually on Granada. There on the screen were the lads. I thought, Bloody hell. What a shock to see John's smiling face. They were playing 'Love Me Do'. They were quite good, though I didn't like the song all that much. The one I remember liking was 'Baby's In Black'.

"But it was seeing them really, not what they were playing, that was what shocked me. I could see they had improved and they sounded better.

"I suppose I should have seen at the time how good they might be one day, but I didn't really. John didn't strike me as someone determined to make it. I always thought John was come day, go day. You know, what will be, will be. He didn't seem all that bothered either way with the group.

"But I should have seen it in Paul. He did have musical talent, that was clear enough, but looking back, I should also have realised how focused Paul was. That should have been the sign, the writing on the wall, that they might go places. But at the time, I have to admit that none of these things ever struck me. It doesn't, does it? It's just what you're doing at the time.

"Not long after that, you could hardly avoid them. They were every-where. A lot of people at work knew I'd played with The Quarrymen. I couldn't keep it secret, could I, though I used to deny it with new people. Someone would always tell them, 'See that Colin Hanton over there on that bench, he used to play with The Beatles.' So they'd come over and ask me if it was true. I'd say, 'They're pulling your leg, take no notice of them,' so that would confuse them."

But why didn't you want to admit it?

"Oh you know what Liverpool people are like. They love taking the piss. Oh here's Colin, he could have been a Beatle. I hated all that. It really got up my nose . . ."

# 9

# Men At Work

If 1963 was the year The Beatles were busy conquering the UK, then 1964 was the year they conquered the USA. Which, of course, means the World. What else after all is there left to prove, once you have proved yourself in America.

In February, 1964, they did *The Ed Sullivan Show*, live, which was watched by an audience of 73 million, breaking the then record for the world's largest ever TV audience.

In March, just to prove that John could write as well as sing, his first book came out. *In His Own Write*, published by the leading literary publisher of the day, Jonathan Cape. It became a bestseller. How that must have amazed and bemused those English teachers who had taught him, or suffered him, at Quarry Bank School.

They made their first film, *A Hard Day's Night*, which again was a worldwide success. On July 10, 1964 they returned in triumph to Liverpool for its northern premiere. They landed at Speke airport and followed a pre-arranged route through the streets of Liverpool to a civic reception in their honour at the Town Hall. It was estimated that 200,000 Liverpudlians turned out and lined the streets, just to catch a glimpse or at least cheer their heroes.

By 1965, they'd had it all, really, fulfilled all the fantasies which had kept them going back in the late Fifties, trailing on buses, hoping for a few bob or at least a free pint. They now had all the money they could sleep with, all the women they could eat, all the fame they could stomach. Unlike some others.

★　★　★

Pete can remember where he was when he first heard 'Love Me Do' on the radio. Not serving teas and snacks that day in the Old Dutch Cafe in Liverpool. He and his wife Beth were on holiday at his sister's house in the south.

"It was a Sunday and they were going through the Top Twenty. Suddenly they played 'Love Me Do' which they announced as the new number 17. I couldn't believe it. We worshipped the Top Twenty in those days. Everyone listened to it, waiting to hear what was up or down. I had imagined that everyone who was on it was a 'Star'. So I couldn't believe The Beatles were on it. They were not what I had imagined 'Stars' to be. So when I heard it, I thought it's fucking John.

"I didn't actually much like 'Love Me Do'. It was sort of flat and repetitive. I preferred 'PS I Love You'.

"When they did *Please Please Me*, their first LP, John played it to me at Mimi's. He was home for the weekend. He had an old gramophone and he played it over and over again. He was so thrilled to have an LP. He kept on saying, 'It's fucking brilliant, fucking brilliant.' I don't think he had believed they could ever produce an LP."

On another weekend, John rang Pete at the Old Dutch caff to say he was in Liverpool, asking Pete to come round and meet him at Mimi's.

"John was clearing out his old papers and drawings and books he'd done as a kid, collecting them all up to take to London with him. I helped him put stuff in sacks and bundles.

"He told me about the great time they were having on tour, all the girls they were screwing, how Mal's job [their road manager] was to pick out the best ones and line them up for afterwards.

"He also went on about America, America, how that was the one they still had to crack. They wouldn't have made it, not till they succeeded in America.

"Then he asked me how I was getting on, how was the job? I said OK, but it wasn't really going well. Business was bad. People weren't spending money, with Christmas coming up. He asked me what I was doing for Christmas, and I said not a lot.

"Out of his pocket, he pulled a brown paper envelope and said, 'Here Pete, this is for you, have a happy Christmas.' It was his wages, still unopened. I said I don't want this. But he said, 'Don't be daft, Pete, take the fucking thing.'

"I didn't open it till next day. When I did, I found there were ten crisp £5 notes, £50 in all. At the time, I was earning about £10 a week. So it was a lot."

The reason John was scratching around amongst his old drawings became clear when *In His Own Write* was published.

"He showed me the proofs in advance and I recognised quite a few of the drawings and some of the doggerel. He said he had wanted to

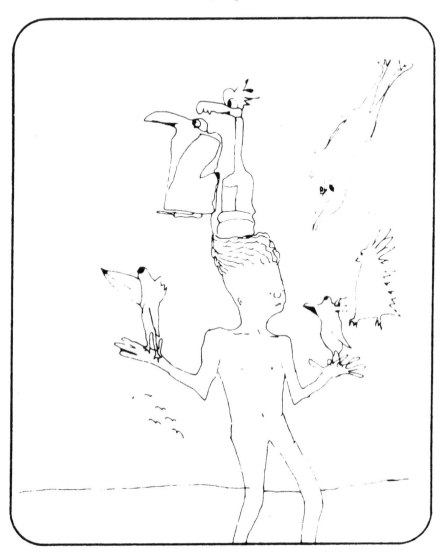

(Image from IN HIS OWN WRITE by John Lennon published by Jonathan Cape. Used by permission of The Random House Group Limited.)

dedicate it to me with the inscription 'To Pete, Who Got it First' but then he thought Mimi might get offended if his first book was dedicated to me.

"But if you look at the dedication page, you'll see there's a drawing of a curly haired fellow with some strange birds perched on his head and arms.

That's me, the curly hair bloke. It was John's way of dedicating it to me without hurting Mimi's feelings. I felt very flattered."

During another visit to Liverpool, at the end of 1963, John invited Pete and Beth to come to London after Christmas to see their first Christmas Show to be held at the Astoria, Finsbury Park.

John also said that Pete must get out of his caff and do something better. Was there anything he wanted to do? Pete said he quite fancied running a betting shop.

"They were just starting to spring up all over the country and sounded a good idea, if you could afford one. John said he'd fix me up with some money, anything to get me out of the lousy caff. He said he'd tell Brian to let me have a couple of thousand to get started. I said Brian wouldn't like that. He said, 'Fuck Brian. It's my money. I'll do what I like with it.'"

A few weeks later, Pete went round to Brian's office, NEMS in Chapel Street, to pick up a cheque for £2,000.

Brian wasn't there, but Pete was led into Brian's office to wait for him. As he waited, the phone rang, so Pete picked it up. An American voice asked for Mr Epstein. Pete said he wasn't in. "Tell him it's Ed Sullivan's office. Mr Sullivan would like to speak with Mr Epstein."

Pete had never heard of Ed Sullivan, but took the name and telephone number and wrote it down. When Brian eventually arrived, and after some inconsequential chat, Pete casually gave him the note.

"Brian was ecstatic. He says do I know what this means, do I realise who Ed Sullivan is? I had no idea, of course."

Pete not only got his cheque for £2,000, there and then, but an offer from Brian of a job as his PA.

"I didn't think he really meant it. It was just out of all the excitement, but he said no. He'd been impressed at how I'd answered the phone and taken the message – as if anyone else couldn't have done it.

"I did think about it, well for a few moments, but with getting the £2,000, I now had the chance to start my own business. That was what I'd always wanted. I never wanted to work for someone else. So I turned his offer down."

But the week after Christmas, Pete and Beth did go down to London to watch The Beatles perform at Finsbury Park, just to see how they were getting on in London.

★　★　★

After graduation from Cambridge in 1963 with a 2.2 in Modern Languages,

Rod went off to Germany for a year to teach English at the Berlitz language school in Regensburg in Bavaria. It was partly putting off trying to decide what to do in life, but at the same time he thought that learning German, to add to his French and Spanish, would be a useful thing to do.

Most of his weekends in Germany were spent playing music. On Friday nights, he played in the Old Blackfeet Jazzband in the cellar of a pub. On Saturdays, he played guitar in a mainstream band in a converted crematorium. Sounds a bit like his Quarrymen days, from the venues if not the music.

"I asked some of the German students I was teaching if they had heard of The Beatles. Because they had played for so long in Hamburg, they had become well known in Germany, so I'd been led to believe. But not one of them had heard of The Beatles, not in 1963."

Back in Liverpool in 1964, he went to see Mr Pobjoy, his old headmaster, a social visit, during which he told him he didn't know what to do next. Pobjoy suggested teaching. With his foreign languages, he was sure Rod could always get some sort of teaching job. There and then, Pobjoy picked up the phone, rang a colleague at a neighbouring Liverpool school, and Rod was taken on. In those days, it was not necessary to have a teaching certificate or diploma to be hired as a teacher in a state school. A degree was sufficient, though the pay was slightly more if you did have teaching qualifications.

Rod taught modern languages in several Liverpool schools for the next three and a half years – while at the same time spending a great deal of his spare moments making music. He played the fiddle in a Ceilidh band and helped to form The Bluegrass Ramblers, playing mandolin and fiddle. They did an audition for Hughie Green's *Opportunity Knocks* TV talent show, but opportunity didn't knock.

In 1968, Rod decided he'd had enough of teaching. He could see himself stuck at it till he was 60, but what else could he do? He was aged 27, unattached, with no responsibilities. In theory he could go anywhere, do anything, try anything legal, just to get out of teaching.

"I applied for a job at Ford motor works, a manual job on the production line. When I got interviewed, and they saw I'd been to Cambridge, they thought I was either mad or an anarchist. That was a fear at the time – that I might be trying to get in to sabotage the plant."

Today, of course, it is not unusual to find graduates, even from the smartest universities, employed in the humblest of jobs, hence the joke: "What do you say to someone with a PhD from Cambridge?" Answer: "A Big Mac and French Fries please . . ."

Anyway, Rod was turned down. He then answered an advert for a job as a locust control officer in Saudi Arabia, but didn't get that either. Having left teaching, and failed to get another job, he ended up in the dole queue at Garston, scene of so many excitements in the early Quarrymen career.

"A lot of people didn't believe I'd gone to Cambridge. I never mentioned it, but if it ever came out, I'd be asked the same questions – how did a scruffy bastard like you come to go to Cambridge? 'I passed the bloody entrance exam.' That's all I could say. So mostly I kept it very quiet.

"On the whole, I'd say it's been a disadvantage in life, having gone to Cambridge. People become suspicious of you. They think you must be cleverer than you are, that you'll be after their job.

"I was good at languages, had a talent for it, but it's just like having a talent for gymnastics. It's nothing special.

"I would say that some of the stupidest people I've ever met, with the least common sense, were people I met when I was at Cambridge.

"If I had stayed in an area where a Cambridge degree mattered, such as teaching, or then gone into another area with people from similar academic backgrounds, like the law, then that would have been fine. Cambridge would have been a definite advantage.

"But I eventually found myself moving into an area where a degree didn't matter, where no one was bothered about what sort of education you'd had. That's why I was always able to keep it quiet I'd been to Cambridge. People change their attitude to you, if they know. So from then on, I didn't let them know . . ."

★　★　★

Eric did well in the merchant navy, passing all the appropriate exams, and between 1958 and 1964 he rose through the various officer grades until he reached the heights of Second Mate. Then he had a big decision to make.

When he'd first joined up, he had the same girlfriend he'd had from his Quarrymen days. On his first home leave, he went out with her again. But on his next leave, he found she had chucked him and was now going out with one of his old friends from Quarry Bank – whom she later married.

After that, he didn't have a regular girlfriend for some years, allowing him to concentrate on his naval career, but eventually he started going out with Relda, a Liverpool girl from a Welsh–Scottish family, whom he met while on leave at the Mardi Gras Jazz Club in Liverpool. She had a good job, working for Globe Insurance. When they got engaged, Eric realised it was time to give up the sea.

"I had seen too many marriages and relationships collapse. You can't have a happy marriage and be at sea. I was still enjoying it, and even today, I often think of the many good memories of the life I had at sea, but I knew I had to leave.

"I had become a navigation officer, but I realised my sort of expertise would not translate to any sort of shore job. So I knew it would be very hard, once I came ashore."

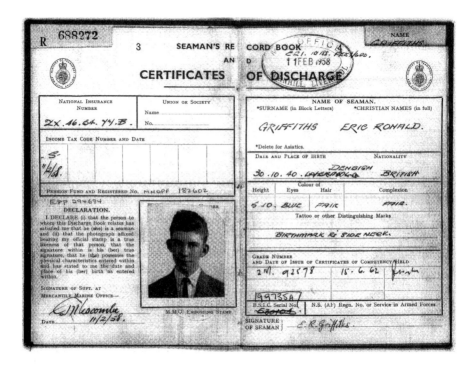

They got married in 1964 at St Peter's Church in Woolton, of course, the ceremony being conducted by the Rev. Pryce-Jones, who was still there. Eric had not been in the Sunday School with John and Pete, as he only arrived in the area aged ten, but he had been in the church youth club. "We had to go to a certain number of church services before he would marry us. I remember looking at my watch and thinking, how long is this going on. I'll never get to the pub before it closes . . ."

Eric then had great trouble finding any sort of job. He sold encyclopaedias for a while, was a central heating salesman, drove a van carrying spares.

"In the navy, I had been responsible for the lives of many men and millions of pounds worth of navigation equipment. I was on £1,300 a year at sea, quite a lot in those days. On shore, I was getting a third of that and being either ignored or looked down upon, especially when I turned up somewhere driving a van. But it was an interesting experience, taught me some valuable lessons about handling people. I like to think I would never be dismissive or rude to people doing apparently ordinary jobs."

He worked in the Ford motor works, in a glue factory, followed by 12 months with Littlewoods mail order company. In all, he had three years in various jobs. While The Beatles were conquering the world, he, like Rod, was still trying to find a little niche, a little role for himself.

Then in 1967, aged 27, he chanced upon a new career. At Littlewoods Pools, he did a work study course, realised he quite enjoyed it, and in 1967 applied for a job at the Home Office as a works study officer. He was accepted and found himself working in the prison service.

Eric's job was to analyse the work which prisoners were doing in prison, whether sewing mail bags or making clothes. He had to study the time spent, the amount produced, where it was used or sold, and suggest what other things they might be doing. The work took him round the country for a few years, from Market Harborough, where he was mainly employed at Gartree Prison, to Halsted in Essex.

"My hairiest moment was at Albany Prison on the Isle of Wight. There had been a riot by prisoners and one of their complaints had been the works incentive scheme. They were mainly making things out of timber. Anyway they all decided to strike and I was sent in to get them back to work. The team leader responsible for Albany had had a heart attack. I had to pick up the pieces.

"The prison staff just seemed to disappear, leaving me to address 60 prisoners on my own. Some of them were pretty nasty customers. There was one huge guy who was in for cutting off women's breasts. He didn't like me, I could see, and he and some others were slowly backing me against a wall. But then two London mobsters came forward to help me. They stood side by side with me as I finished my talk. I finally did persuade them all to go back to work. It turned out the mobsters had been at Gartree where I'd been helpful to them in some way.

"After that incident, I could do no wrong in the Governor's eyes . . ."

So well done, Eric. Could have been nasty if he had been forced into a corner. But then life for The Beatles was often just as hairy, trapped in a corridor at the back of a stadium or in a hotel bedroom by thousands of

American or Japanese teenagers screaming outside, wanting to do, well, who knows what with them.

★   ★   ★

In 1963, Len's mother died. He thinks this was the final straw which made him give up his articles and any hope of becoming a qualified architect, though for a while he did keep on with a course at the Liverpool College of Building. He then got a job with Birkenhead Council, in the architect's department, as an architect's assistant. By this time he was going out with Sue, a student nurse.

Sue had once been asked out by Ringo Starr, while at a Butlin's holiday camp in North Wales. "But I said no. He was too ugly." She later went out with Clive Walley, brother of Nigel Walley, The Quarrymen's original so-called manager.

"He had boasted that his brother had been in The Quarrymen, then when I started going out with Len, he said he had been in The Quarrymen. I thought, What is going on? I'd never heard of The Quarrymen.

"I hadn't even heard of The Beatles, when I first started going out with Len. I was probably the only girl in Liverpool not to have heard about them. This must have been, let me see, 1962. As a student nurse, doing 42 hours a week, all you do off duty is sleep. You are out of touch with most things."

They got married in 1965 and found a flat in Broad Street, Liverpool. Two sons quickly came along, Robert in 1966 and Jonathan in 1968.

Sue was born and brought up in a tough part of inner Liverpool compared with Len and his suburban school chums. She had also become a committed Christian, a member of a Pentecostal sect called The People's Church. Len had always had a vague spiritual attitude to life, or as others might have put it, he'd always been a bit of a dreamer. He became as committed to the sect as Sue, attending their local church services and was soon going to meetings and gatherings all over the country.

Not long after they got married, while still in the full flow of her religious fervour, Sue decided to burn all Len's Quarrymen photos – some of them never seen to this day, including one of them wearing tassled shirts. A bit drastic, Sue. It wasn't the tassles, was it?

"Our church at the time was preaching the wickedness of pop groups, especially The Beatles. They were said to encourage young people to sinful behaviour. We had to rid ourselves of all connection with that sort of life. In my case, what happened was that at a prayer meeting, I asked for prayers for Len who was poorly at the time. One of the elders advised me to get rid of The Quarrymen connections. So that's why I burned all Len's Quarrymen relics."

Len, at the time, being equally involved in the Pentecostal movement, didn't object. And he didn't put much value on them anyway, thinking they would never be of any interest to anyone.

"We then met someone who told us about this Pentecostal church down in Kent," says Len. "I was so impressed by the joy he obviously felt, that we decided to go there and join. Oh yes, Sue and I agreed. We shared our faith together."

So in 1971 Len gave up his steady job with Birkenhead council, packed their two young boys into the back of their Vauxhall Viva, and all four drove off to Kent, looking for joy.

★ ★ ★

Colin also got married in 1965, to Joan, his aunty, at St Dunstan's Church of England in Wavertree. Joan was brought up C of E and Colin RC, but he had mostly given up going to mass or taking confession.

They bought a terraced house off Penny Lane for £2,400. In 1967 their daughter Alison was born, followed 18 months later by Christine.

At work in the Guy Rogers furniture factory, Colin was promoted to a prototype upholsterer. The money wasn't much more, but it was considered a better, more desirable job. "You worked more with the designers. They would design and draw a new suite and you would have to make it, so it was interesting, yeah."

In the summer, though, they were often laid off as the factory went on to short time. "This happened every summer. People saved up to buy their new suites in time for Christmas. So we were always busy pre-Christmas and slack in the summer. But what they did at Guy Rogers was put everyone on a three day week. Oh, we were miles ahead of Ted Heath in doing that.

"No one lost their job, as such. You just got less money and had two days off. So what I'd do was look around for a foreigner. I usually got one or two to tide me over, like."

The use of the term 'foreigner' is interesting. It means unofficial, freelance work, outside your normal employment. I'd always thought it was a purely Carlisle term, not Liverpool. "In Glasgow," said Colin, "they call it homers." Thanks, Colin.

On July 10, 1964, Colin had a dental appointment in town . "I'm pretty sure it was a Friday. [It was.] I'd arranged the appointment for late Friday so I could get off early from work at Guy Rogers in Speke then rush home and change before going to the dentist.

"I had a Morris Traveller at the time. My route took me up King's Drive, over the hill and along Menlove Avenue, through Penny Lane, up Smithdown Road, up Upper Parliament Street.

"When I got to Menlove Avenue, by the Derby Arms, there was a lot of people standing around. I thought, This is funny. As I drove on, I saw more crowds, just standing waiting. I was confused by them, wondering what was going on.

"At Penny Lane, I saw The Beatles banners. I had forgotten this was the day they were coming. And I hadn't anyway realised this was the route they were going to take on the way from Speke to the Town Hall.

"You know what Liverpool crowds are like, when they're standing around waiting for something to happen. Any car that happens to go past, gets a big cheer or a wave. So all the way to Upper Parliament Street, till I got to the dentist, I was being cheered and waved at.

"I was in good time, so when I'd parked, I walked back to the junction of Upper Parliament Street and Smithdown Road – and was just in time to see the lads crawling past in their stretch limo.

"John and Paul were leaning out of the window on the side nearest me. I don't know why I did it, but I found myself shouting out their names. Sort of involuntary. Obviously, they couldn't hear me. And I'm sure they didn't see me either. Or were even aware that I still existed . . ."

# 10

## Pete Goes South

Pete's first experience of The Beatles' London life was at Christmas time 1963, invited by John to see their first Christmas Show at Finsbury Park. He and his wife Beth arrived on Boxing Day at the flat which John had taken in Kensington. John had already gone over to the theatre, so Pete had to make his own way there.

"I took a taxi, but even miles away the traffic was hopeless, so I got out and walked. As I got near, the whole place was pandemonium, the streets packed with screaming teenagers and flustered bobbies trying to cope with an hysterical mob.

"On stage, The Beatles were in their grey collarless Pierre Cardin suits and their hair uniformly styled in mop tops. They looked like four cuddly toys – a bit different from the scruffy blokes who had played in the Cavern.

"During a pause between numbers, John grabbed the microphone and shouted, 'Hi ya Pete!' I screamed and waved back. I knew he couldn't possibly have spotted me, being so short-sighted, but the stage manager had given him a signal when I arrived."

After the show, Pete went backstage, had drinks, then left with John to go home in his Rolls Royce. "We had to run the gauntlet of fans to get to it. When we got in, the Rolls was literally covered with girls, crawling all over it, trying to get a hand through a window to touch John. 'This is the life,' I said to John. 'No it's fucking not,' said John. 'One of these days one of these fucking maniacs is going to get hold of me and tear me to fucking death.'

"I knew from the old days that John didn't actually like physical contact, even from his family and close friends. Most of all he hated strangers touching him – yet here he was, surrounded by thousands, wanting to get at him."

Each evening, Pete went to the show, then afterwards, he and John would go round the clubs till the early hours.

"About four o'clock one morning, we were desperate for an early breakfast. The only caff we could find was one at Kensington Air Terminal, quite near his flat. We had eggs and bacon as we watched all the travellers arrive to fly off somewhere.

" 'Let's get on a fucking plane,' said John, 'the first one that we can get on.' I said, 'Don't be daft, John. You've got a concert tonight.' 'Fuck the concert,' said John. 'Let's just fly off to the Canaries for the day, have a couple of hours sun, then fly back.'

"It was the sort of daft idea he'd always had, but now he could fulfil his daftest fantasies. So I thought, 'Why not?' Better than going back to work in the Old Dutch Caff.

"John told his chauffeur to take us out to London airport. When we got there, we asked what was the first plane out – and it was Manchester. Manchester! That's when we decided it was a bit daft after all. So we came home and went to bed . . ."

On New Year's Eve, George and Ringo called on John and they all set off for a party given by a new, thrusting millionaire called John Bloom who had made his money from washing machines. (I remember him well. I once went for drinks at his private apartment behind Grosvenor House Hotel and was later invited to his wedding, which I went to, for the laughs and the free food, and found myself sitting at a table beside his bank manager who didn't really know him either.)

"John had met John Bloom somewhere, probably in a club, and he'd told John that if they gave him a million pounds, he could give them back two million in a month. That was typical of John to believe this. He was a sucker for any sort of miracle worker. He didn't give Bloom the money, but they agreed to go to his party.

"We got dropped off at what we thought was his address, but we couldn't find his place. We saw in New Year's Eve, still wandering round the streets in Mayfair.

"John got spotted by a posh looking woman in a fur coat coming out of a hotel. 'It's you,' she screamed. 'It's a Beatle. Wait till I tell everybody . . .'

" 'You silly fucking cow,' said John, 'acting like this at your age, you should be fucking ashamed of yourself.'

"The woman didn't take in what John was saying. She just chuntered on about what she would tell her husband.

"John said that was typical. 'People are so blinded by the image, they don't listen to a single word I say.' "

Pete enjoyed his week living it up in London, but then returned to reality in Liverpool, back to work behind the counter of the Old Dutch

Caff. Unlike Colin, he was recognised by them that day when The Beatles did their triumphal return.

"They actually went past the Old Dutch. Ringo spotted my face in the crowd and shouted, 'Pete, Pete.' The others turned round and I could see them waving at me through the back window as they drove on." Lucky Pete.

Which he was, because he had the £2,000 which John had let him have to open a betting shop. What happened to it, Pete?

"It's a long story. It took months to find a suitable site, till at last I saw one near Anfield football ground. I thought with 50,000 people going past every Saturday afternoon, it was bound to be a good location.

"I had to go to the magistrates court to get a licence – and as my luck would have it, a local Anfield cleric turned up to oppose it. He didn't want such a dubious enterprise near his church. I said, 'Let's do a deal. I won't open my shop on a Sunday if you don't conduct your services during the rest of the week.' The magistrate wasn't amused – and my application was rejected."

Yes, but what happened to the money?

"Dunno. Just went. I did buy myself a car and the rest sort of just went . . .

"Yeah, I did tell John later. He said, 'Fucking hell, Pete, I would have done the same myself with two grand in my pocket.' "

As The Beatles went on collecting more fame and fortune, John brought up the subject again of helping Pete to start a proper business and get him out of the Old Dutch caff.

"He said money was raining on him, so it was about time I had something that would make money for me. I should find something really good. Something around £20,000."

So Pete looked around again, this time for an existing shop. He's not quite sure why he fancied a shop, but his mother had one and it seemed an easy enough business for someone with no qualifications to get into, if you had a bit of money.

At first he looked in the Liverpool area, but didn't see anything he liked. He was on holiday on the south coast, staying with his sister Jean and her husband, when he came across a little supermarket for sale on Hayling Island, near the Isle of Wight. It was really a general store, selling everything from hardware and post cards to food and drink and also included a post office. It was primarily a seasonal business, aimed at the summer tourist trade, when it did very well, then went very quiet in the winter. But the location was pretty, a nice place to live.

"It was a fucking sight prettier than Liverpool. And it had a flat above, which was another attraction. At the time, we were still living with Beth's parents in Liverpool. I'd never even heard of Hayling Island till then, but we both jumped at it. It seemed good value, for £20,000."

It's always hard to equate old values, to compare the prices then and now. In 1965, you could have bought a house in Hampstead for £20,000 which would be worth £2 million today. But that's probably an extreme comparison. In 1965, a top executive or top barrister on £20,000 would be on £500,000 today. In 1964 I bought my first Mini Minor for £500. Today, the average small car is almost £10,000. Let's just multiply by ten and say it was like giving someone £200,000 today. In other words, John gave Pete a massive amount of money.

It wasn't exactly a gift, as John implied when he mentioned it during my research on the biography, nor was it a loan in the normal sense. One of The Beatles' accountants checked out the shop first, to make sure it existed, and was a reasonable buy – then it was purchased in John's name. He always therefore owned it, but took no share of the profits or received any rent or any interest. That had been clear in the document drawn up between John and Pete. All the same, a remarkably generous act, which could easily have been wasted. But as John told me, he didn't care.

Pete and his wife Beth took it over at Easter, 1965. They lived in the flat above which was where they had their son Matthew, born in 1967.

The shop did well so Pete decided to expand and open a clothes shop as well. To do this he borrowed another £9,000 from John. He put in a manager – but it didn't work out and he sold the shop. But the super-market itself continued to thrive and do good business.

★   ★   ★

One of the attractions, for both Pete and John, about Pete moving to the south coast, was that Pete was now living relatively near, compared with Liverpool. By car, he was just an hour away from where John, Cynthia and son Julian now lived in a mock Tudor mansion called Kenwood on a private estate in Weybridge, Surrey. Ringo was just down the hill. George was not far away in Esher. Paul was the only one who had stayed in London, buying a house in St John's Wood, not far from Abbey Road.

Pete spent many weekends with John at Kenwood, observing and hearing about all the things happening in his life since he had left Liverpool. "On the 1965 USA tour, they had this house full of starlets and models. John said he fucked one under the stairs, one in the bathroom, one on the kitchen floor. In one night, he fucked seven of them. So he said.

"It was during that trip they met Elvis. The Beatles wanted him to come to their hotel but he refused, so they had to go to his place. John was dead excited about meeting one of his all-time heroes. Elvis just grunted when they arrived, and then watched television. But John loved Colonel Parker, Elvis's manager. He told them all about his days as a lion tamer. John thought Parker was a real showman, a great character, but meeting Elvis was a non event."

That's Pete's memory of what John told him at the time. A bit different from the memories which Paul, George and Ringo recalled thirty-five years later for *Anthology*, published in 2000. "It was one of the great meetings of my life," said Paul. "I think he liked us."

Beth, Pete's wife, often went up with Pete for the weekend. At George's house one evening, after a party with all four Beatles, Beth took off all her clothes and threw herself in the pool. "George responded by switching on the spotlight over the pool and we all cheered." As if they had never seen a naked woman before? Just a laugh, says Pete.

Another time he went with The Beatles to a party held by Lionel Bart, creator of *Oliver* and other musicals. "He lived in this amazing palace in Chelsea, crowned with turrets. There were antiques in every room. He had his own cinema. One of his lavatories was in the shape of a carved wooden throne, with carpeted steps leading up on to it. There were also lots of strategically placed one-way mirrors."

If they stayed in, over the weekend, Pete would just muck around with John, playing with his toys, chatting, playing silly word games, just as they had always done. When John wrote 'Help', Pete says that "I do appreciate you bein' round" was a reference to him.

John liked to stay up late while Cyn liked to go to bed early. "By 1965 their marriage had settled into a state of peaceful co-existence. They had little in common, but at that stage, I wouldn't have said their marriage was unhappy. The only row I remember between them was when Cyn wanted to buy a Porsche and John was against her having such a fast car. In the end he relented.

"John didn't do much with Julian. He spoiled him with expensive toys, but he had a low tolerance level. He'd put Julian out of the room and say he was working or 'talking to Pete'.

"During my visits, I got to know the other Beatles as well. I grew very fond of George. In fact he originally wanted to put money into my super-market, but John did it on his own.

111

"The one I found hardest to really know was Paul. He was always friendly and charming with strangers, but he played his cards close to his chest.

"Paul was the one Beatle who posed any challenge to John's authority in the group. John did see him as a more or less equal. He admired and respected him for his self-discipline and all-round musical facilities – which John thought he was relatively lacking. But John never forgot that The Beatles had started out as his band. Sometimes it irritated him when Paul appeared to imagine otherwise.

"But until about 1968, I never witnessed or heard about any serious disagreement between them."

Pete also got to know The Beatles' wives and girlfriends, but didn't care much for Jane Asher. "She seemed aristocratic, as if she was cut from finer cloth than the other Beatles' women.

"John preferred it when I came on my own, without Beth. 'We don't want the women hanging around,' he would say. One of his favourite phrases was 'women should be obscene and not heard'."

By the end of 1966, John was becoming less interested in going out. "He immersed himself in books about Christianity or the Dead or Tibet or Freud, looking for new ideas and philosophies all the time. He was really bored, that was the main thing. He thought he'd become Nowhere Man, which was why he wrote the song.

"For a time, John gave up alcohol and meat. When he caught me stuffing my face with steaks and burgers, he'd say, 'You know that's someone's mother you're eating.' I once caught him going through the Bible for clues to Christ's eating habits. He was convinced Jesus was a vegetarian, but he couldn't prove it.

"Just for amusement, for something to do, he wanted me to commit a robbery with him. He knew that The Beatles could now enter any building in the world, just walk in, and be welcomed. So he thought he'd steal the Crown Jewels. Just walk into the Tower of London and take them.

" 'No one would ever suspect The Beatles, Pete,' he said. 'We are allowed in anywhere.'

" 'Yes, but how do I get out afterwards,' I said. 'You can do what you want, John. I'll come and visit you in jail.' "

One escape, from the boredom of being a Beatle, was drugs. "They first got going on LSD through George's dentist. After that, they were at it regularly."

And how about you Pete, as a good shopkeeper, just visiting, did you take the odd trip? "I didn't at first. I was scared of drugs. It was police training, I suppose. I associated drugs only with low life, not with wealthy, clever people. But after about a year, John finally talked me into it. I joined John and Terry Doran, another of John's friends, on an LSD trip during Julian's fourth birthday celebrations.

"After that, John and I tripped together regularly. He used to appear in my bedroom in the morning with a breakfast tray containing a cup of tea and a tab of acid. John saw acid as a godsend — a magical key to the uncharted regions of his mind. It did bring enthusiasm back into his life and inspired him to write some of his most brilliant songs.

"He loved getting in references to drugs and sex. In 'Day Tripper', they didn't think at first they would get away with the title or 'She's a big teaser, she took me half the way there.' Everyone knew it meant prick teaser. But it wasn't even banned by the radio stations.

"The first Beatles song composed in my presence was 'You've Got To Hide Your Love Away'. In the original version, there was a line saying, 'I can't go on feeling two foot tall.' When John sang it to Paul, he accidentally sang 'two foot small'. He paused to correct himself then laughed and said, 'Let's leave that in. All the pseuds will love it.'

"I suppose the song I was most intimately involved with was 'Eleanor Rigby'. I was at Kenwood one week when they were all there, The Beatles and their wives. After dinner, we went upstairs to this little room which was John's sort of recording studio. Paul as usual had brought his guitar and began strumming. 'I've got this little tune here. It keeps popping into my head.' And he played it to John.

"This was 'Eleanor Rigby', but he said he hadn't finished it. So we all sat around, throwing in suggestions. Ringo came up with the line about 'Father McCartney, darning his socks in the night.' Everyone liked that.

"Then Paul said hang about, his Dad will think it's him, darning his socks. He'd better change the name.

"Various people suggested other names. I noticed a telephone directory lying about so I picked it up and went through it. One name that amused us was McVicar, but it didn't quite flow with the rest of the line. So I asked him to try Father McKenzie.

"Paul still didn't know how to finish the song. I suggested he had 'Eleanor Rigby' dying and Father McKenzie was doing the burial service for her. That way you'll have two lonely people coming together in the end — but too late.

"I thought it was a good idea, but John butted in. 'I don't think you quite understand what we're trying to get at Pete.'

"I was upset by this remark and said, 'Fuck you, John.' It wasn't like

John to insult me in front of the other Beatles. We all packed up and went downstairs again. We had a few joints and relaxed again. I began to think perhaps my idea hadn't been so good.

"But when I later heard 'Eleanor Rigby' for the first time, as I was driving along and it was on my car radio, I was thrilled. Paul had after all used some of my suggestions, particularly the ending."

One afternoon, while Pete was at John's house, Pete was idly going through one of the sacks of fan mail which were delivered most days, and mostly left unread, till they were chucked out. But sometimes if they were really really bored, Pete would take a lucky dip, pull one out, read it, and they'd have a good laugh.

"I dipped into a sack which had just arrived and pulled out a letter which happened to be from our old school, from a pupil at Quarry Bank. He said that his English teacher was getting them to read and analyse Beatles lyrics, find out the hidden meanings, what they were really all about.

"This started John off remembering lines we used to recite when we were at school. 'How did that 'Dead Dog's Eye' song go, Pete?' I thought for a while and remembered bits of it – about yellow matter custard, green slop pie, all mixed together with a dead dog's eye . . .

" 'That's it,' said John, and he started scribbling 'Yellow matter custard dripping from a dead dog's eye.'

"And it went into 'I Am The Walrus.' He threw in semolina, thinking of how we were forced to eat it as kids and hated it, and also pilchards.

"When he finished, he turned to me and said, 'Let the fuckers work that one out, Pete.' "

# 11

## Len And Rod Make Moves

Meanwhile, what of the other ex-Quarrymen? Hard to compete, really, for fun and excitement, not just with John's life, but with some of the life Pete was also experiencing, if just at second-hand.

The Sixties for Colin and Eric were times of solid, steady family life, bringing up their children, working hard, not a lot in the way of sex, drugs and rock'n'roll.

Colin was now a senior upholsterer, still employed by Guy Rogers in Liverpool, where he had been since he started work and expected to be for ever, till he retired. Eric, having found his way into the Civil Service, after several years in a variety of jobs, was zooming his way up through the prisons department. But there were some changes of direction and location for both Len and Rod.

★ ★ ★

When Len arrived in Kent, having given up his job and life in Liverpool to follow Jesus, he found that the Old Gospel Church, about which he had heard so much, was in the garden of an old country house.

On arrival, in their Vauxhall Viva, he and Sue got out and knocked on the front door of the main house. Len said they had two little boys in the back of their car, could they come in.

"We got given a good welcome by the two preachers who asked to be called Aunty Ethel and Uncle Fred. He was about four feet six inches, very small. While she was enormous. Together they ran the church."

Len, Sue and their children stayed on the estate for several weeks, doing a lot of praying, being joyous, but not much else.

Slowly their money ran out. They'd had a little house in Liverpool which they'd sold for £3,000. "I'd sold it too cheaply, but I wasn't bothered. At the time, I just wanted to get out of Liverpool as quickly as possible."

He managed to find a job in a little town not far from the church as an assistant in an architect's office. By now the first feelings of joy in their new church and its preachers were beginning to fade.

"We hadn't realised how interested they were in money. They were into prosperity preaching – encouraging all the worshippers to go out and make money. God approved of it, they said. It seemed to us that what they really approved of was having things like gold taps in their bathroom. So we left that church in the end."

They then moved to Devon, to a pretty little fishing village where Len went out to look for work.

He saw an advertisement for a basket weaver. He got an interview, which lasted about five minutes, till they found out he had never weaved a basket in his life. He did some spud bashing instead – picking potatoes in the fields.

What did Sue think of being trailed round the country. "Oh, Sue has always gone with the flow," says Len, smiling.

"I just wanted him to be happy," says Sue.

Len eventually ended up in Exeter, again as an architect's assistant on £3,000 a year. They bought a house, on a mortgage of course, at a cost of £8,000, and went on to have two more children, girls this time. Ruth was born in 1973 and Jane in 1976.

So, settled at last, or so it seemed.

★  ★  ★

In 1968, Rod saw an advertisement in the *Daily Telegraph* for a driver to lead expeditions to Eastern Europe and North Africa. The firm was called Minitrek Expeditions based in Kingston upon Thames. He applied and got the job. His first trip was to go to Russia, despite not having been to Russia or speaking Russian, but he had picked up a bit of Romanian and Italian in recent years, to add to his French, Spanish and German.

He moved south, found a place to live near the firm's head office, on his own, of course, still being a single man, and set off on his first expedition. He drove to Russia OK, got safely back, and then went off on many other trips over the next few years, to Turkey, Morocco, the Sahara and elsewhere.

"You'd be given a twelve-seater minibus, some tents, a stove, some maps, and off you'd go. You didn't have to have been to the country you were going to, though eventually I was visiting the same places. More important was being the sort of person who could cope, who could find his way around in a strange country, who could sort things out when things went wrong. And of course most important of all, you had to bring all the passengers back in one piece."

On Thursday, January 30, 1969, Rod happened to be in London on business for Minitrek Expeditions. He can't remember what for. Probably some expedition he had to arrange or fix.

"I found myself walking down Saville Row, towards the Museum of Mankind. I heard the unmistakable sound of The Beatles coming from the rooftops. They were playing what turned out to be their last live performance. I stood there listening to them in the cold, until I had to leave for my appointment. It was the only time I ever heard The Beatles play live. . . ."

# 12

## Apple Madness

You can take your pick on when and why The Beatles gave up being Beatles. When they gave up touring in 1966, that was an end to one stage. When Brian Epstein died in 1967, that was another watershed, though they had grown away from him by then, from his influence and guidance.

When Yoko Ono moved in with John in 1968, that definitely changed John's life, but it wasn't what caused them to split up. That didn't happen till 1970, when by then there had been rows and petty arguments, both Ringo and George saying they were leaving, then it all turned serious with legal cases and nasty acrimony over Apple and associated management problems.

You could say it all began to change and go wrong when Apple first came along – madly, wildly, marvellously, dopily wrong. What fun that all was, watching it happen, when The Beatles got it into their heads that they could move on from singing and playing to changing the world, at least the business world, applying idealistic, hippy attitudes to running things like shops and other companies.

The origins were cynical and accountancy led, a strategy dreamt up by men in suits who pointed out that The Beatles had approximately three million pounds lying around which was about to go in tax, unless it was otherwise spent.

Tax in those days was up to 90 per cent, so no wonder the nation's wealthy felt sympathy with The Beatles and their 'Taxman' song in 1966. Written by George, who had always felt aggrieved that so much of their money was taken from them. Sometimes illegally, of course. Brian Epstein, to his personal shame, had allowed about one million pounds of The Beatles' money to be moved by some financial wizard to a safe haven in the Bahamas – where it was never seen again.

But when they dreamt up the idea of Apple, as a way of using their money, they were also thinking and believing altruistically. They did want to do some good, to put back something, to help others to achieve the sort of creative and artistic success they had had. No one had actually helped them. No financial hand-outs had come their way. No millionaire had backed their first flutterings. But looking back, they remembered the struggles they had had, the prejudices shown against people like them from the north. So they wanted to make it easier for people like themselves who had no formal training, no official qualifications, but had some natural talent, some unusual ideas, which they felt should be given a chance.

The first visible manifestation of the Apple concept was the Apple boutique at the end of 1967. And who better to run it than a person who in fact did happen to know a bit about running a shop, someone they all knew quite well.

★   ★   ★

Down in Hayling Island, Pete was trying to keep quiet about his fantasy weekends with The Beatles. "When I met people, I never told them I was a friend of John's. It would seem out of context somehow, running the shop and being John's best friend. I didn't want people coming up to me and saying, 'I believe you know John Lennon.' All that bullshit I'd have to put up with. I just wanted people I worked with to be interested in me, not in John.

"But it did come out. I woke up one day to find two reporters from the *People* outside the shop. I don't know how they found out, but I suspect it was the person who had sold the shop. It was my shop, run by me, but they must have known it had been put in John's name. I suppose they couldn't help boasting about it. Anyway, I refused to tell the reporters anything about John."

One day John himself arrived – when Pete was in Liverpool, visiting his mother.

"I'm at fucking Hayling Island," said John on the phone. "What are you doing up there?"

"That'll teach you to ring up first," said Pete.

But he got in his car and drove back to Hayling Island where Beth was plying John with Scotch and coke. He proceeded to give John a tour of the supermarket where John ran round the aisles, stuffing things in his pocket. "I can nick anything I like – and nobody can touch me."

It then came out why John had arrived out of the blue. He had with him an older cousin from Liverpool, Stanley, who was staying the weekend at Kenwood. John had run out of things to do with him, so on the spur of the moment had decided to visit Pete.

★   ★   ★

And then the real call came. Some time later, while Pete was staying at Kenwood, John asked him when he was joining them. "Joining what," said Pete. "Joining Apple," said John. "Just pack your stuff and move to London at once." Pete didn't really know what Apple was, or where he would fit in, nor did he know whether he wanted to actually work with John and The Beatles as opposed to simply being a friend. So he went home to think about it.

"I loved all the toys that went with knowing John, but I liked my ordinary life in Hayling Island as well, with Beth and our son Matthew. I was only earning £25 a week from the shop, but I was living on the premises, with everything thrown in.

"The Beatles were really alien to my world. I remember once they had this idea of all moving to a Greek island, along with all their friends, such as me, our wives and children. We'd live in a commune, in interconnecting houses. John drew me the plans for it. They did look at an island, and might even have bought it, I can't remember where, but the commune idea never happened. Perhaps just as well.

"But the Apple idea was real, so I went home to think about it. I didn't discuss it with Beth – because once I thought about it, I decided to turn it down. I went up to London to tell John. He wasn't at Kenwood, he'd gone to Paul's. So I went there.

"They were all there. Paul threw his arms round me saying it was great that I was joining them. I said to John, 'No I'm not,' and John said, 'You fucking are.' They all said I was – and they all seemed thrilled. I still wasn't sure what Apple was or what I'd be doing. But John had told everyone I had agreed. I suppose I was flattered that they all seemed pleased.

"That evening John told me they were going to start a chain of clothes shops all round the world. A group of young Dutch fashion designers called The Fool had crept into their lives. They thought their hand-woven clothes made out of silks and satins and velvets were marvellous. The first Apple Boutique was going to be in London, and I would be in charge of it. I said I didn't know anything about clothes. 'Just have a go,' said John. 'If you don't like it, fuck it, we'll find someone else.' "

Pete arranged for his mother, who for many years had had a shop in Woolton, to come down and manage his supermarket. He would stay in London during the week at John's, leaving his wife and son at home, but would eventually find a flat in London.

Three weeks later, having made all these arrangements, he was told by Neil Aspinall (once The Beatles' roadie, today Apple's MD) that he would have to go to his first board meeting. None of The Beatles turned up, though they were all directors.

"I had to go to Hilly House in Mayfair and there were all these suits sitting there, lawyers and accountants and stuff. Clive Epstein [Brian's brother] was also there. He'd inherited Brian's shares.

"I had no idea what was happening. They all just seemed to mumble but I heard Clive discussing a proposal for Beatles birthday cards – for which The Beatles would do the drawings. Everyone agreed it was a nice idea. Then more mumbles. I said I didn't know what was going on. One of them said, 'Thank God you're here.' Then they all fucked off. Alistair Taylor [Apple's Office Manager] was left behind and he poured us out a whisky. That's when it dawned on me that I was in charge. It looked as though I was supposed to set up the whole Apple empire.

"Eventually, they created different departments – Apple Films, Apple Records, Apple Publishing, Apple Electronics as well as Apple Retail, the one I was to run. Nothing was happening in the other departments – except several people had been given huge salaries and told they were doing Apple Films or Apple Music or whatever. They were on huge salaries – £25,000, even £30,000 a year – but they were producing nothing – just ideas.

"I found I was on only £2,500 a year, though I had been promised 1 per cent of Apple Retail, when it started making money.

"I looked at houses to rent in London, so Beth and Matthew could come up, but they were all about £20 a week rent. I couldn't afford that out of my salary. So I either stayed at John's or at Neil's in London."

Pete's first task was to get Apple Boutique stocked and staffed and ready for opening. They decided to use a building at 94 Baker Street which some of their accountants had bought as a long-term investment.

"I wasn't the manager. I just had to get it ready for opening. But it was total madness. I had four bosses for a start, giving different orders. Paul would come to the shop and tell me where he wanted a partition. Almost as soon as we had done it, John would arrive and say, 'What the fuck's going on here?' He'd then want the partition taken down.

"There was so much back stabbing and status seeking as Apple took on more and more people, often just people they'd met in a club or a gallery. Then there were the suits, pushing around their bits of paper, sending memos. Most of them didn't have a fucking clue. I'd come from running a little supermarket to find I was supposed to organise something which was taking on the size and complexity of ICI.

"The Beatles wanted the shop to be a beautiful place where beautiful people could buy beautiful things. They also wanted everything to be for sale. So if a customer fancied a light fitting or display case, that was for sale as well. Imagine trying to stock for that.

"The Beatles thought they could do anything and everything. They saw things in black and white. All very simplistic."

Pete did try his best, and also tried to look the part. He even managed to get into beads, grow his sideboards long and have a droopy moustache, as we all did, tra la, in the late Sixties. He put in fifteen hours a day, but even so, the original opening date was put back a month as they still didn't have enough stock.

He went off on a trip to New York, his first to America, along with another Apple executive to look at stock, a possible site for a New York Apple Boutique and also set up what was supposed to be the first of a chain of Sgt. Pepper Discothèques. Naturally, with all that to discuss, they got the big treatment from everyone they met.

"During our five days in New York, I don't think I was sober. As roving ambassadors for The Beatles, we were wined and dined and constantly supplied with drugs and voluptuous girls. We picked up a pair of beautiful black girls one evening and took them back to our hotel. The one I ended up with was stunning – except when I was screwing her, her wig fell off.

"When I later told John all this, he said why hadn't he gone with me.

"I only spent 25 cents in cash on the whole trip – and that was checking in my coat at some exclusive club. But when the hotel bill came in, the extras came to $1,000. The two hookers we'd taken back had run up this massive bill after we'd fallen asleep. They were ordering champagne, steaks, strawberries and ringing their friends round the world.

"We kept our fingers crossed that the Apple accountants wouldn't query this astronomical bill – or tell The Beatles. But it was never mentioned."

On his return, one of Pete's final jobs before the opening was to paint the outside of the Apple Boutique the way The Beatles wanted it – in psychedelic colours. The weekend before the opening, Pete arranged for scaffolding to be erected and a huge psychedelic mural appeared overnight on the outside of 94 Baker Street. Traffic stopped on the morning of the opening on December 5, 1967, with huge crowds coming to gape. At the opening party, there were so many special guests and assorted gatecrashers that half the goods in the shop were trampled underfoot.

"George did tell me on the opening night that I'd made a good job of it. 'You know, I really wasn't keen at first when the others told me they wanted you to run Apple.' I asked him why. 'Because I always used to think you were a bad influence on John.' I told him I must be slipping up then."

Three weeks after the opening, Pete bowed to pressure from Westminster Council and agreed to have the mural removed. "They threatened to send over their own team of workmen to repaint it all white – and bill us accordingly. But I got it done. I surrendered."

Apple Boutique was packed over Christmas and did a roaring trade. "Things were flying off the shelves as fast as we could replenish our stocks – the trouble was that a lot of it was flying off without the benefit of a cash transaction. Our tuned-in, turned-on staff were loath to apprehend shop-lifters – and they also had few scruples about helping themselves to stuff that caught their fancy.

"Apple's blend of idealism and lunacy meant that none of it was ever going to be profitable. When they set up Apple Records, they put out an advert which said: 'This man has talent. One day he sang his songs into a tape recorder and sent the tape to Apple Music, 94 Baker Street, London W1. If you were thinking of doing the same thing yourself, do it now. This man now owns a Bentley.'

"To no one's surprise, except perhaps The Beatles, we were inundated. Thousands of tapes arrived from all over the world. People also sent novels, screen plays, poetry, art work. Some of it was delivered in person. It was utter chaos. No one at Apple had bothered to think up a system of sorting out the submissions. So they just lay in piles, till they were chucked out.

"Magic Alex, over in Apple Electronics, was working on a flying saucer and a new kind of paint which would render objects invisible to radar. His laboratory mysteriously went up in a fire. Two of the earliest computers were bought for £20,000. No one could work them, so they were left to gather dust in Ringo's garage.

"After about seven months working with Apple, I became totally disillusioned with it all. And it wasn't even fun any more. I told John I was giving up. I'd had enough."

A new head of Apple retail was appointed, but Apple Boutique closed down shortly afterwards, on July 30, 1968.

The previous evening, The Beatles and their girlfriends had been in and got first pick of any of the stock they fancied. The next morning, the staff were told they could give away everything. Their give-away closing down sale had been kept quiet as The Beatles didn't want traders from Carnaby Street to come round with white vans. But news soon got out, by telephone and word of mouth, and Baker Street was soon so full of people that the police had to be called to handle the crowds.

Altogether, in those eight months of madness, during which the Apple Boutique was open for business, it lost a reported £200,000. "I can't remember now exactly how much, but it was a lot," says Pete. "What I can remember was that we later had to pay purchase tax, even though we'd given away the clothes."

# 13

## Pete The PA

But, ah ha, that wasn't the end for Pete and The Beatles. When he told John he was leaving Apple Boutique, John wasn't at all put out. Instead he offered Pete a job as his PA.

"What's a PA?" asked Pete.

"Piss Artist," said John.

Having resigned from Apple, Pete started the next morning as John's personal assistant. His somewhat nebulous duties included driving John around, sorting his post and paying his bills, but most of all it meant being John's companion.

"One night, after a few joints, a bit of LSD, we were sitting around at Kenwood playing tapes when John suddenly said, 'Pete, I think I'm Jesus Christ.'

" 'You what?' I said.

" 'I'm Jesus Christ. I'm back again . . .'

" 'Oh yeah,' I said. 'What are you going to do about it?'

" 'I've got to tell the world who I am.'

" 'They'll fucking kill you.'

" 'That can't be helped,' said John. 'How old was Jesus when they killed him?'

" 'I reckon about 32.'

" 'Then I've got at least four years to go,' said John. 'First thing tomorrow morning, we'll go into Apple and tell the others.' "

Next morning, John was still convinced he was Jesus, and so Pete contacted Apple to arrange an emergency board meeting. All four Beatles turned up, plus Neil Aspinall and Derek Taylor, their press officer.

"Right," said John, sitting behind his desk. "I've something very important to tell you all. I am . . . Jesus Christ. I have come back again. This is my thing."

The Beatles looked rather stunned, but said nothing.

"It was totally surreal," says Pete. "I found myself half laughing and thinking fucking hell. But no one cross-examined him. No plans were made to announce the Messiah's arrival. There was a bit of muttering, then silence, till somebody suggested the meeting was adjourned for lunch.

"In the restaurant over lunch a man came up to John and said, 'Really nice to meet you, how are you?'

" 'Actually,' said John, 'I'm Jesus Christ.'

" 'Oh, really,' said the man. 'Well, I liked your last record.' "

The matter was not referred to again, but later that same night, back at Kenwood, John said to Pete that he fancied having a woman around. Cynthia had gone away on holiday at the time. Pete said he wasn't interested. He was shattered and wanted to go to bed.

"I think I'll give Yoko a ring," said John. "I'd like to get to know her a bit better, and now's a good time."

Yoko was contacted at her flat in London and persuaded to jump in a cab, with John telling her he would pay for it. When the cab arrived, John found there was no money in the house. The Beatles, like the Queen, did not carry money.

"He asked me for the money. As a joke, I said no. 'Come on, Pete,' he said. 'You'll get it back. Put it down as fucking expenses.' Which, of course, it was.

"Yoko appeared shy and nervous and mumbled a lot so I couldn't hear what she was saying. After about half an hour's awkward chat, I went to bed and left them to it . . ."

Pete had met Yoko before, after John had first met her at the Indica Gallery, over a year earlier.

"Nothing much happened at that first meeting. I assumed she was just a 36-year-old Japanese lady artist whose interest in a young multi-- millionaire was that he might finance some of her future exhibitions. We gave her a lift back to her flat in Park Lane. I drove and John and Yoko sat together in the back of the car. As far as I can recall, she and John didn't exchange a single word, then we dropped her off."

Next morning, when Pete got up, he found that John was standing in the kitchen in a kimono-style dressing gown, eating a boiled egg. Pete asked if he'd, er, had a good time, as mates do.

"He said, 'Yeah, Pete, it was great.' The way he said it, I could see that something unusual had happened. He said he and Yoko had not slept all night.

"He asked me if I was busy that day. I expected he wanted me to drive him shopping or up to Apple. But what he said was, 'Pete, I want you to find me a house.' I said he already had a house. He said he wanted another house – to go and live in it with Yoko.

" 'Just like that?' I said.

" 'Yeah, just like that. Thi is IT. This is what I've been waiting for all my life. Fuck everything. Fuck The Beatles. Fuck money. I'll go and live with her in a fucking tent if I have to.'

"He then ran back upstairs. He said he couldn't bear to be away from Yoko for another minute . . ."

Yoko moved her belongings into Kenwood while Pete was asked to take her shopping, driving her up to the West End to get some new outfits.

"As we drove around, I filled her in on who each of the Beatles were and gave her a crash course on Apple.

"John asked me to go out to Italy, where I think Cyn was, and tell her he'd fallen in love with someone else. I refused. I'd always got on well with Cyn. So Alex was sent.

"The day Cyn returned, she found Yoko and John sitting together having breakfast, the curtains closed, surrounded by dirty dishes. Yoko was wearing one of Cyn's nightdresses."

"Oh, hi," was all John said, according to Pete. And that was it. End of marriage. Cynthia moved out.

Pete spent a whole week looking for a house for John and Yoko, contacting several estate agents, visiting likely-sounding country estates, though he was not quite sure what he was looking for. "If you like it, Pete, I'll like it." So John had told him.

He eventually found a Gothic mansion with its own minstrels' gallery and ancient organ which he was sure John would love. He took John and Yoko to inspect it, driving them in John's new custom-decorated Mini Cooper. Both John and Yoko were dressed all in white, which they had resolved to wear from now on.

"We went round it and John said he loved it – but next day, he said Yoko didn't like it after all. I said, 'Fuck it. I'm not looking at houses any more. You get all the brochures, you look at the pictures, you go and look at them yourself.' "

Did you feel threatened, Pete, when Yoko came along, that your days with John were numbered?

"Oh no. I couldn't have been more pleased by Yoko's arrival. She had a galvanising effect on John. I'd say she was the best thing that had ever happened to him. She wasn't just the love of his life, she convinced him he was an artist, which he'd always wanted to be. John rediscovered his convictions through Yoko. It brought out the child in him again. You could even say that Yoko brought John back to life."

And how did you personally get on with Yoko?

"I sincerely believed that I did my best to make Yoko feel welcome at Kenwood – and I would like to have been able to say she extended the same courtesies to me. But unfortunately her possessiveness and jealousy or insecurity, call it what you will, meant that she couldn't bear to see John enjoying a close rapport with anyone but herself."

But it must have been hard for her, finding that John didn't just have a wife but a male friend, living with him, someone who had known him all his life, who knew all about him, shared the same memories, jokes, references. You had a past with John which she didn't know anything about.

"Yeah, I can see that, but I honestly was pleased by her arrival. I knew it made him less dependent on me, which was a relief."

Over the next few weeks, says Pete, Yoko changed from being a timid little mouse into a tiger, insisting on being with John at all times, going to Apple meetings, even sitting with him at Abbey Road, in the actual recording area where wives or girlfriends had not been allowed before.

Pete eventually found his own place to live nearby and didn't need to stay at Kenwood with John, unless requested. He took over a house at Esher, bought by John, where Cyn's mother had lived. "I don't know why John was so good to Mrs Powell – she never liked John."

Pete's wife Beth and son Matthew moved up from Hayling Island at last, to live with Pete, who was still working for John, despite Yoko's arrival.

"I was at Kenwood one morning, having stayed the night, when I found John and Yoko happily having breakfast together. John said he wanted to be driven up to town for an Apple board meeting in half an hour. I burst into song, singing, 'Yoko, Yoko, it's off to work we go . . .' John laughed out loud at this stupid pun, but I could see from Yoko's steely look that she wasn't amused by me as much as John was.

"Yoko tried to manipulate John and everyone she could. Being John's PA, that was just a title. I wasn't a dogsbody. I was just a mate who hung around with John. I never took orders from John so I wasn't going to take them from Yoko. But she was soon treating me like a servant to order about. That's when it got hard.

"She rubbed lots of other people up the wrong way. John used to say, 'Even my best friends have turned against Yoko.' "

Pete's first row with Yoko happened while he was driving them, in his own car, back from Abbey Road where they had been recording 'Hey

Jude'. John and Yoko were now living in Ringo's flat in Montague Square, in central London, while waiting for their new house to be ready.

"I got lost, as I didn't know central London very well, and she started screaming at me. 'Get me home, get me home.' I told her I wasn't her fucking chauffeur. I said I was doing her a fucking favour and if she wasn't happy she could get out and walk home. John intervened and said, 'Pete, Pete, easy easy, she's dead tired.'

"But that incident did annoy me. I thought back to just nine months earlier, when I'd been at Apple and she'd come to my office begging for £2,000 for some project. Now here she was trying to boss me about."

Not long afterwards, John asked Pete, as a favour, to come and help clear up the flat, saying that he was very busy and Pete was the only person he could trust to go through his personal stuff.

"When I got there, the place was a mess, papers and dirty dishes and dirty underclothes everywhere. I thought, What the hell am I doing? Why the fuck can't Yoko stay home one afternoon instead of running after John all the time and clear the place up herself? Anyway, I did it.

"When they came back, John said, 'Thanks, Pete. You've done a great job.' I said to him, 'Who the fuck do you think I am, John? It's Pete Shotton. Don't you remember me. I'm not here to clean up your dirty underpants and your girlfriend's soiled knickers. I'm Pete, remember?'

"John looked a bit stunned by this outburst. I then said I'd had enough, I was resigning as his PA. I'd remain his friend, but I didn't want to be employed by him any more."

But Pete did go round to Montague Square one more time, on October 18, 1968, a social call, keeping in touch.

"I found John in the throes of vacuum cleaning, much to my amazement. 'Thank Christ you've come,' he said. 'We've had a tip-off that the Drugs Squad are about to raid us. They'll have their fucking sniffer dogs and they're bound to find fucking something. For Christ's sake, Jimi Hendrix used to live here.'

"I helped John clear up as much as possible, shoving things in bags, when Yoko appeared. 'I don't want him here,' she screamed. John said they needed all the help they could get, but Yoko said no, they could handle it by themselves.

"So I left. I took some stuff with me to dump, but to my regret, I must have missed a vital bit. That was the day John got busted for possessing cannabis. He got fined £171 which gave him a police record that created so many problems for him in the next few years."

And that, finally, was the end of Pete's working life with John – a mad year, starting with Apple and ending as John's PA. It also brought to an end Pete's intense, close friendship with John, which had begun in childhood and continued right throughout the Sixties, observing his Beatles life from the inside. From then on, Yoko was truly installed by his side, not Pete.

★   ★   ★

Looking back, Pete, did you ever think you were just a hanger-on, which is presumably what Yoko must have thought about you?

"No, I was never a hanger-on. If anyone was doing the hanging on, it was John. He hung on to me, always had done. He always made me feel special, made it clear he was desperate for my company, especially when he was depressed and fed up, which he was for many years.

"He used to say to me, 'I don't want to be a Beatle any more, stuck in a bag marked Beatle. I want to open the bag and let The Beatles out. I want to be myself.' But he couldn't. He felt stuck, couldn't go out without being pestered, yet he didn't know what to do with the rest of his life.

"So I was vital to him at many times. I didn't go on about him being a Beatle, treating him like a star, asking him dopey questions about The Beatles. I wasn't interested in all that. We just mucked around as mates, as we'd always done.

"He hung on to me all those years because he was afraid to be on his own. Especially when he went out. He always needed someone.

"When I was out with him, he never put me down. He'd highlight me, if anything, introduce me as his mate.

"We were once in the Revolution club, in London, and we met Jimi Hendrix. We were at the bar and Jimi came across to talk to John. So we were three in a row, with John in the middle. I was about to have a smoke, so when I got out my packet, I leaned over in front of John and said to Jimi, 'Would you like a ciggie?' As we did, in those days. You don't offer people cigarettes today.

" 'Piss off,' said Hendrix, very nastily. He hadn't realised I was with John. He thought I was just some punter, trying to hassle him. I grabbed Hendrix and said, 'Who do you think you're fucking talking to?' John calmed me down and explained I was with him, his friend, staying at his house. Hendrix apologised. We shook hands and it was all OK.

"When I first started going to Kenwood, it was astounding to me, seeing the sort of life John led, but it wasn't really flash. He had the big house, and painted Rolls and all that, but he wasn't really showing off. It was all a laugh. When we went out it wasn't champagne and lobsters and saying, 'Everyone have a drink on me.' The Beatles weren't like gangsters.

We went to ordinary restaurants and ate ordinary food, nothing fancy.

"But, of course, the life of The Beatles wasn't ordinary. They grew to expect their whims and wishes to be instantly answered. They couldn't wait for anything. Neil and Mal were the whipping boys, not me. They were always getting bollockings. Mal would be shouted at, told he was sacked, which could have him in tears. Then the next day, it was all forgotten.

"John did have a very simple approach to life. He once said to me, 'Life's very simple. If it gets too bad, just kill yourself.' That was typical of his simple solutions to anything – without thinking out the consequences, the effects it would have on your family and friends, or even how and where you would do it. Just do it. That was John's thinking.

"At the same time, he was good at changing his mind – and admitting it. Most people don't like to admit they've changed their mind, or done something contradictory. If you pointed it out to him, he'd say, 'So what? I've changed my mind.'

"In many ways, he didn't change at all. Just things grew to be on a bigger scale. The sort of stunts and jokes he did as a Beatle were much the same as the daft things we'd done as boys.

"The whole bed-in business was one gigantic piss-take. He rang me up from the bed in Amsterdam and said, 'It's bloody brilliant, Pete, we've got the whole world coming into our bedroom to talk to us on radio and television – while we're in bed. I'm just lying there,' he said, 'a daft cunt in bed, and they are taking down every word I say. You wouldn't believe it, Pete, it's one big fucking laugh.' "

Yes, but there was a serious point behind the laughs.

"Of course, but it was still a piss-take. Just because you have a serious point, you don't have to make it seriously. That's the bit he liked – knowing people wouldn't know whether to keep a straight face or not. He kept a straight face, but was laughing inwardly all the time. It was like that incident at school, when we enrolled the two lads from the Institute into the art class. John kept a straight face then, but he was pissing himself.

"There's one minor little incident I'll always remember. One day at Kenwood, not long after Yoko had moved in, there was a call from the David Frost programme which I took. I went upstairs, knocked on their bedroom door, and John shouted, 'Come in.' John was in a sort of alcove, getting dressed, and I could see him and he could see me.

"Yoko was on the bed – naked. I didn't want to stare at her, did I, lying there naked, when she was my best friend's girl? So I just fixed my eyes on John, not looking at her, and told John about the message and he said OK, he'd ring them later. Then I closed the door and went out.

"Many years later, I happened to be reading John's last interview, the radio one with Andy Peebles. In it, Yoko says how upset she was when she first met John and his best friend ignored her. She said he came into their room once and just ignored her and talked to John.

"John then says, 'That was just Charlie, we've been into all that enough times already.'

"I knew that he meant me. He just said Charlie because he knew the interview was going out on the radio. But that hurt me, that did. She hadn't realised how awkward it had been, seeing her naked. I'd just wanted not to do anything which embarrassed her."

# THE SEVENTIES

# QUOTES TO COME

You already know a bit about what each Quarry Man did. Yes, it was Eric who became a Civil Servant. But can you identify these quotes to come? Which person will soon be saying these words?

| | John | Pete | Rod | Eric | Len | Colin |
|---|---|---|---|---|---|---|
| 1. "All I really want to do is watch the trees change colour." | | | | | | |
| 2. "His death preyed on my mind and I was off work for a week." | | | | | | |
| 3. "Life was hellish for two years." | | | | | | |
| 4. "I just needed to relate to the earth." | | | | | | |
| 5. "I'd been gutted by BSE." | | | | | | |
| 6. "My first impression was – who are these fucking old men?" | | | | | | |
| 7. "To say I played the guitar is stretching it a bit . . ." | | | | | | |
| 8. "Common sense is not very common." | | | | | | |
| 9. "I've kept them on top of the wardrobe." | | | | | | |
| 10. "I haven't gone through life crying for 15 minutes every morning because I could have been a Beatle." | | | | | | |

# 14

## Post Beatles

The Beatles split up in 1970. Everyone had a hard year. John wanted a divorce, but so did the others by then, apart from Paul, who would have liked to have gone on, still married to the other Beatles. It ended in recriminations, law suits, slagging off each other, oh, awful stuff, how could they have stooped so low when they had been so high? Disintegrating just like any other run-of-the-mill, formerly happy unit. And so they went their own ways.

John and Yoko got married in Gibraltar in 1969 and went to live in their new mansion near Ascot, Tittenhurst Park. They formed The Plastic Ono Band, got themselves photographed naked for the cover of their *Two Virgins* album which delighted us all. John took to defending causes of various sorts, specific ones like the Hanratty murder case, and took to his bed for a more general cause, in praise of peace. He recorded 'Give Peace A Chance' in 1969, which became a peace anthem, and in 1971 he did *Imagine*. Cynthia got remarried.

In September 1972, John departed for New York with Yoko, never to return to the UK. There, he got involved in several political protests and peace campaigns and fought long and hard to get his Green Card which would allow him to stay in the USA.

In 1973, he went off for a long weekend to California with his secretary, May Pang. It lasted a year, most of which he spent drunk, stoned or just confused. He returned to New York and Yoko in January 1975. Their son Sean was born later that year – on October 9, 1975, John's 35th birthday.

He produced his tenth album as a non-Beatle in 1975, *Shaved Fish* and then said, "That's it, I'm taking a long break. I'm having the next five years off work to play with the baby."

In 1976, John finally got his Green Card, by which time he had settled down to semi-retirement and domestic seclusion, turning himself into a house-husband, looking after Sean.

His retirement lasted almost six years, during which time he made no records and didn't do much at all, apart from bake bread. "All I really want to do is watch the trees change colour."

So that was the Seventies for John. New country, new home, new wife, new family.

★ ★ ★

Rod finally made it in 1970, aged 29, the last of The Quarrymen to get married. His wife, Vivien, was one of his ex-passengers, whom he had met while leading an expedition to Turkey. They moved to St Albans and Rod left Minitrek Expeditions and went to work for the YHA, but still in the same line of business, organising their Adventure Holiday programmes. In 1975 his first child, Sophie, was born, followed by Jonathan in 1975.

During the Seventies he worked for various other travel companies, including Paris Travel, Villa Flight and Yugotours. In his spare time he was still playing music, appearing on the fiddle at informal, unpaid sessions in Chalk Farm, London, at a pub called The Engineer. He also studied at the Polytechnic of Central London in his spare time to gain a postgraduate diploma in marketing.

But a few years after the birth of their second child, it was clear to both of them, so Rod says, that their marriage had crumbled.

What went wrong?

"Just being incompatible, I suppose. If the moral climate in the late Sixties had been different, we'd have lived together for six months or so before we got married. We'd have found out quicker that we weren't suited and packed it in. By being married, then having children, it took us longer to find out. There was no one else involved. I was probably just impossible to live with."

Rod, of course, was referring to the moral climate under which most people at the time lived, not the life which certain rock stars managed to create and inhabit for themselves.

He says the final parting was amicable. He contributed to the upbringing of his two children and saw them at regular intervals. His wife kept the house but by a piece of good fortune, Rod was also able to depart the marriage with a small amount of money. Unusual for Rod. In his life, he has rarely been smart when it comes to money matters. It came about because at the time of their marriage break-up, planning permission had been granted for a new building to be erected in part of their garden. They were able to sell the plot for a reasonable sum.

136

With that money, Rod was able to go off and look for a small flat to live in and start a new life for himself, on his own.

★　★　★

In 1972, the year John moved to the USA, Eric also moved to another country. He was rewarded with promotion in the Civil Service and found himself in Edinburgh, where he became Head of Planning at the Scottish Office. It meant organising and planning workshops for all the Scottish prisons which, at the time, catered for around 3,500 inmates.

He and his wife Relda arrived in Scotland with two sons, Timothy and Matthew, born in England. They went on to have a third, Scottish-born son, Daniel, born in 1973. They lived in Edinburgh for five years then bought a house in Fife, just across the Forth from Edinburgh.

Eric then got another promotion, another bit to his title, when he was made Head of Planning and Production for the prisons in Scotland. So, he'd done pretty well for an ex-merchant navy man, ex-salesman, ex-van driver, ex-skiffle player. Eric was now an important man in a suit.

But as the Seventies went on, he grew to be a trifle frustrated about his chances of moving up another grade.

"I was far from the traditional civil servant and I made a number of enemies along the way. I don't think it was the lack of a degree that held me back. I had reached the highest grade for my discipline I could in Scotland. In those days there was no transfer between Professional and Administrative grades. To advance further, I would have had to move to London. No thanks."

Unlike Rod, Eric had moved into a field where these things tend to matter, where promotion goes to the already chosen, the ones marked out early on as the right stuff. However, as Head of Planning and Production, Eric had done jolly well.

He had to deal at times with parliamentary and ministerial questions, including having to draft an answer for Mrs Thatcher, the Prime Minister, in reply to a question in the House of Commons about Scottish prisons.

"On one occasion I drew the short straw and had to accompany the Secretary of State for Scotland to a meeting in Inverness. At the meeting, he was asked why the Scottish Office was not supporting a certain tourism initiative. He had no briefing and so turned to me and said, 'Mr Griffiths, what do you know about this?' Oh shit, I thought. In the distant past I remembered reading something about the Scottish Office refusing funding. I also remembered advice from a battle-worn Glaswegian Principal about briefing. 'Make it short, make it sound good and, if necessary, make it up.'

"Very few people in those days had a clue about European financial assistance, so with a straight face I told the Secretary of State that there were problems with EC funding on projects such as this. He turned to the worthies and said, 'There are problems with EC funding on this project.'

"I was very relieved that the EC was a total mystery to all the people at the meeting. In the Civil Service, you never say, 'I do not know.' "

But Eric was still stuck at the rank of Civil Service Principal. He'd decided the obvious thing to do, if he ever wanted to reach the heights of Assistant Secretary, was to go on more courses, get himself further experience, more qualifications and take on some extramural activities.

One thing about the Civil Service is that they are good at providing courses for their staff. So that did at least give Eric a bit of variety in his Civil Service life as the Seventies rolled on.

★　★　★

Len was quite well settled in the Seventies, after the wanderings of his Pentecostal phase and his change of jobs and geography. He and his wife Sue had their own house in Exeter and four children, two boys born in the Sixties, Robert and Jonathan, followed by their two daughters, Ruth and Jane, born in the Seventies. Jonathan, when he reached his teenage years, turned out to be a bit of a handful, but not too worrying, or so they hoped.

Len was still an architectural assistant, from which there was no real promotion, but he was now an experienced senior, working for a well-respected local firm called Louis de Soissons. French by name and origin, but very much a West Country firm, with good commissions for work on local hospitals and schools.

★　★　★

Colin, alas, who had appeared from the beginning of his working life to be completely settled, not to say sorted, received some very bad news in 1979 about Guy Rogers, the furniture people with whom he had worked as an upholsterer since leaving school in 1955.

"We'd been taken over by Dykes of Glasgow some time previously. I don't think it was that Guy Rogers was doing badly, but Dykes collapsed, went into the hands of the receivers, and Guy Rogers went with them. Everyone lost their jobs.

"I had been there 24 years, longer than the bosses even. I knew every brick, every bench. I expected I'd be there till I retired. So it was very frightening, having to come home and tell Joan I'd lost my job.

"We all got some redundancy which came to £3,000 in my case, but it meant I had to look for other work."

He and his wife Joan did at least have their own little terraced house in Liverpool near Penny Lane, with the mortgage almost paid up, but they also had their two young daughters still at school. Alison was aged 13 and Christine 11 at the time Colin became unemployed.

Colin read all the job adverts in the trade press, looking for something local, but with no success. Then he saw one for a prototype manager in a furniture factory called Englanders, in Derbyshire. A long way away, but times were hard, few options around, so he applied and got the job.

After long discussions and thought, he and Joan decided that it would be best not to move the girls at this stage in their school career. It would be unfair on them to have to settle in a strange area in a strange school. Instead, Colin would commute to Derbyshire. He'd find local digs and live there during the week, coming back to Liverpool and his wife and family at the weekends. Not a perfect solution, but he would give it a go for a few months, perhaps a year or so, to see how it worked out.

★   ★   ★

Pete, the bold Pete, the man who had had such an exciting, fun-filled, brain-bashed, celebrity-drenched time in the Sixties, had to create a new life for himself in the Seventies.

John was off and away with the fairies, plus Yoko, then to the US of A, out of range now for social calling by Pete, out of his daily life at last.

Pete had bought the Esher house, owned by The Beatles, where he was living with his wife and son, getting a mortgage and paying the market value. He didn't need to rush back to Hayling Island, as his mother was still running the shop. But what was he going to do next?

"I was just so relieved to be finished with Apple and all that. It was John who'd talked me into it. Yes, I had some good times, some laughs, some amazing experiences, saw and did things most people will never do in their lives, but I wasn't happy there. It's not what people think of you that matters – but how you perceive yourself."

Beth, his wife, hadn't much enjoyed their life in Esher so far, what with Pete rushing around after John. She still didn't know most of her neighbours, felt lonely and out of things.

Pete, now that he had more time on his hands at home, decided to organise a big party for the whole street. He went round each house, sticking invitations to Quill Cottage through letterboxes. He was worried few would turn up, as he didn't know his neighbours, or their names, but most of them appeared. Pete made a huge, strong punch, which got them all going, and discovered that most of them didn't know each other either.

One of his neighbours and new friends turned out to be working in insurance and had an idea for a new way of selling insurance over the phone. He suggested to Pete that he should have a go at it. He said that Pete was friendly and personable, just the person to set up a sales team. Pete said he knew nothing about insurance, but agreed to go on a short course and try it out. He found he was good at it, receiving a percentage of the sales of everyone in his unit.

For the next three years, Pete and his team sold insurance with great success – till, like Colin, there were sudden changes made above his head, out of his control. His insurance company was taken over by a bigger firm, based in France, and they didn't want the direct sales side, which was then closed.

Pete was out of a job, but he did get a fairly generous handshake of £20,000, much more than Colin.

Meanwhile, his marriage to Beth had failed. He says it was nothing to do with those years working with John. He doesn't like to go into the precise reasons, except to say it was amicable and they remained close friends.

Beth and their son Matthew moved back to Liverpool while Pete decided to sell the Esher house and return to Hayling Island and the supermarket.

In 1977, Beth died of cancer. Matthew then came to live with Pete in Hayling Island. Pete then met another woman, Stella, whom he married in 1981, thus providing a stable family home for Matthew.

But on the job and career front, he was still looking for something new to do. His mother was coping well with the supermarket, so that wasn't a problem.

Pete then bought a betting shop. This was the fantasy he had first had in the early Sixties in Liverpool, when John had let him have £2,000 to find one – but he never did and just wasted or spent the money.

"It was an accident really. I was in this betting shop, putting a few bob on the horses, and I asked the owner what it was like running a betting shop. I said I was thinking I might buy one. He said I could have this one. He was fed up with it. So I bought it from him."

★   ★   ★

In the autumn of 1973, Pete read in the newspapers, as we all did, that John had left Yoko and gone off with someone. It was the time when Pete and his own wife were separating, so he felt for John, whatever he might be going through. He decided to ring John, at his Dakota apartment, and find out what had happened . . .

"John said to me, 'Don't believe all you read, Pete. It's not like they say in the papers.'

"He said it was just that Yoko and he had been getting on each other's nerves, so they'd decided to have a break for a year. A couple of weeks apart was no good, he said. It would need a year to test the strength of their feelings for each other.

"I asked him where Yoko was and he said, 'Oh, just screwing around somewhere.' I was surprised he was in the flat as the papers had given the impression he'd been thrown out. I asked him how he felt about what had happened and he said, 'I'm not exactly over the moon, but it's got to be done.' "

★   ★   ★

In the summer of 1976, Pete went on a long holiday to the USA with a friend, Paul Hepworth, taking in 29 states in ten weeks. At the end of October, they arrived in New York. After a stroll in Central Park, they realised they were passing the Dakota building and Pete said that was where John lived. His friend said Pete should pop in and see John. He might be upset if he ever heard Pete had been in New York and not called on him.

So Pete went up to the front entrance to the Dakota – and got the bum's rush from the security guard on duty who naturally had not heard of Pete. But he did manage to leave a note for John, plus his phone number.

Within an hour, John had rung Pete, telling him to come over straight away.

Pete was ushered up and John met him at the door of the flat, baby Sean in his hands. He looked trim, very fit and healthy. Pete was told to take his shoes off before entering the apartment. The first thing Pete noticed was an all-white £100,000 carpet he recognised from Tittenhurst Park.

" 'This is fucking fantastic,' said John. 'I was at my Japanese lesson today and I had to learn a new word, sho-ton. It made me think, now I wonder how Pete's getting on these days. Then I got home and found your note.'

"He said first of all he'd had to ring his numerologist, to ask if it was OK to see me. I said, 'You had to ask permission to see me?' He sort of flushed up, like a child."

Yoko floated around in the background, not saying much, while John and Pete chatted. John had booked a table for them all at a local Japanese restaurant, so after Sean had been put to bed, all three walked a couple of blocks to the restaurant.

Pete was surprised that John wasn't hassled as they were walking, but John said he never was, not in New York. People might say they loved his records, or offer him a joint, but he didn't get pestered.

At the meal, John ate only brown rice and raw fish. That was all he was eating now. He told Pete he should try it. "You'll live to a hundred and fifty." He declined Pete's offer of a cigarette. At one time he, like Pete, was getting through three packs a day. He later gave Pete a book called *Sugar Blues* by William Duffy, which frightened Pete to death with its account of the dangers of eating sweets, thinking back to all those Palm Toffees he and John had scoffed as kids.

"During the meal, John was in excellent form, warm, funny and at peace with himself and the world. It was the real John Lennon, the one I always knew was there. He seemed to have got over the 'ex-Beatle' thing, didn't seem bugged any more.

"He talked about being a house-husband, looking after Sean, and only mentioned any of his music once. This was when he talked about 'Woman Is The Nigger Of The World', a title he'd got from a remark by Yoko.

" 'Yoko is so far ahead of anyone else,' he said. 'When I first heard that phrase, I didn't understand it. Now the whole world's coming round to that point of view.' I said I was a feminist, before he was.

"John paid the bill – in cash. I'd never seen him carry cash before. And he worked out the 15% tip exactly and added it on the bill. He boasted that he was trying to do everything right these days."

Back in the apartment, they all watched a TV docu-drama called *Sybil* about a psychotic girl. They had it on so low that Pete could hardly hear it. "When I asked them to put the telly up, John said it would wake Sean. I said he was right at the end of the apartment. 'I don't want to risk it,' said John. 'The baby comes first.'

"When the TV programme finished, me and John chatted for a few hours, drinking tea. He said he'd given up alcohol for ever. He told me about his Japanese lessons and also his numerologist.

"This numerologist had said his body was out of synch with the rotation of the planet. To reset his cosmic clock, Yoko said he would have to travel halfway round the world. So he had been to Hong Kong, on his own, without Yoko. She'd made him go alone. I was amazed – and so was he. He'd done the bookings, organised everything, something he'd never done before. He'd loved it, checking into hotels on his own, walking the streets on his own.

"I jumped up at one stage when I saw something crawling on the wall. It was a cockroach. John said not to worry. They're all over New York.

"He did mention his lost weekend in California, about the time he was hanging out with some Hell's Angels who were all maniacs.

"It was almost light when I left, but John said he had to be up early in the morning for his Japanese lesson. He said we must do this again, before I left New York.

"I didn't hear from him for a couple of days, so I rang him at the Dakota, on the private number he had given me. In the background I could hear Yoko shouting something and John saying, 'Look, Yoko, he's fucking coming over and that's it.'

"John didn't realise I could hear all this. When he came back on the line and said, 'Come right over, Pete,' I thought, Fuck, here we go again. After all these years Yoko is just the same about me. Then I thought, What the hell? I'll go anyway.

"When I got there, all three of us went out for dinner, to the same Japanese restaurant. But the atmosphere was totally different. They were both uptight. They hardly spoke to each other or to me. John looked pale and drawn, not as fit and healthy as he'd looked three days earlier.

"We didn't talk about the old days or personal things this time. Just about the occult and mysticism. 'Still searching then, John,' I said. He told me he'd seen a flying saucer from his window at the Dakota.

"He brightened up a bit when we got back to the apartment. I left after a couple of hours. Once again, he said he had to be up early for his Japanese lesson.

"As I put on my shoes, I gave Yoko a goodbye kiss. It was just being cheeky, really, knowing what she felt about me.

"But John shook my hand warmly as he took me to the lift. As I got into the lift, he shouted, 'Give my love to England.'

"And that was it. I never saw him again . . ."

# THE EIGHTIES

# 15

## The Death Of John

In August 1980, John started work on his first album for six years, *Double Fantasy*, as if to indicate that his self-created period of domestic and private isolation was over. It was virtually finished in October, in time to serve as a fifth birthday present for Sean and a 40th birthday present to himself. It was released by Geffen Records, in the UK and USA, on November 17.

John and Yoko and Sean were still living in their Dakota apartment on the seventh floor, though by now they had bought some adjoining apartments as well, which they used for storage. The main rooms were still white, as Pete had noticed. One room was devoted to Egyptian art and artefacts, including a mummy. On the wall of one corridor was a painting which John had done aged 11 at Dovedale Road Primary School in Liverpool.

They had also bought houses in Florida and Long Island, and a farm with a herd of prize Holstein cattle. These were holiday homes and rural amusements for their retirement years. John had kept his weight down and appeared fit and well. He was making plans for a tour and interviews to promote the new album.

On December 8, John and Yoko went off in the morning to a recording studio where John was helping her on a song called 'Walking On Thin Ice'. As they left the Gothic archway entrance of the Dakota, a young and ardent John Lennon fan called Mark David Chapman thrust a copy of the *Double Fantasy* album into John's hand and asked for his autograph.

A normal enough, mundane enough occurrence which had happened to John for almost 20 years – one which he had longingly hoped for, when younger, if and when he ever got to The Top. He did not, of course, always oblige, if he was in a bad mood or his mind otherwise engaged.

On a train to Bangor, North Wales, on August 25, 1967, on the way to meet the Maharishi, fans were shoving autograph books through the windows as the train stopped at various stations. The Beatles tried their best to sign them all, apart from John, who quickly got bored. When it resulted in tears, I signed John's name instead.

On this occasion, John was courtesy itself and signed his autograph for Mark David Chapman, so no offence given there, and went off to the recording studio, New York's Hit Factory, leaving Mark David Chapman with his autographed record and his collection of John Lennon tapes.

Mark David Chapman, who has gone into history with all three of his names intact, decided to wait outside the Dakota building. It proved a long vigil, but then fans are used to such experiences. Fans need dogged devotion. Fans can also, by definition, be fanatical. Who knows what his thoughts and feelings were about his hero, as he stood there, waiting.

John and Yoko did not return till quite late, about 10 o'clock that evening. As they entered the Dakota building, Mark David Chapman took out a .38 revolver and shot John Lennon dead.

★   ★   ★

Most people in the so-called civilised world, then alive and concentrating, remember where and when they heard the news, just as people remembered the death of John F. Kennedy. Thousands gathered in Central Park to pay their respects. Yoko called for a round-the-world silent vigil.

There was sadness in the UK, yet tinged with some surprise at the scale and intensity of the reaction to his death. Many people in Britain had grown to think of John as something of a harmless eccentric, an oddball who had gone off with that funny woman to do funny things. A hero from our Sixties, but now more of a recluse, about whom we hadn't heard much, who didn't appear to be doing anything, held in affection, in our memories, but not quite an icon.

On his death, we realised that in America, and elsewhere, he had become a Legend, a spiritual leader, a symbol of our age, an inspiration for the Vietnam generation. 'Give Peace A Chance', which he had written almost 11 years ago after a bed-in in Montreal, had become a world anthem.

His sudden and tragic death highlighted his life and music, which perhaps in the UK we had come to take for granted. It also brought about the definite end of The Beatles. For ten years, since their split, there had been endless rumours and suggestions of a reunion. They had died emotionally in 1970. In 1980, there was the first burial.

★   ★   ★

Len was at work on the day of John's death, in the offices of the architectural firm, Louis de Soissons, at 12 Baring Cross in Exeter. He was still working as an architectural assistant, busy that day on the refurbishment of Torbay hospital.

"Someone in the office went home for lunch. When they came back, they said they'd heard that John Lennon had been shot. I was totally shocked.

"It was strange, because I'd had no contact with John since 1961, when I'd met him that time at the Pier Head, coming off that boat. Yet I was so upset. I went home, telling people in the office that I had 'flu.

"His death preyed on my mind and I was off work for a week. I took it as sick leave.

"When I felt able to return, someone subsequently found out in the office that I had known John, that I had been in The Quarrymen. I hadn't told anyone at work. I don't know how they found out. I never went around telling people such things."

Why not? Living in the south-west of England for the previous 10 years, yet still with a strong Liverpool accent, people must surely have said to you, 'Oh, yeah, you're a Scouser, I expect you knew The Beatles.'

"When that happened, I did say I'd gone to the same school as Paul McCartney. But I never mentioned I'd once played with them. If I had, they would have made the obvious remarks. 'Oh, so you could have been famous, Len. You could have been rich, Len.'

"I didn't want that sort of conversation. I didn't want to draw attention to myself. It would have been embarrassing, to mention my Quarrymen days."

Because they were a pretty crummy, amateur group?

"No, not that, though I was always a bit embarrassed about playing the tea chest bass. I was embarrassed at the time – and I am now. If I'd ever told people I'd been in The Quarrymen, they would have asked which instrument I played. I couldn't say I was on vocals, which I was at the time, in the background. But we only ever had one mike, at most, and John had that, so you only ever heard John singing. Anyway, he was the lead singer. Everyone knows that. So if it came to questions about The Quarrymen, I'd have had to admit I was on the tea chest.

"You've also got to remember that in 1980, people hadn't really heard of The Quarrymen, unless they were fanatical Beatles fans. There wasn't the general knowledge about them that there is today, with all the books and research. Most people would not have understood what I was on about, if I'd said Quarrymen."

Len had, of course, followed their career since last seeing John, knew all their tunes and albums, though personally he had always preferred Elvis Presley.

He was aware of their fame and fortune, but says he never envied them, even when he was out of work. All he was jealous of was the fact that they had found fulfilment in their work, had made the most of their talents, which he felt he never had.

"I suppose what happened the day John died was that I felt part of my own life had died."

★ ★ ★

Eric had little interest in The Beatles or their lives after he had left The Quarrymen. Apart from that moment on board ship in 1963 when he'd heard 'Please Please Me' and told some of the cadets, he never revealed to other people that he once knew them. He just couldn't see the interest, for him or anyone else.

"If someone had said to me, 'Oh, I once played with John Lennon in The Quarrymen,' my reaction would have been, 'So what?' That's how I would have replied.

"I've never liked people trying to get reflected glory, so I wanted none myself. I really could not envisage anyone in their right mind being interested in me."

So all those years only Eric and his wife knew about his Quarrymen days, and she wasn't much interested either. Living in Edinburgh, working in the Civil Service, he had grown away from all the people who had once known him at Quarry Bank School.

"I suppose I could have picked up the phone and talked to John, had a chat about old times. As you get a bit older, you do think back to your roots. But I never did. Once someone becomes famous, there's a barrier set up. You don't want to break it down, in case it looks as if you're only doing it because they've become famous. It was only ever a passing thought, which soon went out of my mind."

So what were you doing, Eric, the day that John was killed?

Eric gave me a blank look. He didn't even know the date or year. When I told him, he wound back through his life and worked out that he must have been at Sunningdale that day, on a Civil Service course, one which he hoped would catapult him into the Administrative grade.

"It was a six-week course, and very intensive. I came back to Edinburgh on the Friday evening, talked non-stop to Relda about what was happening, then went back again on the Sunday night. It was like living in a cocoon.

"I must have heard about John's death, but I honestly can't remember where or how or who told me . . ."

★   ★   ★

A non-event, then, for Eric, but Colin can clearly remember where he was. Not at home with his wife and daughters in Liverpool. It was a weekday, so he was in Derbyshire, where he was working at Englanders furniture factory, living in digs during the week with Albert and Pearl in South Normanton, coming home to Liverpool for the weekends.

"The radio was on at work, as it always was, when suddenly the news came over that John had been shot dead. My first reaction was disbelief. You can't take it in when someone you know has been shot.

"Everyone else heard it, of course, and someone said to me, 'Oh, you come from Liverpool, don't you? Did you know him, then?'

"I was always getting that. This time I said, 'Yeah, I did actually.' Saying it made me sort of feel a bit funny.

"I went to find a phone and rang Joan from work. They were very good about that sort of thing, letting you use the phone. She'd heard the news.

"I thought of going home to Liverpool, there and then. I don't know why. It just seemed the thing to do, to be home at a time like that. It was like the Hillsborough disaster. Anyone from Liverpool felt they should be there. Anyway, Joan said stick it out till the weekend, so I did.

"Joan did try to get me a ticket for the Memorial service to John in Liverpool Cathedral, but it was too late. All the tickets had gone . . ."

★   ★   ★

Rod was working in London at the time, still in the travel business, as assistant to the Managing Director of Ugotours. Their office was in Regent Street and Rod came in each morning on the train from Hertford to Finsbury Park where he got on the tube to Oxford Circus.

"When I got to work, various of my colleagues were talking about it. One or two knew of my connection with John. It wasn't a sort of WOW!, you knew John Lennon thing. It was more a bit of an office joke. No, perhaps not a joke. It just amused some of them in the office. They also knew I still played music.

"To me, though, John had become a remote figure, from another part of my life. It was a shock, but not quite the shock it might have been. My mother had died just two months before, and I was drained of emotion.

"His death had nothing like the effect of a death in 1963. I had per-suaded this friend from Woolton, Graham Heap, to go on holiday with me and some pals to Spain. We rode there on his Lambretta scooter. He'd just graduated from Liverpool University. He died from drowning, on a beach in Spain. He couldn't swim. I wasn't with him at the time. He was buried in St Peter's churchyard. It was a terribly tragic ending.

"By 1980, I'd become more philosophical about death, accepted it more. John's death was sudden, of course, and he was still young. But even so, I wasn't as devastated as some people were who had known him.

"What struck me most was thinking that this was what they had always feared. They rode the tiger and one day the tiger would turn round and bite them. Yet it hadn't happened that way. The years of mass lunacy were over, when they'd had the screaming mobs. When often, as in the Philippines, they'd been in danger, when things had got out of control.

"Now, that mad life was over, things had calmed down – then suddenly lightning had struck when least expected. Not in a mass audience, or a mob situation – but one to one, on John's own front doorstep.

"They had survived the years of mass lunacy, and now suddenly a lone lunatic, when least expected, had crept out of the darkness.

"Those were my thoughts that day. Not original, I'm sure. Others must have been thinking much the same."

★   ★   ★

Pete was at home in Hayling Island. He was still running his supermarket and also the betting shop, but still vaguely wondering what he really wanted to do. He had been taking longer and longer holidays in the USA, since that time when he visited John, and had grown to love the American way of life and business.

"I was asleep, in bed, when the phone rang. I've always tended to go to bed late and sleep late. A friend rang to tell me the news about John. I couldn't believe it. So I switched on the radio and TV, and it was true.

"I was stunned, didn't know what to do at first. Then I decided I wanted to be with someone who knew John as well as I had. So I jumped in the car and drove to Friar Park."

To see George?

"Yeah, I've always felt fairly close to George, more than Paul. I just felt we could both comfort each other.

"I got to his house shortly after midday. George had also just got up, having been awakened with the news. He wrapped his arm round my shoulders and we went silently into his kitchen and had a cup of tea.

"I told him I just wanted to be with someone, communicate with someone who would understand. He said he knew what I meant.

"We spoke quietly, just for a bit, not saying much, then George left the room to take a transatlantic call from Ringo. He was in the States somewhere.

"After about an hour, some musicians started to arrive. George had arranged a recording session for that afternoon. I asked if he was going to cancel it and he said, 'No. There's nothing to gain by it, there's nothing else we can do, we just have to carry on.'

"So I left, leaving George to get on with his music.

"All the way home I thought, What a life. What a fucking life. And what an end. What a fucking end . . .'"

# 16

# Times Of Change

The rest of the Eighties, for the five remaining original Quarrymen, became a time of change and upheaval for each of them. In varying degrees.

Len, who had been most affected by the death of John, experienced the most dramatic change, and who is to say that there was not a remote connection in his mind, triggered off, perhaps, by dissatisfaction with his lot when he saw John's life coming to a sudden end.

It was being made redundant that set it all off. This happened in 1984, while he was still living in his house in Exeter with Sue and his four children, still working as an architectural assistant in the firm of Louis de Soissons. It had happened before, of course. It's the nature of the architectural business that when there's a property or building boom, work floods in, architects need all the assistants they can get, especially people with experience who are quietly and calmly reliable and amiable, who will copy out drawings neatly, go to the draggy meetings with dreary planning officials and keep clients at bay, or at least happy.

"There wasn't the work coming in, so I was one of those they let go. I just sat at home, watching the war on TV."

Which war was this, Len?

He does tend to be pretty calm, not to say casual, in his reaction to many things, including current events.

"Can't remember which war. But it was on all the time, night and day. 'I counted them in, I counted them out.' Oh, yeah, that was it. You're right. The Falklands War. The war gave me something to do each day for a few weeks. There was a lot going on . . ."

Len eventually got another job, working in the Devon County Council architect's department, still based in Exeter.

"It was a good enough job, but they wouldn't put me on the permanent staff. I just got temporary contracts. They said, 'You're doing a good job, Len, we'll make you permanent soon,' but they never did. I was about to reach the age of 45. That seemed like, well, a sort of watershed. So what I thought I'd do was emigrate . . ."

Bit of a drastic step, especially with four children still of school age?

"It was reaching 45 – that was what was so important if you were thinking of emigrating. At the time, you couldn't get an assisted passage over that age. They only wanted people under 45.

"But the main thing was, I'd got fed up with the job and fed up with England."

They decided upon New Zealand because Sue's father had emigrated there some ten years earlier, after he had been made redundant from Liverpool docks. Her younger brother was also there. They all seemed to like their life in Auckland, though Sue's father had recently developed angina. That was another reason for going out there, in case she never saw him again.

Len asked his in-laws to send copies of the Auckland newspapers so he could look at the job adverts. He spotted one for an architectural assistant in Wellington which paid 40,000 NZ dollars a year. Sounded good, so he wrote off with his CV and some of his drawings. The firm, Morrison Cooper Associates, phoned back – and offered him the job. He got them to put it on paper. He needed proof that he had a proper job to go to, in order to get all the right papers and his passage paid.

"I hadn't really expected to get the job. I'd just applied on spec. But I took it as a signal, that we were meant to go to New Zealand. I had to go up to London, for the medical. That was a worry. I had awful 'flu that day, but I passed it."

Robert, their oldest, was aged 19 at the time. He was sitting his 'A' levels when the idea of New Zealand had first come up. By the time it was all definite, and they were ready to go, he'd started at the University of Wales at Lampeter. He therefore decided not to go with them.

Jonathan, aged 17, was not doing very much. "He was a punk at the time, and driving us mad. He'd left school with no qualifications at all. He didn't want to come either. He preferred to stay in England and be a punk."

Ruth, 13, was at a local comprehensive and not very happy there. She was being bullied by an ex-girlfriend of Jonathan's whom he had chucked and she had decided to take it out on Ruth.

"This girl was even threatening Ruth with a knife. I went up to the school to complain, but the head didn't believe me. So Ruth was quite pleased to leave the school, get away as far as possible – for her own safety as much as anything."

Jane, aged 11, was in her last year at primary school. It therefore seemed as good a time as any for a change in her life, as she was about to change schools.

"Well, it was sad to split the family, and leave the boys behind. But I liked the idea of a new start in life for the rest of us . . ."

It was Len and Sue's first time on a plane. Rather surprising in 1987, for a couple well into their forties, when cheapo package hols had become so common and Len, on the whole, had been in regular work for the last 20 years.

"I'd never managed to save enough money for holidays. But really, looking back, I was never interested. I suppose if I'd had money, then an interest in holidays would have been sparked off. That's the effect that money has – you want to spend it. When you don't have it, you learn not to think about it."

So, in 1987, Len and Sue and their daughters sold up everything they had and flew off to New Zealand, for a new life, in a new country.

★　★　★

The big change in Colin's life was also set in motion by being made redundant. That had happened in 1979 and he had then taken the job in Derbyshire, staying in digs, then returning at weekends to his wife Joan and daughters in Liverpool. Not exactly a satisfactory way of living or working for someone in his forties.

But after nine months, he heard about a local job going, at a furniture factory in Runcorn called Loungecraft. He applied and was taken on as a prototype manager, the same job he'd had in Derbyshire. He was then promoted to works manager, in charge of a staff of 25. He was doing very well, till in 1985 there was another upheaval. It wasn't a matter of a firm going bust this time but of being relocated. The whole company was moving to Glasgow. He could have gone with them, but decided not to. Unlike Len, he felt that at his age – 47 by now – he didn't want to move anywhere, nor did his wife and two daughters. They were all too settled in Liverpool.

Instead, he decided to go freelance as an upholsterer, working for himself, not in someone's factory any more. He started off with a very good order from a seat manufacturer who had a contract to build seats for a bus company in Coventry. Colin had to provide the upholstery for several hundred bus seats. He rented space in an industrial unit and took on five workers. Was he about to become the Guy Rogers de nos jours? The new Cyril Lord even.

It all went well, and profitably, for over a year – till the seat manufacturer lost its contract with the bus company. Colin, as the sub-contractor, lost all his work, at a stroke. He paid off four of his workers, hoping something else might turn up, but he was still stuck with the rent and overheads for his unit which was now far too big and expensive for his use.

"I had so little work coming in that it didn't even cover the costs of the unit. I got in a terrible state. I didn't know what to do. I was stuck with all these expenses I couldn't get out of.

"Life was hellish for two years. I'd go to bed, fall straight asleep exhausted, then wake up at four o'clock with a blinding light in my head, as if a searchlight had just been switched on. And that was it. No more sleep. So I was exhausted each morning, even before the day began. I felt I was having a nervous breakdown. I went on valium in the end, trying to calm myself down and get some sleep.

"Joan was very good, through it all. She always tried to comfort me, saying I'd get through it in the end. Which I did. I eventually managed to get rid of the unit, and that was when things got better all round. I stopped worrying as much. But it was a terrible time, the worst by far in my life."

Having got rid of his unit, and his remaining worker, Colin then went as slim and economical as possible, working totally on his own this time. He rented the back of a shop from a friend, at a very small cost, and opened for business as a modest, jobbing upholsterer, waiting for house-wives to bring him their favourite sofas or chairs so that he could re-upholster them.

★   ★   ★

In Edinburgh, Eric's problems were not economic or financial. He was well rewarded and well regarded in his job as Head of Planning and Pro-duction for the prison services in Scotland. Even reorganisation, privat-isation of various bits, did not really affect him.

But what was bugging him was that he was still stuck at the Civil Service rank of Principal, unable, so it seemed, to progress to the heights of an Assistant Secretary.

He applied sideways, for other Civil Service positions, hoping that might swing it, but without any luck. He went on further courses, but nothing materialised.

By 1985, he decided he had gone as far as he could in the Civil Service. He felt on top of his work, knew how to solve most of the recurring prob-lems, could run his department almost in his sleep. He didn't want to leave, as it was a good job with a good pension at the end, despite his feel-ings of frustration.

So what did he do? He bought a launderette. It was a matter of elimination. He wanted a little business to run in his spare time, get rid of some of his energies, but one which would not be too onerous or worrying. It also had to be near his home, so his wife could help supervise it when he wasn't available. He'd picked up a bit of knowledge of the dry cleaning and laundering world through his prison work. The Scottish prisons ran their own laundries, making them the biggest in Scotland.

The launderette he bought was called Launderama, a leftover name from the Fifties launderette boom. He would have liked to have changed it, make it more modern-sounding, but decided not to. It cost him £12,000 for the business – not the freehold of the premises – and it came with a staff of four.

It did so well that he bought another, this time in Leith. Then he opened a dry-cleaning shop, from scratch, in Murrayfield, near the rugby ground. By the end of the Eighties, Eric was faced with an interesting and unexpected dilemma. Should he jack in the Civil Service and become a launderette mogul? Or what?

★   ★   ★

In 1985, Rod was also getting fed up with his day job. His marriage had collapsed some time previously, and in 1982 he'd got divorced. He was now a single man which gave him more time for his real passion in life – making music.

He was now playing guitar in a Tex-Mex band called The Armadillos, who appeared at folk festivals and folk clubs throughout England and Wales. The Bluegrass Ramblers were revived and he played for them as well. "We had some brilliant musicians – Bob Winquist, Rick Townend, Alan Ward and my young sister Rosie on bass. She also featured as an Appalachian clog dancer."

The band was pretty successful, playing at the main bluegrass festivals and supporting big name US bands when they were over here, such as The Johnson Mountain Boys. They played the 100 Club in Oxford Street, the Half Moon in Putney, appeared on radio and produced a cassette of their own numbers which they sold to fans after their performances.

But, alas for Rod, this was all in the margins of his life, in his spare time from work and at weekends. It did make him a few bob, provided some free drinks, but not enough to live on.

Life in the mainstream music world had moved on since the days when Lonnie Donegan and other skiffle groups could sell millions of records, get to number one and become national names. Not that Donegan himself made as much money as people might have imagined at the time, as Rod later found out when by chance he met him.

"I never realised that for recording 'Rock Island Line' Donegan received only £5 for his session's work – and no royalties afterwards. What a rip-off, eh . . .?"

From time to time, over the years, the occasional folk singer had done well, and mass revivals were always being promised, but not much happened. When new musical styles came along, they were things like punk groups, which didn't last long, or were heavily electronic, using canned sounds or rhythms which, of course, folkies did not approve of. They prefer real music on real instruments.

Rod's day job was still in the travel industry where he had been for 17 years now, with various firms. He had long given up leading expeditions himself. "I'd become stuck behind a desk all the time, organising other people's expeditions or working for idiots above me in the hierarchy."

In 1985, he decided to give it all up. But what could he do? As a graduate who had done several years of teaching in the past, teaching was the obvious thing, but he didn't want to go back to teaching foreign languages.

He thought about all the new skills he had picked up in the last seventeen years, wondering how he could use them, and realised there was a new subject, just coming in, which he should be well qualified to teach – tourism. Various colleges and polytechnics were now offering it. So he became a lecturer in tourism and marketing at Uxbridge College.

Around the same time, Rod found a new woman in his life, Janet, who worked for Marks & Spencer. They met at a singles club and set up house in Uxbridge. Together, they shared a new passion in their lives – windsurfing.

So the Eighties ended for Rod with a new career, a new woman and a new, terribly healthy open-air interest, far better than all that hanging around smelly, smoke-filled cellars or back rooms of nasty, noisy pubs.

★ ★ ★

In the early Eighties, into Pete's life again came Billy Turner. He was a friend of his and John's from Liverpool, who went to the Institute and along with Len enrolled as 'new boys' at Quarry Bank in John's art class. Now you remember him.

Like Pete, Len and Eric, he had left grammar school at 16, not knowing what he wanted to do in life. Like them, he had gone into what were traditionally thought to be careers or industries that held out advancement and security. Unlike the others, Billy had stuck to it.

Billy went into cotton, one of Liverpool's long established industries, in which Paul McCartney's father had spent a lifetime. Billy started at 16 as an office boy, worked his way up and by the time the Lancashire cotton industry was collapsing, he was up, up and away, becoming managing director of a cotton firm in Hong Kong, making a lot of money, living the affluent life. Then he had a heart attack at 38 and was subsequently made redundant. That's modern life.

"He came to see me in Hayling Island," says Pete. "All depressed. His marriage had collapsed, not just his job. He'd had a huge amount of money to pay his ex-wife, plus the costs of his big house which he'd bought in England, with a gardener and staff and other expenses.

"He brought with him a list of all his overheads – from his gas and electricity bills to his household staff. I took it from him – and tore it up. I said, 'What you do first is sell the house. That's most of your bills stopped. Then you start again.'

" 'You imagine you are just leaving school, with nothing, having to begin at the bottom. Except that you have already been a success – you know what it's like to succeed and the thing you know about success is that all it takes is common sense. So you can do it again.'

"We sat down and thought of what he should go into. I wanted to help him. I had some capital, having sold the supermarket, and some money left from when I was paid off by the insurance company. John had helped me to get started in my shop. I wanted in turn to help Billy."

The new venture they settled on was a fish and chip restaurant, Long John Silver's, at Hyde on the Isle of Wight. Pete found it, checked it out, decided the situation was excellent and put up 40 per cent of the money. It did good business and proved so successful that when, just three years later, they received an offer they couldn't refuse, they sold it for a handsome profit.

Pete was so encouraged, nay excited, by this turn-up in his business life that he began to think that the restaurant business was the one to be in, not betting shops. He had been to the USA several times, since that meeting with John, and was greatly taken by what he had observed.

"What impressed me in America was the casual eating – ordinary people, just casually going into a restaurant for a meal. When we were young, back in the Fifties, people hardly ever went to restaurants. When you did, it was planned about six months ahead. And once in a restaurant, everyone spoke in whispers. In America, the restaurants were all so casual and relaxed. I also liked the style of food they sold – big steaks, burgers, apple pies, lots of ice cream.

"So I started looking around for a restaurant for sale which I could turn into an American diner. I eventually heard about one not far away, in Southsea. It had been open for only eight months but was said locally to be doing great business.

"I went to see the agent selling it and I was sure the bills and invoices I was shown didn't tell the whole story. So I sat outside in the car for about two weeks, checking the people going in and out. That convinced me business was good. Then I went to see the owner, talked myself into going back with him to his own home, just to see how he lived. It was palatial. That was proof he was doing well.

"We had made a profit of £50,000, Billy and me, from the fish and chip restaurant. With that, and a bit of borrowed money, we bought the new restaurant. We only had to change it slightly, as it was already on the American model. It was called Fatty Arbuckle. I liked the name. Me and John used to call people that, if they were fatties. I didn't know at the time that there had been a real Fatty Arbuckle – some fat American comedian, I think, who'd come to a nasty end."

Fatty Arbuckle, the restaurant, proved an immediate success. Pete and Billy started looking for another. Billy had evolved into the management man, running the actual business, day to day. Pete was the ideas man, the creative one.

"One night when I was in the restaurant, there were a couple of drunks causing trouble, refusing to pay the bill. I got involved, grew pretty angry, which I can do, and told them I was going to sue them if they didn't pay. They'd been well treated, looked after, had a good meal. They could have no complaints. But still they refused to pay.

"There had been a couple eating at a table who'd been watching this scene. After the drunks had left, they came over and said they'd be willing to be witnesses, if it ever got to court. They'd testify the blokes were drunk and disorderly. So I took their names, thanked them for their offer.

"A few months later, I did find another restaurant, to be our second Fatty Arbuckle. It was in Bournemouth. I was wondering who to get to manage it. I thought of this bloke who'd offered to be our witness. Adrian Lee he was called.

"The case didn't come to court in the end, but I'd met him once or twice again because of it. He'd never been in the restaurant business. He was in Customs and Excise, I think. It was all just a hunch. Anyway, I offered it to him – he accepted and he turned out to be a brilliant manager."

The second Fatty was soon doing so well that Pete was looking for a third. That was proving harder than before, trying to find the right place in the right location.

"For some reason I can't remember, I drove out in the country one day to West Meon, a little village I'd never been to before. I was sitting in the pub garden having a drink when I got talking to the pub's owner. I mentioned that I was in the restaurant business. He said he had a friend who was buying a restaurant in Southampton. He told me the street, and the restaurant's name. I knew both – the street and the restaurant. But it was news to me that it was for sale. And I should have heard, as I was in contact with all the agents.

"I finished my drink at once and drove straight to Southampton. I tracked down the restaurant owner and found out how much this other bloke was offering. When he told me, I offered more – and got it. Yeah, I did feel a bit sorry for the poor sod who thought he had it all tied up. To this day, he probably doesn't know how it leaked out."

So, Pete and Billy now had three Fatty Arbuckle restaurants, designed the same, selling the same giant steaks, hamburgers, baked potatoes, American apple pie.

Soon there was a fourth, in Poole. One restaurant had turned into a mini chain, in just five years. Pete was still the creative brains, looking out for new sites, deciding on the style and contents. Billy had moved slightly behind the scenes, becoming the financial and admin man. Adrian, their witness who wasn't, was now the hands-on, day-to-day top management man, looking after the staff.

They were taking in a lot of money, could prove it from their books, but a small chain needs big money for the next leap forward. They didn't have the track record or financial clout of the long-established chains, and in the fast food world, there are lots of them, with a lot of money.

Did they want to go on anyway, or should they stick at four Fatty Arbuckles?

As the Eighties ended, we therefore have the unexpected sight of both Eric and Pete moving into the big money. Possibly. Maybe . . .

# 17

# Len And New Zealand

Len and Sue and their two daughters, Ruth and Jane, arrived in Auckland and went to stay with Sue's parents. Their flat wasn't very spacious, so it was a bit cramped for all of them, but they knew it would only be for a while, till they found their own place.

Sue liked Auckland right away but Len's first impression was that it wasn't quite how he had imagined New Zealand would be.

"It was like the American West – with big flashing advertising signs in all the streets. I hadn't expected that. But the countryside around was nice."

They also hadn't quite grasped the geography of New Zealand, when contemplating the move back in England. Wellington, where Len had secured his job, is on the same island as Auckland, North Island, but there is about 300 miles between them. Yet one of the attractions of emigrating to New Zealand had been for Sue to be near her parents. She wanted Len to cancel his Wellington job, find something in Auckland, but Len felt he couldn't. He'd signed a contract and it was thanks to this contract that they'd got their passage out.

Their life savings at the time were £37,000, all of it from the sale of their Exeter house. After a couple of weeks, Len went out and bought a Mazda car and they all headed south for Wellington, spending a couple of days on the journey.

They arrived in Wellington right in the middle of the rush hour. Len stopped the car in what turned out to be an illegal parking bay, trying to work out where he was, wondering what to do next. A policeman appeared and got out a parking fine to slap on their car window. "We've just come from England," pleaded Len. The cop let him off.

They had nowhere to go, not having booked any accommodation in advance, but managed to find a cheap guest house. Next day, Len contacted some local estate agents about buying a property.

"The agents took us to these timber shacks. I said I'm not living in this sort of place, I'm used to bricks and mortar. They were terrible. I then discovered that getting a mortgage would mean paying 19 per cent interest – far higher than in England. It was better to put our savings in the bank and get 12 per cent interest which was enough to pay the rent on a cheap flat.

"So that's what we did, but it was all so depressing. During those weeks I spent trailing round looking at properties, I cried my eyes out a couple of times."

Len's work turned out to be equally depressing. He found that his office was on the 14th floor of a multi-storey concrete block. It was also open plan, which he wasn't used to. Several of his colleagues were Japanese, who naturally talked to each other in Japanese. The systems in the office and the management hierarchy were also different from England.

"The construction engineer, for example, was superior to the architect. I hadn't come across that before.

"But it was being on the 14th floor, that depressed me most. I hated being so far from the ground. I used to bunk off all the time, as if I was back at school. I'd say I was off to the toilet, then go to the lift, go down to the ground floor, go outside and sit in a little garden. Just for ten minutes at a time, that was all, but I was always doing it. I just needed to relate to the earth.

"The rest of the office must have realised eventually what I was doing. They presumably thought some terrible personal tragedy had happened to me, which I was trying to get over. But no one ever said anything, not to me directly."

After a month of work, the whole of his office, like the rest of Wellington, closed down for two weeks for a national holiday. Len and Sue and the girls decided to set off in their car to explore the coast. "The swimming was very good – apart from the jellyfish."

But back at work, he felt just the same. The break hadn't really helped. He still felt depressed, disappointed, unhappy, regretting what he'd done.

After just four months in New Zealand, Len decided that was it. He was packing up and going home. Except that there was nothing physically to pack up. All their worldly goods, furniture and personal belongings had still not arrived by sea from England.

"It arrived a few days later at the docks. I managed to track it down quickly and told them, 'Don't unload. It's going straight back to England . . .'"

Len gave in his notice at work. His boss tried to persuade him to stay, saying he hadn't given it long enough, new people often felt like this, he must give it six months at least. But Len was adamant.

And Sue?

"Oh, she agreed with me. Perhaps if we had stayed in Auckland, we might not have come home. We might still be there to this day. But she didn't care much for Wellington, either.

"But the biggest disappointment for me was New Zealand as a whole. I was so surprised to find that New Zealanders were such workaholics. I suppose they have to be, to pay off their 19 per cent interest on their mortgages. I thought they would be much more laid back. I had expected their style of life would therefore be suitable for me, but it wasn't."

He didn't get round to telling the landlord of their flat that they were leaving. They had agreed to rent it for six months, so technically they had two months of their contract still to run.

Instead, they did a midnight flit. Len reckoned that as he was leaving without claiming back his deposit, it was about quits.

So, just four months after arriving in New Zealand with such high hopes and expectations, they were heading back to the UK, with no idea where they were going or what they were going to do.

★   ★   ★

In England, meanwhile, Pete was still wrestling with the problems of expansion. How to go up a notch, reach the next stage. He was determined to expand his Fatty Arbuckle empire, if he could find some way of acquiring new money.

"One day, I was reading an article in a newspaper on franchising. I'd never heard of franchising till then, didn't know what it was. I wasn't even aware that a great many of the McDonalds restaurants are, in fact, franchised.

"The moment I read about it, I thought, This is it, this is the way forward. It all suddenly clicked. I'd been dealing with banks, getting loans to finance each new restaurant, but it was all so slow and time-consuming. This seemed a way of immediately getting new money in.

"I jumped on a plane and flew out to Marbella to see Billy. He'd bought a villa there and was on holiday. In fifteen minutes, I'd explained the idea – then we both flew straight back.

"Setting up the blueprint was harder and took longer than I expected. I was starting purely from scratch. We had to find accountants and lawyers who dealt in franchising. I then had to create the Fatty Arbuckle philosophy and manual – itemising every little thing, from when the ashtrays get cleaned to the size of the steaks."

But they solved all the problems, announced their franchising opportunities, and cash rolled in. They still bought new sites, as before, especially if they came across a really good location, but they were now expanding at twice the rate because they were also selling franchises, giving new people the chance to operate their own Fatty Arbuckle American Diner, putting in their own capital.

Until then, their restaurants had been situated on or around the south coast of England. Now they started moving up through the country, into the Midlands and North.

Pete always checked every new site, whether they were buying it or not. Each Fatty Arbuckle had to be run to their specifications, most things had to be ordered through their head office in Poole, apart from fresh foods which they were allowed to buy locally.

"The beauty of the franchise system was that we took six per cent of their turnover – not profit, turnover – without having to put up any capital."

A vital turning point was the purchase of their biggest restaurant so far, in a large shopping mall in the Midlands.

"This was a major site, right in amongst the big boys, between a McDonalds and a Pizza Hut. Top of the market. I knew I had to have it the moment I saw it. It had been an Italian restaurant which hadn't done very well, but I knew it would be perfect for us.

"The site was owned by a famous property and leisure group. I found out who the appropriate regional manager was, heard what rental was wanted, and said I'd take it. I was told it had been promised to someone else. I said, 'OK, I'll pay a premium – I'll offer £50,000.' I was told sorry, it had been promised to someone else. I then offered a £100,000 premium. Again I was told, 'No, go away and forget it.'

"I lay awake, trying to puzzle it out. What was going on? What was wrong with my money? Then a light bulb seemed to switch on in my head. I knew what I'd do.

"I bought some shares in this property and leisure company. Then I wrote a personal letter to their national chairman. I said, as a shareholder, I'd be coming to the next annual general meeting. But as Chairman of Fatty Arbuckle Ltd, I'd also be asking a question about why they had refused my offer of a £100,000 premium on one of their sites. I was sure all shareholders would be interested to know why they were turning money away . . .

"The day he got my letter, the chairman rang me personally. My premium was accepted.

"No, I never found out what was going on. I can only suspect some private deal was going on which I was mucking up by offering a premium.

Top left: Colin marries Joan, March 6, 1965; top right: Len marries Sue, September 4, 1965; and below: Eric marries Relda, May 31, 1965.

Pete with John at the premiere of *How I Won The War*, featuring a short-haired John, October 18, 1967. *(Courtesy Pete Nash Collection)*

Pete and John at the *How I Won The War* premiere. *(Courtesy Pete Nash Collection)*

Pete, looking very Sixties, at Apple, 1968. *(Pete Shotton Collection)*

Len with Sue and daughter Jane, at her graduation from the London School of Fashion, 2000.

John wearing his Quarry Bank school tie,
New York, September 1980. *(Bob Gruen/Star File)*

Colin, the upholsterer, at work at the
Runcorn Suite Centre, Astmoor, Runcorn.

Eric and Relda en route to the Holyrood Palace Royal Garden Party, 1988.

The Quarrymen reunited in 1997, left to right: Rod, Colin, Len, Eric & Pete.
(*Rod Davis Collection*)

The Quarrymen on the same spot at St Peter's Church – in July 1997 – near where the famous shot with John was taken in July, 1957. (*Ian Crawford*)

The Quarrymen on tour in America, in Maryland in 1998, with Pete at the wheel.
(*Rod Davis Collection*)

The Quarrymen reunited at the Cavern Club, May 1998; left to right: Eric, Pete, Len, Colin, Rod.
(*Rod Davis Collection*)

Pete Shotton with his Aston Martin – note his cute registration number SHO 10.
(*Hunter Davies*)

The Quarrymen answering questions at the Beatles Fan Conference in Orlando, 1999; left to right: Colin, Eric, Rod, Len & Pete. (*Rod Davis Collection*)

The Quarrymen with fellow oldie Hunter Davies at the Quarry Bank school performance, August 2000. (*Hunter Davies*)

"But we got that site, opened it as a Fatty Arbuckle, and it was the biggest and most profitable in the chain, turning over almost a million a year."

★   ★   ★

Len and Sue and their two daughters arrived back at Heathrow from New Zealand in February 1988. They had no plans, no home, no jobs and only £10,000 left of their life savings.

At Heathrow, they hired a car – then sat and thought about what they should do next. Where to go? Should they head into London, look for somewhere to stay, then find a job? Or back to Exeter, from whence they had only recently come? Or up to Liverpool, back to their roots?

They thought about their two sons. Perhaps they should first of all see how each was getting on. Jonathan, by all accounts, was still punking in the Exeter area. Robert was a student in Wales at Lampeter.

While they debated, Len went to ring his dad, Harry, in Liverpool, to tell him they were back from New Zealand. Harry was still living in the family house in Lance Lane, where Len had been brought up, but he had remarried some five years previously. Len had never got on much with his stepmother, but he had written occasionally from New Zealand.

"Hi," said Len on the phone. "It's me, back from New Zealand. How's me dad?"

"Didn't you know?" replied his stepmother. "Harry has passed away."

He had died of a heart attack the day before, while they were in the air, coming back from New Zealand.

Len decided they had better go up to Liverpool, in case there were things to sort out, plus attend the funeral. On the way, they made a detour to Lampeter to see how Robert was getting on. He was in debt, like most students, so Len gave him £300 to help him out. "I thought I might as well, while I still had some money left."

They arrived in Lance Lane, knocked at the front of the family house, where the early Quarrymen had often met and practised. Len's stepmother wouldn't let them in.

"I don't know why, she just wouldn't. I suppose it was because we'd never got on. Or she just wanted to be on her own, not have all of us moving in with her."

It transpired that under his father's will, his new wife was to live in the house for the rest of her life. Ownership would revert to Len and his brother, but only on her death.

They sat in the car and thought about what to do next, then drove across Liverpool to the house of an old friend of Len's called Stan.

Len knocked on his door, while Sue and the girls sat in the car. He didn't want to mention them, till Stan had said he could stay with him, then he'd say, "Er, I also have the family."

"You've saved my life!" So Stan exclaimed as soon as he opened the door to Len. "My wife's just left me. I'm suicidal. Come on in . . ."

All of them stayed with Stan for two weeks, by which time Len, not Stan, had had enough.

"It turned out to be true. Stan was a suicide case. But not just because of his wife leaving him. He was off his rocker and was hell to live with. He was soon doing my head in.

"By myself I might have stood it for a bit longer, but not with my daughters as well. I didn't want to put them through it. So we all moved out."

They contacted a cousin of Sue's in Speke called Dan, who agreed to take them in. By this time Len had found a job. There was once again a mini building boom which meant lots of vacancies for architectural assistants.

They saw a house for sale, a semi in a cul-de-sac near Woolton, not far from where he had grown up, costing £28,000. All they had to put down was a five per cent deposit. They still had enough money for that, just, out of their savings. They then got the girls into local comprehensives.

After the debacle of New Zealand, were they now settled? In work, in a house, in schools?

# THE NINETIES

# 18

## Musical Manoeuvres

The Nineties began with our heroes moving further and further apart, socially and economically. It seemed the chance of them ever meeting up again was more remote than it had ever been.

Len had come back to his roots, but was not in touch with any of the former Quarrymen, not even Colin, the only one who had never left Liverpool, apart from those nine months of digs in Derbyshire. Rod was still in the London area, but taken up with a new woman and a new career.

Pete was concentrating hard on his booming business, now a chairman in a suit, rather than a Sixties hippie with beads or a Fifties scruff with a washboard. His Quarrymen days, his Lennon connections and his Apple activities were now all ancient history.

Eric, in many ways, was the one who had travelled furthest from his roots, throwing off all interest in his former life and connections from almost the moment he had left Liverpool. He must have been one of the few people alive that day John died who wasn't aware of it happening.

In 1993, Eric did the deed at last, making a decision on the topic which had been nagging away inside him for some years. He applied for redundancy from the Civil Service. It was currently being offered, but not precisely at people like him, being aimed more at Prison Governors and Prison officials, not higher Civil Servants. But he applied, and got it. Aged 53, he gave up his salary of £36,000 a year, took a redundancy payment of £60,000, plus a reasonable pension, and was able to devote himself full time to his little laundry chain.

By then it consisted of six units – two launderettes, two dry-cleaning businesses and two dry-cleaning shops, where clothes were received. They traded under the name of Care Clean and employed in all 13 full-time and part-time staff.

Should he now expand? That was the first decision to make. Or should he just sit back and enjoy himself, let the shops tick over, consider himself a retired gentleman. Not unusual, these days, for folk to retire or be retired in their early fifties.

On paper, it did look a nice little business, probably worth around £250,000 at the time, but not exactly exciting, sexy or dynamic. Launderettes were thought attractive thirty years ago, but the public gloss and profits had gone. Not like, say, the restaurant business, which might have its failures but new things, new styles, are always coming along, capturing the public's eye, its tummy and its purse.

Eric did think of selling, but had to admit it would probably take time. His profit margin had always been good, around 16 per cent, but as the years had gone on he was aware it was not considered a desirable activity by the rest of the world. He knew that retired people in the Nineties with money, looking for a nice little business, would rather go for a small country hotel or pretty guest house than some boring-sounding, back-street dry cleaners.

"It's a hard business, with a lot of aggravation. Customers' expectations are often way beyond reality. And you get a lot of people trying to con you. Most people are OK. It's just a handful who try the usual scams."

Such as?

"Well, when they come to collect a garment, they'll say they've lost their ticket, hoping the assistant will let them identify the garment and take it. Next week, they come in again – this time with their ticket and, of course, the item can't be found. It will miraculously have turned into a £1,000 suit and they'll demand the full compensation. That's the sort of thing you had to put up with in the early days, till we created a system to cope with that sort of con.

"But you still get the old tricks – people maintaining there was not a mark on their garment when they brought it in, and now it's ruined.

"I've been taken to court three times, to the small claims court in Edinburgh. And each time I won my case. The last time the Sheriff said I should claim more costs, but I didn't. The maximum you can claim is supposed to be £75."

His profit margin was good because he was specialising in the top end of the market, cleaning silks and wedding dresses, the sort of clothes people don't normally trust to the dry-cleaning chains.

Eric had established a niche, so he decided for the moment to stick with it, let it tick over. Meanwhile he was looking forward to playing a lot of golf.

★　★　★

Billy Turner, the old Liverpool friend who had come back into Pete's life and helped him start the Fatty Arbuckle chain, died of a heart attack in 1993. Pete, in due course, bought all his shares, which meant that he was not just chairman but owner of the whole company.

By 1995 there were 50 Fatty Arbuckle restaurants – 20 owned and 30 franchised. They ranged all over England, Scotland and Northern Island.

Pete moved their HQ from Bournemouth in Dorset up to Manchester, wanting to be nearer the geographical heart of his empire.

"The staff weren't pleased at first, and I was very unpopular, but they found nice places to live in Cheshire – and were soon deciding that they loved it in the North."

The North? Cheshire, to me, sitting in Cumbria, is the Deep South, practically the Mediterranean, but of course Pete had been away from his native hearth since 1965 when he first moved to Hayling Island in Hampshire.

By this time there were 40 staff in his head office and a total of some 1,500. Far bigger than Apple had ever been. The pages of the national papers were beginning to mention Pete Shotton, businessman.

On September 21, 1995, an article in the *Daily Mail* referred to him as the "owner of the expanding Fatty Arbuckles restaurant chain". The *Daily Mirror* of October 6, 1997, in their financial pages, had the headline "Fatty's £6 million expansion". Chairman Pete Shotton was said to be planning to open 20 more Fatty Arbuckles by the end of the year.

★ ★ ★

One of the new places where a Fatty Arbuckle opened in the mid-Nineties was Liverpool. In small print, in one of the local newspaper announcements, Len noticed the name "Pete Shotton, chairman". He did wonder if, by chance, they were related, or could it even be the same Pete Shotton he used to know?

Len and his family had taken a while to settle down on their return to Liverpool. The first minor problem had been that Jane, their youngest, aged 13, was not happy at her new comprehensive.

"She got teased for not having a Liverpool accent," says Len.

Had she acquired a New Zealand accent? Of course not. They'd only been there half an hour. What she had was a Devon accent, having been born and brought up in the South West.

"She also got called a poof," says Len.

Now that was more surprising, but a sign of the times, a sign of play-ground epithets and television soap invective.

In the end, they took her away and sent her to a private school – a Christian-based one, and not very expensive. Len had secured a reasonably paid job in an architect's office so they could pay the fees.

But Len didn't settle long at his new job. "The partner didn't know what he was doing. The job was soon doing my head in. So I left."

He'd only been there six months, but times were still good in the building world, and he soon found another job with a well-known firm of Liverpool architects called Owen Ellis.

Then, once again, it happened. After only four years back in Liverpool, he was made redundant.

Len was on the dole for 12 months and got into difficulties paying his mortgage. Sue went back to work as a nurse, doing nights in an old people's home.

Len eventually got a job as a Day Centre carer, looking after adults with learning and physical problems, taking them on outings, playing games, singing songs to them.

He'd been all his working life in the architectural world, as an assistant, but now he decided he'd had enough, for ever. He'd liked doing the drawings all these years, but the endless meetings had got him down, not to mention doing his head in.

In his mind, in his fantasy world, he had always wanted to be a singer, though without doing much about it. But at least in the Day Centre, he was doing the odd bit of singing, keeping his charges amused, from time to time.

★　★　★

Colin had packed in all interest in playing music when he left The Quarrymen. He had shoved his drum kit on top of the wardrobe – and there it had remained, in their little terraced house off Penny Lane.

As a self-employed upholsterer, things had turned out quite well. He was happier, more satisfied, being totally on his own than being a works manager or, even worse, trying to run his own firm with his own staff and contracts which might, or might not, be cancelled.

His order book had soon filled up. His customers were local housewives, not companies, who wanted their sofas repaired. They provided enough work to keep him occupied and in business.

★　★　★

Rod had continued to play his guitar, plus assorted other instruments, through the ups and downs, ins and outs of his personal and working life, though his new hobby of windsurfing was beginning to compete with music for any spare time that came his way.

In 1996, after ten years as a lecturer in tourism, he decided he'd had enough. He'd never seen himself as a career person anyway, as his life since leaving Cambridge had shown. He considered that Janet, his new partner, ten years younger, was the proper career person in their house. Her job at Marks & Spencer was not on the selling side but behind the scenes, working on the breast screening programme for the company's female staff throughout the country.

"Janet is very sensible and organised. She's also good with money. One of the reasons my first wife gave me the elbow was that my pockets always seemed to have holes in them . . ."

Rod decided to set himself up as a freelance translator, working from their home in Uxbridge. He did a translator's diploma and bought himself a computer. He had been getting some useful French and Spanish translation work, but this source soon dried up and all he managed was a few articles.

Fortunately he had kept in contact with his ex-colleagues from Uxbridge College and got some part-time lecturing at nearby Brunel University.

His fantasy, on giving up full-time teaching and the daily grind of going to work, was that he would be free and able and ready to jump, should anything in the way of musical work come along. But he seemed to be waiting a long time.

With a friend, Doug Turner, he wrote a guitar tutor, so that was one musical project. In 1996, he was asked to do the voice for a talking book version of *The Day John Met Paul*, the rather flowery book by the American writer Jim O'Donnell, about the events of July 6, 1957 at the Woolton Church Fete. Rod spoke it well, his Liverpool accent still intact, sounding a little bit like John, but it didn't make him much money. In fact, Rod, under the name of Scorpion Publications, Uxbridge, produced the cassette himself. Scorpion also published the guitar tutor under the title *Country Fingerpickin' Guitar*. Look out for it.

★   ★   ★

In 1992, Rod met up again with John Duff Lowe – an early, but not original, Quarryman who had played the piano on that first-ever recording session, which resulted in just one copy of the record being produced.

Duff, like Rod, had gone into the sixth form at school. He got two 'A' levels, but he didn't go on to university. Instead, he left the Institute at 18 and joined a local firm of stockbrokers in Dale Street, Liverpool.

"In my lunch hour I used to go to the Cavern to watch The Beatles playing. I met John there one day and he introduced me to someone and said, 'This is Duff, he breaks stock.' A very typical John remark."

Duff later worked for Barclays Bank, then, in 1975, left the Liverpool area to work for Hill Samuel in Bristol. Later he became a financial adviser.

In 1981, by which time Beatles memorabilia and anything connected with them was beginning to command high prices, Duff realised he had the only copy of 'In Spite Of All The Danger', their first record.

He can't remember who exactly gave it to him, but he had had it for as long as he could remember. Colin might have given it to him – or the person Colin had loaned it to. "I always presumed I got it last because I lived furthest away from the others. I lived in West Derby, about four or five miles from Woolton, where John and Colin lived."

He decided he would sell the disc at Sotheby's. "Stephen Pile in the *Sunday Times* wrote about it – and on the Monday, Paul rang my mother in Liverpool, asking me to ring him. He'd put an injunction on the sale of the record.

"When I rang him, I got Linda. Paul was out but I asked if he was not pleased with me. He then rang me and we talked about the old times.

"He said he wanted the record back and I said it was mine to sell. So we discussed it for some time. He said that he owned the copyright of the B-side, 'That'll Be The Day', the Buddy Holly song, and The Quarrymen's song was also his. Even though it said on the disc the song was by Lennon and Harrison, Paul said he had really done it.

"He asked me if there was a guitar solo on it, as he couldn't quite remember, and I said yes, there was. 'There you are,' he said. 'That was George's solo. George created the guitar solo, but I wrote the song. I just put both names on because that was what you did at that time.'

"Anyway, we agreed on a deal. He sent an assistant and his solicitor to see me in Worcester where I was at the time. We went into a private room at Barclays Bank and drew up an agreement. I handed over all the rights to Paul."

For how much? Originally it had been reported that the disc might fetch at least £5,000 at Sotheby's. Today, it must be worth £100,000.

"I'm not saying," says Duff. "It's in our agreement that I don't reveal the precise figure. But it was more than £5,000."

Duff had never played the piano again, since leaving The Quarrymen, till he met up again with Rod in 1992.

They decided to form a group and played a few gigs in a touring show which included Cynthia Lennon and Denny Laine. They even produced a CD. But Duff was still working full time, in finance and banking, and still living in the West Country.

★ ★ ★

Now and again, Rod vaguely wondered what had happened to the real original members of The Quarrymen. The only one he had remained in touch with was Colin. They sent each other Christmas cards. Now and again, when he was in Liverpool, Rod popped down Penny Lane to say hello to Colin and his family.

He did eventually manage to track down Eric in Edinburgh. He wrote to him, saying that he and Duff Lowe were trying to reform The Quarrymen. Would Eric ever fancy playing with them again? Eric said, "No, definitely not."

Rod failed to find out where Len was. He did at last hear that he'd emigrated to New Zealand but was unaware that he had returned to Liverpool.

As for Pete, the last he'd heard was that he'd gone off to run a supermarket in Hayling Island, wherever that was, but he realised that that news was about 30 years old and possibly well out of date.

In the summer of 1994, Rod happened to be windsurfing off Hayling Island. When he'd finished surfing, he remembered that Hayling was the place Pete had gone to, all those years ago.

"I found a telephone box and stood there, going through the directory. There was only one Shotton so I rang and got Pete. I said I was surprised he wasn't ex-directory. Pete was going out that evening, but we agreed I would ring him the next time I was in the area and we'd have a few beers. Next time, when I tried to ring him, he'd taken my advice. He'd gone ex-directory, so I never met him."

Eventually, Pete was contacted about the possibility of a reunion, but said no. So Rod, Duff Lowe and some others did a recording session, but nothing ever came of it. Later, they did another session, and produced a CD, this time called *Open For Engagements*. As a result of this, Rod and Duff Lowe got invited to a Beatles' festival in the USA. Rod saw the enormous interest in the USA in The Beatles, but his fantasy of a revival of the original Quarrymen had come to nothing.

# 19

## We'll Meet Again . . .

The first Beatles Convention in Liverpool, and the first organised Beatles tours of the city, began in 1981. Beatles events were already happening elsewhere in the world, but many folk in Liverpool still harboured a slight resentment, left over from the Sixties, that The Beatles, once they had got to London and achieved international fame, had not appeared all that interested in their home town. Or it could just have been prophets not being raved about at home on the scale of their worship abroad.

It was John's death in 1980 which sparked off a greater increase in all Beatly things. More and more people were coming to Liverpool from all parts of the world, clutching their assorted Beatles reference books and photos, trying to track down houses and places associated with the Fab Four.

Merseyside Council, one of those leviathans of Seventies local government reorganisation, realised there was a market here, money to be made, and set up the Merseyside Tourist Centre which organised the first convention and began training Beatles guides.

In 1986, thanks to Mrs Thatcher, there was further council reorganisation and Merseyside Council disappeared. Its successor was not as keen or as organised in matters Beatly, and so the convention was given over to private hands, to two local lads who had been Beatles guides – Bill Heckle and Dave Jones.

Dave Jones had been a full-time guide but Bill had been doing it part-time. He was an economics teacher at Bebington High School on the Wirral, which he continued to do till 1990, by which time he and Dave had set up their own company, Cavern City Tours, organising the annual convention as well as other Beatles activities and events.

In 1991 they took over the lease of the Cavern Club. The original had long since been demolished but it had been rebuilt and reopened in 1984 on the original site.

In 1996, by which time their company was employing over 50 people, they realised the 40th anniversary of the opening of the Cavern Club, in January 1957, was coming up. They decided to invite as many people associated with its history as possible, including the original Quarrymen. If they could be found.

"The only one we knew at the time was Len Garry," says Dave Jones. "He had come along to various of our annual Beatles events, but he didn't know where the others were."

"It was John Duff Lowe", says Bill Heckle, "who put us in touch with Rod Davis and helped us look for the others. We eventually managed to get addresses for all the original Quarrymen and sent off invitations."

"The response to the party invites was amazing," says Dave Jones. "It was like sending out Kruger bars. People considered it a great honour."

And also a great party. They had managed to get sponsorship from Holstein Pils, John Smith's Bitter, Guinness and Classic Wine, so that for the seven hours of the private celebration party, not open to the public, the 600 or so specially invited guests would get free booze.

Would The Quarrymen turn up?

The invitation was for Thursday, January 16, 1997 at 12 noon. Rod was naturally very pleased when his invite arrived, having kept up his interest in music, still hoping for that breakthrough. As a retired person, he also had the time to go up to Liverpool, not just the inclination.

Len was also pleased, as he had begun to attend Beatles events and still hoped to be seen as a singer, without ever having done much singing for 40 years.

But Eric and Pete, our busy businessmen, had other things in their lives going on. Why should they bother?

Up in Edinburgh, Eric had always declined any invitation to turn up at any sort of Beatles events.

"When Rod had contacted me, asking me to do something, I can't remember what, I'd said no because I was sure no one wanted to meet me.

"I'd even got a call about ten years previously from America, inviting me over to do some Beatles thing. I said, 'No. I'm not interested.' "

When the Cavern invitation arrived at Eric's house it happened to be the Christmas holidays. All three of Eric's sons, then in their twenties, and either working or students, were at home.

"They saw the invitation, which I was thinking of refusing, and said, 'Go on, Dad, you must go, see your old chums.'

"They kept on about it all over Christmas, so in the end I said yes, but I was still wavering, still thinking of changing my mind, but knowing they would be disappointed if I didn't go.

179

"Anyway, when the day came, I set off, driving myself down to Liverpool. Halfway down the M6, in miserable weather, I nearly turned back, thinking, What am I doing?

"When I got outside the Cavern, it was pouring down, awful weather, and I was still thinking, This is a mistake, I won't know anyone. There were crowds waiting outside, just hanging around, to see who had been invited.

"I really went inside because the weather was so bad and because I'd promised Rod. I said I'd meet him inside. I wondered, of course, if I'd recognise him, after 39 years . . ."

★   ★   ★

Pete had never been to a Beatles event either, though he had been contacted by Len, who had eventually tracked him down through the Liverpool branch of Fatty Arbuckle. He'd always refused to go to any Beatles conventions or conferences.

"I knew about them, and thought they sounded pretty pathetic. These people who had once been John Lennon's chauffeur, or his gardener, or had once cleaned his drains, they were all now coming forward and making a living out of it.

"I hate people who make a career out of having known a celebrity. I always wanted to live my own life. After a period when the papers were ringing me up, asking me about John, I went ex-directory, just so no one would ever track me down.

"But this was going to be a reunion of old friends, a private party, not a Beatles event. That's why I'd said yes. But I nearly didn't turn up.

"I was halfway there and I suddenly thought, What am I doing? I must be mad, wasting my time. I really did think about turning back. Then I thought, Well, it might be interesting to see them again, after all these years, see what these old men look like . . ."

★   ★   ★

As for Colin, he says he never got an invitation. If it was sent, as Bill Heckle says it was, he never received it. He suspects it was never sent because he had turned down approaches in the past. "Or they could just have forgotten me."

Rod contacted him a few days before, to check that he was coming. When Colin said that he hadn't been invited, Rod said, "Don't worry. Come all the same." But Colin didn't feel he could. So on the day in question, he went off to work, to do a bit of upholstery.

## A Party to celebrate the
# 40th Anniversary of The Cavern Club

## 12 noon onwards, Thursday, 16th January 1997

The Directors of the Cavern Club warmly welcome VIPs, friends, families, valued business associates and customers to a party to celebrate the 40th Anniversary of the opening of The Cavern Club, **the most famous club in the world.**

As owners of the club and organisers of the Mathew Street Festival, with experience of booking hundreds of bands, it was a difficult task to pick a dozen or so to try to reflect the changing musical tastes and influences that have shaped The Cavern Club over the last 40 years. Today you will be able to trace the earliest roots of the club with jazz sessions by original members of **The Wall City Jazz Band, The Merseysippi Jazz Band and The Ralph Walmough Band, who remarkably were the three bands who opened up THE CAVERN CLUB 40 years ago today!!!** With a fusion of skiffle, the club helped to fashion a new sound and we are proud to have Karl Terry and the Cruisers, Johnny Guitar and Geoff Nugent from The Undertakers, who were amongst the earliest exponents of what

became known as Merseybeat.

The Beatles are synonymous with the Club and we welcome Gary Gibson, the world's greatest John Lennon impersonator, who will pay tribute to one of The Cavern's most famous sons. The '60s and '70s are represented by special reunions of The Hideaways and The Klubs, who played The Cavern more times than any other bands (with nearly 600 performances between them).

Today's scene is reflected by The Cavern house band 'Up and Running', long since the region's favourite band, who will showcase their new album scheduled for release before Easter, and Native Instinct who are The Cavern Club's 'tip for the top'. Friends Professor Burlesque, Status Quid, Dark Horses, Ringer and Persuader, together with Marshall's House Band 'Emperor', help to complete what is, we feel, a very special line up.

Eat, drink, dance and be merry as Liverpool's finest talent takes the stage of The Most Famous Club in the World.
**Happy Birthday, Cavern!**

### PLEASE NOTE: THE COMPLIMENTARY BAR DOES NOT EXTEND TO SPIRITS

"Rod rang me at work and asked where I was. He said Shotton and everyone's turned up, we're waiting for you. I said, 'OK then, I'll be there in two hours.' I went home first to shower and change.

"When I got to the Cavern, I didn't have a ticket, of course. I pushed through the crowds and gave my name to the doorman. He said he knew nothing about it. He wouldn't let me in. I felt really pissed off. So I went to a pub nearby and had a Guinness.

"I was just about to get the bus home, but I rang Joan first, telling her I was on the way home. She said Rod had been on the phone. They were all waiting for me. They'd made arrangements at the door for me to get in.

"I went back again – and still the doorman wouldn't let me in. I thought, I'm too old to be fighting with doormen at my age. I'll just have another Guinness and go home. But as I set off, Rod came out and saw me – and he took me in.

"I recognised Rod, as I'd seen him a couple of times over the last few years. We'd sent Christmas cards, that sort of thing. I recognised Pete, even though I hadn't seen him for 40 years. I didn't think he'd changed so much. I'd always thought of him as a fairly confident bloke. Len was still as laid-back as ever.

"The one who threw me was Eric. I said to Rod, 'Which one's Eric?' Eric's hair was still brown, not grey like mine, but he'd got a weather-beaten, crinkly face. That's what threw me."

★   ★   ★

"My first impression when I saw them all," says Pete, "was, Who are these fucking old men?

"I really didn't recognise Eric or Rod at first, not till I had torn the layers away from their faces. Or Len. He was a big shock.

"Rod had a beard, so that was a surprise. Eric's face seemed to have become carved out of stone. But they both had bright eyes.

"I remember thinking that Colin had aged well. And Rod looked very fit. After a few drinks, I discovered he was now into windsurfing, which was why he looked so healthy.

"But as the party went on, I began to realise they hadn't really changed all that much. Eric was perhaps a bit more strong-willed, less tolerant than I'd remembered him as a boy at school. He was more single-minded, more focused. I didn't know, of course, till we got talking, what he'd done all these years, that he now had his own business.

"Len was still Len. He had the same sense of humour and seemed to laugh at everything, just as he'd always done.

"At school, Rod had been one of the enemy, in a way. He became head boy and all that. I'd always thought of him as a bit of a goody-goody.

"But I soon realised he's got a good sense of humour and he's very tolerant. But he does tend to fuss. He's a bit like a mother hen.

"Colin is one of the sweetest people I've ever met, so kind and considerate. He gets worried if he thinks he's said the wrong thing or upset anyone.

"When I heard about him still being an upholsterer, I tried to tell him he should expand his business, make himself a bit more money, but he said he was happy with himself and his life."

★   ★   ★

And what did the others think of Pete?

"He hadn't really changed," says Len. "Fuller in the face, and fuller in the tummy, but that's about all. And his hair is not so thick and yellow as it used to be. But he still had the same bouncy walk and the same sense of humour. We do laugh at the same things. We laughed so much at something or other that we started choking, getting out of breath. Just as we did as boys.

"I was amazed how confident Pete had become. And amazed that he had become a millionaire businessman. That did surprise me.

"I could relate to Pete easily, on that first meeting, but not so well at first with the others. But then I hadn't really known Rod, Eric and Colin. I was at a different school from them after all. But I always knew John and Pete because they lived near and we knocked around together, apart from playing in The Quarrymen.

"Eric always appeared pretty serious. And Rod, in 1957, just seemed to me to be a swot. And I think he was more interested in skiffle than rock'n'roll. I didn't know much about either of them really, back in the old days."

★   ★   ★

"Rod was the hardest to recognise," says Eric, "with his grey beard and cropped hair. He'd also become trendy which was a bit of a surprise. At school, he'd seemed very square, not with the same interests as the rest of us – by which I mean music, girls and cigarettes."

"Pete hadn't changed much, nor Len. I recognised Len right away. He was always the cool cat. He seemed quite young as well, as if he hadn't really matured with age. Colin seemed more subdued than he was as a boy, but then he was a bit older than us. At the time, he seemed more grown up. He was the one who introduced me to Guinness and cider when I was fifteen."

★ ★ ★

Rod, being ever so organised, and also still a musician, had taken the precaution of putting in the boot of his car a washboard, an old tea chest and his guitar when he left Uxbridge for the Cavern. Just in case. Nothing had been said about playing. After all, they'd been apart for forty years and everyone knew they hadn't gone on to be musicians.

But after several hours of drinking, the suggestion came up that they should clamber on the Cavern stage once again.

Rod said yes, knowing he'd brought his gear, but the others said no, how could they. All the other guests said, "Oh, go on."

"When we were persuaded to play," says Eric, "it was pretty late at night, about eight o'clock, I think. We'd been drinking since about 12, at their free bar, so we were all pretty well oiled. I would never have got up on stage otherwise. I hadn't touched a guitar for 40 years. I'd sold mine, the moment I'd left The Quarrymen. It was on hire purchase, so I wasn't going to keep paying it up if I didn't need it any more.

"But I borrowed a guitar from Garry Gibson and played that. He works as a John Lennon look-alike, and is very good, actually.

"To say I 'played' the guitar is stretching it a bit. Let's say I stood on the stage and held it . . ."

Colin played on some drums, but there were no sticks, so he just banged with his thumbs.

However, after forty years, The Quarrymen were together again at last, and trying to make music.

# 20

## Woolton Fete Revisited

Out of that impromptu performance at the Cavern, while half drunk, half playing and only half there, there came an invitation to play again – back at the venue where it had all begun.

There was another 40th anniversary celebration being organised that year in Liverpool, at Woolton Parish Church where they had played on Saturday, July 6, 1957. The Quarrymen were invited back – for the anniversary garden fete on Saturday, July 5, 1997.

They all accepted the invitation, even Pete, deep in the throes of expansions and dramas with his Fatty Arbuckle empire, and also Eric, the two who had not been all that keen on the Cavern reunion. They had enjoyed themselves so much, reliving memories, getting to know old friends again who at first sight had seemed strangers, that they welcomed the chance of another reunion, for social reasons, rather than musical.

But if they were going to have to play again, they might as well try to play a little bit better this time. Pretending to play someone else's instrument, staggering about, might not go down so well at a church event, though there again, in 1957, they hadn't been all that brilliant. And John had definitely been staggering, according to Paul's accounts.

So they met up once in Liverpool, at Len's house, and did their first rehearsal in forty years. Eric even bought himself a new guitar – just a cheap one, costing £100. No use lashing out for what might be their first and last public appearance in 40 years.

Colin was nervous. "My worry was that we weren't very good 40 years ago, so what would people think of us now? But Pete said if they expected us just to be the same, then we had nothing to lose, did we?"

So Colin was persuaded. He got his old drums down from the top of the wardrobe and prepared to play them in public for the first time in 40 years.

★ ★ ★

The Woolton Fete, organised by St Peter's Church itself and various Beatles fans, was intended to raise money for the restoration of the Church Hall, where John and Paul had first met. It was in bad repair and needed £400,000 to complete the rebuilding work. The hope was that Beatles fans, knowing the significance of the hall, would help.

It turned out to be a much bigger event than The Quarrymen had expected. It received national and international publicity and messages were received from the Queen, Prime Minister Tony Blair, Yoko Ono, Sir George Martin, Cynthia Lennon and Paul McCartney, now, of course, Sir Paul.

The programme for the fete was priced at £1, compared with 3d. in 1957, but the events and itinerary were very much the same. There was a parade of floats at two o'clock round the village, crowning of the Rose Queen at three, a children's fancy-dress competition, stalls and side shows. The Quarrymen were billed to play in the field at 4.15, as they had done in 1957, then in the evening at the Grand Dance in the Church Hall. Tickets for the dance were £15 as opposed to two shillings in 1957, but this time a buffet supper was included. In 1957, there were refreshments, but you had to pay 'moderate prices'.

The only real difference in 40 years was a Beatles memorabilia market which was set up in the Church Hall from 10–4, selling the usual Beatles records, books and souvenirs, now so familiar to all Beatles fans. Who could have imagined that, back in 1957?

As before, The Quarrymen travelled on one of the floats in the opening procession – driven by the same lorry driver who had driven them all those years ago, Doug Chadwick. He was aged 17 in 1957, son of the owner of a small haulage firm, DT and P Chadwick, who had traditionally helped out at the Fete. Doug was now running the family firm, but still had the sign he'd put on the back of the lorry in 1957 which proclaimed 'QUARRYMEN Skiffle Group'.

"I'd been confirmed at St Peter's under Mr Pryce-Jones," so he was quoted as saying in the 1997 programme. "We volunteered to provide transport for the fete, primarily for the Rose Queen. I can remember driving the lorry with The Quarrymen playing on the back. It had an aluminium platform and it did our ears in with all the stamping. But it was good music, for its era."

In the afternoon, The Quarrymen played the same tunes, 'Cumberland Gap' and 'Maggie May', and in the same field. In 1957 it was known as the Scout Field, owned by the Church. Now it's part of the neighbouring Church of England primary school. Surprising that it had not been sold off or built over.

**The Day John Met Paul - 4th July 1957**

**40th** Anniversary Garden Fete
Saturday 5th July 1997
at 3pm

Admission by programme £1

Official Celebration Promoters:
Bishop Martin CE School
St. Peter's Church Woolton
Liverpool Beatlescene
Yesterday Once More

Proceeds in aid of School Funds & Church Hall Restoration

| Programme for the Day |
|---|

**10am - 4pm** Beatles Memorabilia Market in the Church Hall
Admission £2; Music from Liverpool duo "Pool O' Life"

**2pm** The Parade of Floats leaves from Bishop Martin School
to process around Woolton Village

**3pm** The Crowning of the Rose Queen (Miss Charlotte Nixon) by
Mrs. Sally Baxter (nee Wright) the Rose Queen of 1957

**Official opening of the Fete by Mr. Harry Forrest, the Organiser
of the Garden Fete in 1957**

Children's Fancy Dress Competition

**From 3.15pm onwards** - stalls, side-shows, entertainments, dancing,
refreshments, and live music....

**3.15pm** Local talent "Smile" and "Chris Mason"

**4.15pm-4.45pm** The Quarry Men Skiffle Group

**4.45pm - 5.45pm** The music of the Beatles by "Ringer"

**5.45pm-6pm** The Quarry Men Skiffle Group

**8pm** The Grand Dance in the Church Hall
Music from The Quarrymen, Ringer and other guests
Admission by ticket only (£15 including buffet supper)

Don't forget to visit St. Peter's Church which will be open throughout the day
12 noon tomorrow is the Beatles Service in St. Peter's - not to be missed!

"Playing in the field was amazing," says Rod. "The sun shone, just as it did the first time. In 1957, I suppose only about 150 people stood in the field and watched us play. This time there were 3,000. Beatles fans had come from all over the world, specially to be there.

"The evening was brilliant as well, playing in the Church Hall. It was packed. We did 'Twenty Flight Rock', which was the tune Paul had played to John and so impressed him.

"We also played Lonnie Donegan's 'Putting On The Style' which we had played in 1957. What I didn't know that night was that a friend of mine from St Peter's Youth Club, Bob Molyneux, was standing in the audience with his tape recorder. This tape was subsequently sold at Sotheby's for about £70,000. It must be the most expensive tape recording ever."

On the following morning, after a church service in St Peter's, The Quarrymen unveiled a plaque on the church hall to commemorate their 1957 performance and the meeting of John with Paul. All The Quarrymen's names are listed – and spelled correctly, except for Rod's. If you go and see it, and thousands of Beatles fans have done so since, you'll spot straight away that it should not be Rod Davies.

As a result of the reunion, the five Quarrymen decided to make a recording of themselves playing, a CD called *Get Back – Together*. This being the modern age, it was announced and sold over the Internet, using Fatty Arbuckle's website.

Perhaps the most nostalgic moment in the whole Woolton weekend, according to Rod, was when Pete decided to sing a song on stage – for the first time in his life.

Back then, awkwardly clutching his washboard, he was ever so shy and ill at ease, embarrassed about appearing in public, just doing it to please John.

Now, as a successful businessman, and one who had lived so much of John's short life with him, he was not embarrassed at all about singing or showing emotion in public.

"Pete sang 'Imagine', dedicating it to his best mate. He sang it with such feeling that I saw tears in the eyes of the audience . . ."

# 21

## Born Again Quarrymen

And so The Quarrymen were reborn. Five gentlemen of a certain age, all by now in their late fifties, with families and homes, some with grey hair and tummies, started getting invitations to play in public, after a gap of forty years. Not just play, but record and tour, things they had never done before, in their previous incarnation.

Back in the Fifties, they had never dreamt of or yearned to go on the road, to turn into pop stars, have crowds queuing, girls screaming, which John and Paul had always wanted. Pete, Eric, Len, Colin and Rod knew at the time it was just a schoolboy craze, a bit of fun with their mates, and that they would soon move on and into real life.

Len did realise later on what he had missed, or at least neglected, wishing he had used his talents better and become a singer. Rod had tried, had kept it up, harbouring notions and desires of playing professionally, but his attempts at playing in various bands and producing tapes and CDs had not led anywhere. But Pete, Eric and Colin had never for a moment harboured any desire to play again in public.

Now, thanks to the worldwide passion for Beatles conventions, conferences and all things Beatly, they found themselves in demand, being requested not just to play, but to be themselves. Twenty years, even ten years previously, few people would have been interested in seeing or listening to five old blokes from another age who, just by chance, once knew someone who later became famous.

Their Beatles connections had mostly been an embarrassment to them in the previous decades. They had never wanted new people in their life, at work or play, to know about it, fearing they would go on about it or that they themselves might appear to be boastful or, even worse, not believed.

The Beatles, during the last 30 years, had found themselves in a similar situation. They, too, didn't want people to go on about The Beatles, were bored by the same old questions. They considered the new generation of Beatles Brains as pretty pathetic anoraks, arguing over trivial facts and details, and the conventions and conferences all fairly tatty or simply cheap moneymaking.

When doing The Beatles biography, the hardest part was making them think back to what it was like. They had little interest in the past, where they had been, only in today and tomorrow. They had kept very few old photos of themselves, old programmes, posters, documents, letters. I picked up some handwritten songs from the floor of Abbey Road which they had let lie there and asked if I could have them, knowing the cleaners would otherwise burn them. (They are now safe in the British Library and in my will, they go to the nation.)

But as the years went on, the three remaining Beatles, now also in their fifties, became more interested in where they had come from. Didn't find it quite so embarrassing to talk about having been a Beatle. In 1996, when their *Anthology* came out – the CDs, TV series, videos and stuff – it showed that they were now quite enjoying themselves, talking about their past. They'd also started collecting Beatles memorabilia themselves, especially Paul who has now got his own private Beatles museum. One of the reasons for high prices at auctions is because a representative of The Beatles or of Apple is often there, or thought to be there.

The Beatles, with age, realised that something remarkable had happened to them many years before. Something that was unlikely to happen to them again, or possibly to anyone, in the same way. So why be embarrassed? Why not enjoy it?

In a similar, if more modest, way, The Quarrymen decided to lie back and enjoy it when unexpectedly they found themselves in demand. Even Pete, running his restaurant empire, agreed to take some time off to play again with his old friends.

Unlike The Beatles, nothing like it had happened first time round to the five original Quarrymen. This was a totally new experience, being invited by strangers wanting to meet them, talk to them, touch them, treat them as special.

We are, of course, not talking mega audiences, mega events. They were still going to be part-time players, fitting in whatever was to come with the rest of their lives. Colin and Len in particular could not afford to take time off work, unless they were being paid enough to cover their loss of earnings.

But they all decided to go with the flow, to accept any interesting offers to play at Beatles conferences. If nothing else, it would be something new, a chance perhaps to stay free in a hotel, a chance to sell their new CD to adoring fans. There might even be groupies. A bit late in life, but you never know.

**Rod Davis**
**John Lennon's**
**Original Quarrymen**
www.quarrymen.co.uk

Scorpion Publications
PO Box 616, Uxbridge, UB8 2YP England
telephone 01895 847504

email davispain @ compuserve.com
http://ourworld.compuserve.com/homepages/davispain

"They'll probably all turn out to be aged 59," said Pete. "But at our age, you can't be choosy."

Anyway, bound to be a few drinks, some fun, a lot of laughs. And so they set off. Pop stars, second time around . . .

★   ★   ★

The Quarrymen's first reappearance in the world at large, after their Woolton Fete performance, was at Derby in November 1997. They were invited to take part in the Derby Beatles Convention and performed at the Derby Playhouse on Sunday, November 9. In between numbers, they were interviewed on stage about their early days.

They discovered, when making their CD recording, that Len had a surprisingly good rock'n'roll voice, so he was allowed to be lead singer, the role John had originally filled. He was thus able to give up his tea chest bass, which he'd always disliked playing. Pete took it over, along with his washboard.

Several hundred people turned up to watch them and afterwards they sold quite a few copies of their CD.

In the audience at the Derby show was Jonathan Bailey, who had been head boy at Quarry Bank when John, Pete, Eric and Rod had been in the fifth form. He had booked The Quarrymen for several school dances, including the Prefects' Dance. They had not seen or heard of him for 40 years, so they were quite surprised to discover his present-day job – Jonathan Bailey had become the Bishop of Derby.

Rob Molyneux also turned up, the schoolboy who had taped The Quarrymen's performance at Woolton Fete – the tape which was later sold at Sotheby's.

Then, in the evening, there was a third surprise appearance – Nigel Walley. As a member of John's gang, he had been an original Quarryman, filling in now and again on tea chest bass, before becoming their first ever manager. He came up to them and claimed that he still had them under contract.

For their last number, 'Twenty Flight Rock', he was pulled on stage with them and invited to stand on the tea chest as it was being played, a trick he used to do 40 years earlier. Wisely, at his age, he declined.

★　★　★

For their second appearance, they were invited abroad, doing better in a way than The Beatles at the same early stage in their performing career.

On April 11, 1998, The Quarrymen appeared at The Beatles Unlimited Festival at Utrecht in Holland. Rod drove from London, Eric flew from Edinburgh while Pete, Len and Colin flew together from Liverpool. Their plane was delayed during a lightning storm and they didn't get to their hotel till five in the morning, feeling pretty pissed off. If this is playing abroad, they thought, perhaps we are too old for it.

But they all enjoyed the next day. They were filmed practising by Dutch TV, did a live radio programme in Hilversum, walked round the old city of Utrecht and were offered some interesting-looking white powder which naturally they declined, being sensible senior citizens.

The convention was being held in the Vredenburg Music Centre where over 1,000 Dutch Beatles fans gathered. The Quarrymen took part in a Beatles quiz where they disgraced themselves by not knowing the answers. The audience turned out to know more about The Quarrymen than The Quarrymen themselves.

Then, later that year, the Call Came. After only one year on the road, and after only three public appearances, they got the ultimate invitation, one which The Beatles and Brian Epstein had spent years dreaming about. They were invited to perform in America.

Not just to hop over and appear in the USA, but go on a ten-day proper tour, doing one-night stands in real venues, including a New York appearance and invitations to appear live, on coast to coast national television.

Fortunately for posterity, Rod kept his own diary of their historic tour, which began on July 1, 1998. Over to you, Rod.

### Wednesday, July 1, 1998

Collected band's US Visas at 1pm in Chiswick and dashed home to finish packing. Off to Heathrow, fortunately only five minutes away by car, with my suitcase containing my clothes and a collapsible T-Chest bass, my guitar, a spare guitar and four huge boxes containing 200 CDs apiece!

Free champagne courtesy of United Airlines in the VIP lounge and then a desperate scramble to get on the plane! A chance to get our heads down for what would be the only three hours' sleep out of 24!

Arrived at Kennedy Airport at 9pm local time, but by the time we had negotiated with the customs over the CDs (and lost!) the crowds of screaming teenagers must have all gone home to bed! After a brief meeting with Thom Wolke, who put the tour together for us, we were off in our Hertz rental maroon people carrier with tinted glass for a hectic three hours' drive up the coast to Foxwoods Casino Resort, which claims to be the biggest casino in the world and is situated on an Indian Reservation in the middle of a forest! Eventually got to bed about 6am our time, knowing we had to be up early.

### Thursday, July 2

Up and breakfasting on a huge American breakfast after about three hours sleep. Chased up the CDs with the US Customs. Caught a few more zzzs then soundchecked in the Cinedrome 360. A quick press conference at 3pm and then off we went for some photographs and an attempt to recreate The Beatles 'pillow fight' photos! We had a very appreciative audience for our gig and we enjoyed meeting them in the interval and after the show, some very big Beatles fans among them! We talked to the *Daily Express* who had sent someone up from New York to meet us, then off to bed, to be up at 5.45am.

### Friday, July 3

Having made it to reception by 6am, delayed for half an hour, because we had lost the parking ticket for the van and some pernickety lady was monopolising the sole reception clerk. Found the ticket in Len's pocket and hit the road across Connecticut to Poughkeepsie and its 105.5 WPDH Classic Rock Radio station, where we had a real laugh with the DJs. Pete Shotton told some outrageous stories which should have had us arrested by the nearest traffic cops! (And I don't mean the ordinary kind of traffic, either!)

Drove down the beautiful Hudson River valley to try and find our motel, which was unfortunately overbooked so we had to settle for the Watergate Inn which suffered certain shortcomings (at least it wasn't bugged!). However, we were too tired to argue, so after a few more winks of sleep we were off to play at a millionaire's party in the late afternoon. A splendid house by a private lake, with people swimming and playing volleyball and enjoying a barbecue. One lady cried when I sang 'Worried Man Blues'. She said her father used to sing it to her when she was a child! The other band members had a less complimentary explanation for her tears! Dinner afterwards at the Rock'n Horse Steak House, where the waitress Roberta told us some very funny but totally unrepeatable jokes!

*Saturday, July 4*

We moved to a more salubrious hotel and went for lunch at Tarrytown overlooking the Hudson. No booking today, no red-blooded Yanks would be seen dead listening to a bunch of Brits on July 4. Funnily enough, I had turned down a booking in London playing bluegrass for an American company on the same day! We decided to drive down the Hudson to Yonkers to watch the big firework display but traffic terrible so turned back and found a convenient bar which sold draught Guinness and Sam Adams. A quiet Fourth of July!

*Sunday, July 5*

Back up the Hudson to Boscobel, a beautiful wooden mansion overlooking the river and West Point Military Academy. We played half in and half out of a marquee (because of the heat!) in which a Shakespeare play was to be presented later! (Quarrymen, warm-up act for Bill Shakespeare!) Most of the audience kept well away from us, but we realised that this was because they were trying to keep in the shade, and not for any other reason! When we finished, we dashed down the road to Peekskill where Pete Seeger was playing for the 150th anniversary of Dains Timber Yard! At the end of his set we were invited up on stage. I got to play his 12-string guitar, a great honour, and Pete sat in on banjo as we played 'Midnight Special'.

In the evening we were invited to the house of the lady who had organised our lunchtime gig and we lounged around her pool! She entertained us to a marvellous dinner, the highlight of which was baked beans cooked in Bourbon!

This made *Blazing Saddles* look like the proverbial vicarage tea party!

*Monday, July 6*

Off to New York Radio WFUV at 0830 at Falmer University where we had a great time with DJ Darren DeVivo and played a couple of numbers on his show. Back to our hotel for a short kip, then back to Greenwich Village and the Bottom Line Club. We soundchecked and then went for a meal. Pete and Colin were interviewed by the man from the London *Times!* Back to the Bottom Line for the first house, it seemed to go very well, once again an audience full of Beatles fans which included Mark & Carol Lapidos who organise the Beatlefests in the US (we'll be at their Chicago bash on 14/15/16 August). Jim O'Donnell who wrote *The Day John Met Paul* was in the audience for the second show, very appropriate this, as it was, of course, the 41st anniversary of the meeting of John and Paul! Again we had a ball but the lack of sleep was beginning to catch up with us!

*Tuesday, July 7*

We found ourselves a hotel near Central Park, recommended by Jim O'Donnell (thanks, Jim) as Ray Coleman's favourite hotel and we piled in there and left Pete Shotton to catch up on some sleep! The rest of us went off to Mike McCann's syndicated radio show, Hot Wax Fax, where we played and chatted with a very genial Mike. Then came a real high spot – George Gunby of 'Yesterday Once More' had suggested we get in touch with Kevin McCarthy, the manager of Shea Stadium! Kevin invited us over and even found a couple of cricket bats and a cricket ball! So the Quarrymen played cricket at Shea Stadium and had our photos taken with our guitars on the spot where The Beatles played. Then we enjoyed a few beers in the Mets dressing room, as used by you know who! As we left the stadium, manager Kevin presented us with NY Mets hats and souvenirs!

Back to the hotel and off to ABC News TV studios where we eventually taped our eight minute or so spot, with an interview and a quick blast of 'Twenty Flight Rock'. This, however, was not due to be broadcast until about 4am so we went and found a bar off Broadway which sold Murphys and had a few beers until our clip came on. By that time we were feeling rather ribald so the comments were flying and I'm sure the rest of the customers in the bar didn't know what to make of the five laughing idiots watching the television! We strolled home across Broadway as dawn was breaking, buying some souvenir T-shirts en route!

*Wednesday, July 8*

We had hoped for an easy day, easy that is, apart from the 250 mile drive down to our last gig in Maryland. However, Japanese National TV wanted to interview Pete Shotton about John Lennon's drawings so we had to put off our departure until late afternoon. It poured with rain most of the way and we had more than our fair share of sea mist.

Arrived in the little town of Easton, Maryland, and drove up to the Avalon Theatre where we were welcomed by the manager, Ellen General and her husband, John. The Avalon was built in 1921 and is now a beautifully restored art-deco theatre! After a real Maryland seafood meal in the restaurant we were taken to our accommodation in luxurious guest villas in the nearby Marine Engineering College.

### Thursday, July 9

Len, Colin and I were up at 6am again to do two radio shows! Len on his own and Colin and myself at 'The Duck' radio station, in what looked like a shack in the middle of a field! However, DJ Karl proved to be a real nice guy and Colin and I went into the Scouse humour routine and we had a big laugh!

Back home to catch up on some more sleep! In the afternoon our hosts laid on a barbecue for us – striped sea bass – at the edge of the water and we met some great people. However, we had to drag ourselves away as our transport arrived to take us to the theatre. Pete, Eric and Len piled into the long black 1958 Cadillac convertible with white upholstery and Colin and I had to slum it in the 1933 Rolls Royce! They belonged to an Austrian multimillionaire who was just delighted to use his cars for such an occasion. Johannes and his sister Elisabeth drove us into Easton in considerable style! After this, we were so hyped up that we had a great time on stage, we only hope the audience enjoyed it half as much! They certainly seemed very appreciative and nobody actually threw anything!

After a few beers we hit the hay, ready for the drive back to New York and the plane home!

### Friday, July 10

Via a factory outlet store we eventually made it to JFK – "heavy traffic on the Jersey turnpike" – those American TV programmes will make much more sense now! One last interview for a new Beatles biography and a swift farewell to our man in the US, Thom Wolke, to whom we owe our grateful thanks! We even managed to sell a CD to the clerk on the airport check-in desk!

We reached London totally spaced out, with an offer of a gig in Las Vegas in January, and talk of recording in Nashville or Sun Studios, Memphis ringing in our ears! It has taken me a whole week to come down! We had a fantastic time and met some wonderful people. We can't wait to go back! Our thanks go to all those who helped revive The Quarrymen, especially Jean Catharell and George and Kath Gunby for inviting us to the 40th Anniversary celebrations of the day John met Paul at Woolton last year.

★   ★   ★

Thanks, Rod. Nicely written. Perhaps next time cut down on some of the exclamation marks.

During that tour, as Rod indicated, there was quite a bit of media interest.

*US Today* on July 6, 1998 had a front page story with the headline "Pre Beatlemania strikes with 10-date US Tour". It listed the personnel, the venues and what they would be performing.

"The group, which plays at New York's Bottom Line tonight, is dryly modest about its own historical importance. Says Davis, 'We're basically five old guys who know someone who became someone famous.' "

On July 8, the *New York Post's* rock critic, Dan Aquilane, described how they had waited 40 years between gigs and now had wrinkles and grey hair. "No one in the group is a great musician, yet The Quarrymen are like five charming uncles who play music together at every family party. They can carry a tune and when they're not singing, they are able to entertain the clan with all the intimate details of the family's history."

One paper said they were the 'Pre fab Beatles', a joke probably better understood in the UK than the USA.

The *New York Times* didn't quite enjoy the joke and Jon Pareles gave them a rather catty review. "Only in the Fifties could such tepid music have galvanized teenagers; even in England, skiffle quickly gave way to plugged-in rock. For The Quarrymen at the Bottom Line, the band member's self-deprecation between songs was well earned. But their music was never intended to be much more than a hobby."

# LIFELINE

A QUICK READ ON WHAT PEOPLE ARE TALKING ABOUT

## Pre-Beatlemania strikes with 10-date U.S. tour

The band that became the Beatles has just made its American concert debut.

Reunited 41 years after the late John Lennon invited Paul McCartney to join the Quarrymen, five other members of the Liverpool band kicked off a 10-date stateside tour Thursday at the Foxwoods Resort Casino in Mashantucket, Conn.

By Stan Godlewski

**'Pre-fab' Five:** The Quarrymen — Colin Hanton on drums, Eric Griffith, background left, Len Garry, Rod Davis and Pete Shotton — perform '50s rock 'n' roll but no Beatles songs.

Performing a set of '50s rock 'n' roll standards — but no Beatles songs — are lifelong Lennon friend Pete Shotton (washboard), drummer Colin Hanton (who recorded with Lennon, McCartney and then-new Quarryman George Harrison), guitarist and singer Len Garry (who played a primitive bass in the original band), guitarist Eric Griffith (whom Harrison replaced) and banjoist Rod Davis.

The group, which plays at New York's Bottom Line tonight, is dryly modest about its own historical importance.

Says Davis, "We're basically five old guys who know someone who became someone famous."

198

**POP REVIEW**

# Meet the Quarrymen, Minus the Famous Alumni

**By JON PARELES**

From left, Eric Griffiths, Len Garry, Pete Shotton and Rod Davis.

Every career has to start somewhere, and John Lennon's started when he was playing skiffle music with the Quarrymen in the late 1950's. A mock footnote came to life when the Quarrymen performed on Monday night at the Bottom Line.

Beatles fans may recall that it was at a Quarrymen show in St. Peter's Church hall on July 6, 1957, that Lennon first met Paul McCartney. Mr. McCartney and George Harrison went on to join the Quarrymen, replacing all of the group's members except Colin Hanton on drums. And after a final drunken debacle of a performance in 1958, Mr. Hanton put away his drums for 40 years, until the Quarrymen reunited for the 40th anniversary of the Cavern Club in Liverpool. The band stayed together to play a benefit for St. Peter's Church, made a CD and have started a second career.

At the Bottom Line, they strummed acoustic guitars and sang their 1950's repertory, mostly songs from Lead Belly and Elvis Presley. Their set, with reminiscences between songs, was a souvenir from a turning point in British pop, when Lonnie Donegan had a hit with "Rock Island Line" and English teen-agers discovered the joys of jug-band music and three-chord guitar. Lennon convinced a friend, Pete Shotton, to put a string on a tea chest like a washtub bass. Len Garry, Eric Griffiths and Rod Davis joined the group on guitars.

Skiffle wasn't just an embrace of amateurism. It was also an infatuation with America as reflected in blues and folk songs: the exotic allure of hopping freight trains and winding up in jail. Only one song the Quarrymen played had lyrics set in a Liverpool, and its tune looked to American ragtime-blues. For most of the set, they played mild-mannered versions of old songs from "Worried Man Blues" to "All Shook Up" to "Come Go With Me." Mr. Garry has soaked up Presley's singing; Mr. Davis did an English approximation of blues slides. Only in the 1950's could such tepid music have galvanized teen-agers; even in England, skiffle quickly gave way to plugged-in rock. For the Quarrymen at the Bottom Line, the band members' self-deprecation between songs was well-earned. But their music was never intended to be much more than a hobby.

<hr />

# A pre-Fab Four reunion

**Dan Aquilante** *Post Rock Critic*

**W**ITH more than 40 years between gigs, the Quarrymen (the band that would become The Beatles) woke like rock 'n' roll Rip Van Winkles for a club performance at the cozy Bottom Line on Monday.

Paul McCartney and George Harrison, onetime Quarrymen members, were absent from the reunion, and on the stage — out of the way, over to the right — was an empty stool. Maybe it was just forgotten furniture, or maybe the Quarrymen had it placed there to honor their mate, the late John Lennon.

For years, these guys have been little more than footnotes in rock history. One of the band members, singer and guitarist Rod Davis, perhaps expressed it best when, in explaining the group's contemporary relevance, he said, "We're basically five old guys who know someone who became someone famous."

And at the Bottom Line, the "Why the Quarrymen?" question was answered in the rambling, yet often wonderful between-song patter when these "five old guys" recalled the heady days of pre-Beatlemania, when they were all teen-agers.

The music they played then (and still do) is skiffle, a cross between blue-eyed R & B and country, with hints of folk and rock. There wasn't a single Beatles tune in the program — that is, unless you count the countrified "In Spite of All the Danger," written by McCartney and Harrison as the "B" side to the Quarrymen's 45-rpm demo covering Buddy Holly's "That'll Be the Day" in 1958.

The tunes the Quarrymen chiseled at the Bottom Line were the same ones that Lennon, McCartney, Harrison and the other Quarrymen played from 1957 to '59. They were all teens then, making music and being in a band just because it was fun.

More than 40 years later — under the wrinkles and gray hair — the band mates bickered and had fun like teen-age pals again as they reprised most of those same old songs. Standards such as "The Rock Island Line," "The Blue Moon of Kentucky," "Good Rockin' Tonight," "All Shook Up" and "Twenty Flight Rock" (the tune that Paul auditioned for the band with) were the highlights of the show.

Although the famous Beatles breakthrough song, "Love Me Do," was written on Lennon's Quarrymen watch, it wasn't recorded until five years later. So "Love Me Do" would have been fair game for this concert, but the band maintained its distance from the work of the Fab Four. As Lennon's life-long pal Pete Shotton, who played the washboard, said to the crowd, "By now, you probably realize that if you've come to hear a Beatles sound-alike band, you've come to the wrong place."

No one in the group is a great musician, yet the Quarrymen are like five charming uncles who play music together at every family party. They can carry a tune and, when they're not singing, they relate the intimate details of the family's history.

The producers of VH1's "Storytellers" should take note: The Quarrymen have the chops and the tales for a shot on the series.

Paul McCartney and George Harrison didn't attend, but three-fifths of their old Quarrymen band members — Len Garry (from left), Pete Shotton and Rod Davis — performed their skiffle music spiced with between-songs banter Monday night at the Bottom Line.

199

# 22

## Pete Packs Up . . .

During that first year of the reborn Quarrymen, Pete was fitting in the washboard with being chairman of the Fatty Arbuckle restaurant chain. And as befitted a chairman, he already had quite a few trappings and outside interests to keep himself amused, such as his BMW 850i, his Aston Martin Viraga and his large yacht, a Fairline Squadron 59, with four cabins and eight berths. Strange that he should have been prepared to rough it on the road with the other four Quarrymen.

When they were staying in a particularly crummy motel, Len used to threaten to take Pete's photo, looking all scruffy and knackered after staying up late, then send it to his staff back at Fatty Arbuckle.

But Pete did enjoy it. He had not acquired any airs and graces over the years, gone all Southern or lost his Liverpool accent. The attraction was not the music but the social life, being with some old mates from Liverpool again, who shared the same sense of humour and memories, with whom he was able to be relaxed and informal.

What he liked best was staying up late and drinking and talking. He'd always been a late-night person, and had remained so, unlike the normal executive in a suit who likes to be at the office bright and early in the morning. By its nature, playing in a group, big or small, is evening work, and by its nature, the fun often goes on and on, long after the music has stopped.

He was finding it easy enough, balancing the two lives, and had no intention of giving up either. With The Quarrymen, he was just one of them, an old mate, not a company chairman.

"I hated it in 1957, being on stage," says Pete. "I always tried to hide at the back. I was so shy and tongue-tied. But this time round, well, you can't keep me down."

On stage, even though he was playing the humble washboard, Pete had become the main talker. Rod did a lot of the boring, organising work behind the scenes, arranging dates and booking places, trying to shift their

CDs, while Pete had become the public face of The Quarrymen.

Over the year, they evolved their own music and talk show, interspersing skiffle and rock numbers with stories about their early days with John and Paul. It all looked and sounded very natural, five unaffected blokes, enjoying themselves, not smooth and professional, with people butting in, getting things wrong, arguing amongst themselves about what to do next.

Eric, despite his successful Civil Service and businessman career, didn't look quite at ease when it came to his turn to talk on stage. Rod also looked nervous at times. Len was, of course, too laid-back to worry about the talking bits, preferring to sing, at long last. Colin, on his drums, preferred to take a back seat, as is the role of drummers, but when it was his turn to tell a tale or two, he did it surprisingly well.

Pete had the best stories to tell, of course, having known John so intimately, but he told them well, fluently, amusingly. He was always good value when it came to TV, radio and press interviews, if he could be bothered, if he wasn't, let's say, being a bit temperamental and moody. Just as John himself could be.

But then, in July 1998, one of Pete's lives came to an end – and it was his company chairman life, not his washboard life, which suddenly ceased.

It all happened just as they were going off for that American tour, but the root cause began the previous year, at the height of the BSE crisis when British beef found itself banned for being susceptible to a disease known as bovine spongiform encephalopathy. In all 5 million cattle were slaughtered. The total cost to the country was estimated at £20 billion.

"BSE had a terrible effect on us and all restaurants specialising in steaks and burgers," says Pete. "Turnover dropped by 20 per cent almost at once. It took months for any recovery."

Pete at this time was still in the full flush of expansion, with plans for dozens of new restaurants and new sites. The really big boys, like McDonalds, can cope better with blips and sudden market changes, ride out any storms, but smaller chains find it much harder. So Pete got pretty depressed.

"My main bank, the NatWest, always believed in us, but the BSE scare made major new borrowings rather more difficult.

"I suppose the biggest effect was that it changed my outlook – it made me see that no matter how well you are doing, unexpected things, out of your control, can knock you back.

"Around that time, we were having talks with some venture capitalists, who were very keen to find us more investment money. They weren't worried about BSE. They could see how healthy our business was. The idea was for them to raise capital for us – then one of them turned round, to my surprise, and said they'd like to buy us out. This was Alchemy Partners – the venture capitalists who later hit the news when they were in negotiations for the take-over of Rover.

"I'd been gutted by BSE. When it happened, I had 11 deals in the pipeline which I wasn't able to complete. But, I still had no intention of selling, until suddenly Alchemy offered me a deal I couldn't refuse. I thought, Fuck it, Pete, take the money and run. So I sold out to them."

As Fatty Arbuckle was a private company, the precise details never came out. It was, anyway, a complicated deal which involved shares and options. In the initial stage, on July 3, 1998, so the *Daily Telegraph* business pages reported, Alchemy paid £5 million for a major stake in the firm. Later Pete sold the rest of his holding. The estimates of Pete's share varied between £10 and £20 million. He's not saying, except to admit, yes, he ended up a 'fucking multimillionaire'.

It meant he had more time now to spend on the road with his old mates.

# 23

# The Quarrymen Tour The World

The Quarrymen's second visit to the States was the following month, in August 1998. They were special guests at the Chicago Beatlefest which took place over a long weekend, August 14–16, at the Hyatt Regency O'Hare. They took part in a question-and-answer session, sold lots of their CDs, got to meet hundreds of local Beatles fans. "Thousands, actually," says Rod. "We were told the figure was about 9,500."

In November 1998 they went to Dublin at the invitation of The Beatles Fan Club of Ireland – 35 years to the day after The Beatles made their one and only appearance in Ireland. They played to a packed house at the Olympic Theatre. On the bill was another group called The Quarrymen – a well-known Irish group who specialise in Beatles music.

They also appeared on Irish radio and TV, both RTE and Ulster TV. Pete did a long radio interview about the time he flew by helicopter with John and Yoko to the remote Irish island, Dornish Island.

Then, later, in November 1998, they went to Cuba, which was where I met them. The main event was the Third International Beatles Convention held over three days in Havana, a very serious, academic affair compared with the much more commercial Beatles gatherings in the USA and Europe where a major attraction is selling Beatles souvenirs, books, records, tapes. There was none of that in Havana. Instead we had learned lecturers reading out their written papers on the inner meanings and motivations of The Beatles. There were also Cuban groups playing Beatles music and old Beatles Sixties videos being shown from *The Ed Sullivan Show* and elsewhere. One of the sponsors of the convention was the British Council and the British Embassy in Havana.

The Quarrymen were amazed by the knowledge and enthusiasm of the Cuban Beatles fans and the musicianship of the Cuban bands. Their final concert attracted an audience of 1,500, their biggest and probably most appreciative audience so far.

While in Havana, they went to several parties, saw the historic sights and buildings, drank a lot of rum, smoked a lot of big cigars.

In January 1999, they returned to the USA, to Las Vegas this time, to play at the Palace Station Casino.

"We were met at the airport by a white stretch limo," says Rod, "and got chauffeured along the fabulous Las Vegas Strip to the Casino where our names were up in lights. We couldn't believe it. And it was on the biggest illuminated sign in the whole of Nevada. A bit different from sitting on the back of a lorry in Woolton . . ."

From Las Vegas they flew to Canada where they did a show in Vancouver. During their Canadian trip Len got nasty toothache. They met lots of ex-pat Brits, some of whom came originally from Woolton and Speke. They did a live TV show in which Colin, for once, didn't wear his tie. That had become one of their running jokes on tour, mocking Colin for always turning up wearing a collar and tie, even on stage while playing his drums.

On their last day in Canada, they spent the evening relaxing at the Irish Heather Club listening to the Irish music and attempting to reduce Canada's Guinness supply. "It was an advert saying 'Drink Canada Dry'," says Pete, which made them over-indulge a trifle more than usual.

In July 1999, they played at the Cavern in Liverpool, a proper performance this time, as opposed to their impromptu, drunken playing at the 40th anniversary party in 1997.

In August 1999, they made their fourth American tour, taking in New York, Orlando and Boston. In New York, they strolled round Strawberry Fields in Central Park and were guests at a major baseball game at the Shea Stadium between the Mets and the Houston Astros. They were meant to play a few numbers before the game began, but this was cancelled. Instead, they were featured on a giant video screen as their CD was played.

In Boston, they drank a lot of Guinness, just for a change, did some college radio at MIT and played a venue called Johnny D's. In Orlando, they attended another Beatlefest. By now, they were meeting up again with Beatles fans and organisers they had met at earlier US tours.

If it was October, it must be Belgium. They visited Mons on October 9, 1999, for a Beatles Day and were interviewed before a French-speaking audience. OK for Rod, of course, with his degree in Modern Languages, but a bit confusing for the others.

Pete didn't make this Belgium trip, as he was ill, the first time so far all five did not appear together. A great loss to the Belgian brewing industry, so the others agreed.

In March 2000, they made their fifth American trip, this time for the

Metro Beatlefest in New Jersey. Again, Pete didn't make it. His paper-
work was not in order. Or was he beginning to get fed up?

★   ★   ★

All these tours and appearances increased the sales of their CD and also
resulted in them acquiring a large following of Quarrymen fans – not just
Beatles fans – all over the world. They had two websites, to keep their fans
up to date with any new excitements in The Quarrymen's life. A Quarrymen fan mag appeared in Germany which was wholly devoted to them
and an internet comic strip began in Spain, based on their characters. They
were experiencing, in a minor way, some of the fame and exposure which
The Beatles had enjoyed.

They were even heard in a film, though you had to be pretty quick to
catch them. The director, Michael Lindsay-Hogg, used The Quarrymen
playing 'Come Go With Me' over the closing credits of his 90-minute
film *Two Of Us*, about Lennon and McCartney, which had its world premiere in the USA on the VH-1 TV channel in February, 2000. Wow.

Not bad, for just three years part-time, rather amateur, very occasional
playing. Could they go on, get even bigger or, like The Beatles, would it
end in tears?

# 2000

# 24

# The Quarrymen Get A Bit Fed Up

From the outside, what a nice thing to have happened to five old codgers. A fantasy made real, something millions of ordinary senior citizens would doubtless like to happen to them, for their names to come up on some bizarre celebrity lottery and whisk them off round the world to exotic places they would never otherwise visit and give them a taste of fame and excitement, but nothing too demanding, mind, nothing too exciting, steady on now, we are talking of chaps of mature age. But come on, what fun. Don't you envy them?

Instead of being nobodies, going nowhere, every day doing the same old boring thing, or shuffling around the house, most oldies would love to have thousands of young people across the world, many of the female persuasion, desperate to meet them, hear them, learn about the trivia and minutiae of their lives. Yeah, sounds good.

But anyone who has ever thought about this fantasy for more than two minutes, considered the real lives of our dearly beloved pop stars, can soon imagine some of the possible drawbacks.

Right from the beginning, during that first 10-day USA trip in 1998, our heroes quickly discovered that touring is not quite as glamorous and exciting as it might appear. In fact, it can be a right drag, especially for old fellas not used to such things, having to travel long distances, checking into some motel late at night, sharing a room with others.

Eric says he did enjoy that first 10-day US trip, especially the Bottom Line Club. "Though we did have a couple of horrendous bookings as well," he adds.

But soon afterwards he began to get fed up with going to so many similar Beatles conventions which, of course, was inevitable. Their claim to fame, or any interest, is their Beatles connection, so most invitations were to appear as part of some Beatles event. Now and again they did manage a one-off gig, in a hall or club, without having to take part in Beatles quizzes or be questioned yet again by Beatles fans, but these were rare.

The irony, of course, is that none of the five had ever been a mad Beatles fan, the sort that joins the fan clubs, collects the souvenirs, reads *Beatles Monthly*, turns up at Beatles conventions. But for their Quarrymen connections, none of them would ever have turned up at any Beatle event.

"Being part of the panel with the same people, being asked the same questions and hearing us give the same answers can be pretty boring," says Eric.

He was also beginning to dislike the attention that he and the other Quarrymen were personally receiving.

"When people treat us like gods, which very often they do in America, I feel very embarrassed. I think, What on earth are they doing that for?

"I do find it hard having to chat to people afterwards. I don't really know how to respond to their emotions. But you have to say something, if they've queued up for an hour to buy our CD and get our autograph. I try to be as polite as possible but really I'm glad when it's over."

He also found it awkward to be asked endless questions about The Beatles, their career, their discographies, where they were, what they were doing each year of their lives – as if he would know, or even care.

"In Utrecht they were having a Beatles quiz. We were asked to go on stage at the end of it and be the final judges, decide which were the right answers. We said, 'We won't know the answers. We're not Beatles freaks.' They said, 'OK, then, we'll tell you the correct answers.' So they did.

"But that evening, we all went out on the town – and we all forgot every answer. Next day on stage we got them all wrong . . ."

What about the actual playing and appearing? That must surely have been fun for them, though it was sometimes hard to tell, particularly with Eric, standing stiffly, half crouching over his guitar, looking awfully serious, as if he was getting very little enjoyment out of it all.

"Oh, I do enjoy myself on stage. I just look that way because I'm concentrating. Rod is always telling me to smile."

Colin also looked worried on stage and found the travelling hard. "I don't know how The Beatles did it for 10 years, touring the world. The worst part is getting up at six in the morning and travelling all day."

Even the laid-back Len found being on the road for 10 days harder than he expected. "The singing's easy. I love that. But getting on with everyone else, when you're with them so close, that can be a bit more difficult.

"Then the mix-ups, flight delays, people trying to rip you off. I now know what The Beatles must have had to put up with in Hamburg. It didn't get them down. They learned from it. I have to admire them for that.

"At our age, though, it's not so easy. Humping all the stuff in and out of hotels, spending hours in vehicles, roughing it on the road, that's OK when you're 20, but not so much fun at our age."

Unlike Eric, Len was enjoying The Beatles events, some more than others. He prefers them when they're all informal, with Beatles fans milling around in the same big hotel.

"I loved the Chicago one because you could just sit around all the time, under the stairs, in corridors, in halls, just play the guitar and sing. That was great fun. No hassle or boring bits.

"I didn't really like Cuba. I prefer it when it's more like us all sitting together round a camp fire reminiscing. Cuba was more like being in a university lecture hall. God, it was so boring. I walked out of most of The Beatles lectures.

"Ernesto, the organiser, tried to get me up on stage to give my own lecture. He had been going on about the influence of Cuban music on The Beatles. I thought this was mad, but then I remembered an incident I'd totally forgotten. John used to sing when we were on our bikes together as boys. And at one time he was always singing this song called 'Rock And Roll Samba', or 'Cha Cha'. I can't remember the words properly, but I can still hear him, belting it out as we cycled along. It went something like, 'Cuban Queen, have you ever seen . . .', then something about 'the beat of the Cuban conga, Creole Queens dancing the samba.' Something like that. It must have been a popular song at the time. We'd sing it together, on our bikes.

"Anyway, when I mentioned this to Ernesto, he was dead excited. It proved his thesis, so he thought, so he wanted me to get up on stage with him and tell the story. I said, 'No way. Not me. I don't do that sort of thing. I think it's all very boring.'

"After Havana, I did enjoy going to the seaside at Varadero with Sue. There wasn't much to do, but it was a pretty beach. We did get a good holiday out of that trip, so that was good."

Like Colin, Len did have the problem of still being an ordinary working man, having to fit in tours with annual holidays, if possible, which, of course, did not always suit wives and families.

"I can take time off work, if I ask in advance," says Len, "but it's unpaid, so unless I'm going to earn more going with The Quarrymen than working, it's not really worth it."

Sue usually went with him, taking time off from her own work. To keep an eye on him, with all those adoring fans?

"Oh, the women don't worry me," says Sue. "Len is more interested in singing than that sort of thing . . ."

Rod was enjoying it all, with few complaints, but then he had always wanted to play more music, to have a chance to do proper tours. He was also retired from full-time work, so there were no other distractions, and the extra money, however small, was useful. He enjoyed doing a lot of the background organising, getting their visas, printing out their itineraries and other details on his computer, keeping a website up to date.

He also thought the others were enjoying it as well. "Colin and Eric have both come out of their shells since 1957. They were very quiet then. Now they don't mind talking on stage and talking to the fans afterwards.

"Pete has turned out wonderful on stage. He's just playing a crappy old washboard, but he has a stage presence. He's so good at telling a story on stage. He just loves it."

That was what Rod believed, or liked to believe. Pete wasn't quite of the same opinion.

★   ★   ★

Surprisingly, Pete didn't mind any slumming, trailing round the dodgy or cheap motels. Despite his wealth, Pete had remained very much a local Liverpool lad, with no airs and graces or pretensions.

Nor did he really mind having to play the humble instruments on stage, the washboard and the tea chest bass. He'd never had any illusions about being a musician, though he was beginning to think he should perhaps take guitar lessons, turn himself into a proper player. But there were two aspects of being with The Quarrymen which were beginning to get him down. One of them he shared with Eric.

"Most Beatles fans are great, but some can be obsessive. What did it for me was Orlando, at their Beatlefest. We were all stuck in this hotel, in amongst all The Beatles fans, unable to escape them, in the lifts, the corridors, the lavatories. They are a tribe unto themselves. And they want to ask you questions all the time. But if they like it, that's all that matters."

His other gripe was with The Quarrymen themselves. They were becoming less and less interested or inclined to go out and play after their gig was over. He wanted them all to go out drinking, find a nice place to eat, visit the clubs, see the sights of whatever town they were in. They preferred to stay in their hotel.

"I suppose to some of the others, a big flash hotel, with room service and stuff, is a treat for them. They're not used to it. But not to me. I've done all that.

"I hate being stuck in the hotel for three days, with all these Beatles obsessives. I wanted us to go out, stay up late and enjoy ourselves. But they didn't. I began to think, What a waste. All this fucking way, just to stay in a boring hotel which might be anywhere.

"When it all began, I saw things like our American trips as a stepping stone to having a good time – three days out with your mates. Wow. But they didn't see it that way. So we ended up trapped in these hotels – just like The Beatles themselves got trapped.

"Unlike them, we could easily leave our hotels, be ourselves, not be recognised. We can escape from The Beatles-obsessed fans. We're not known to the rest of the world.

"So there was no excuse for us *not* to go out, but the others were rarely interested. That really pissed me off.

"What was the point of being abroad? I wanted it to be an experience, but we weren't experiencing anything . . ."

Eric was also coming to the same opinion, though not quite as strongly, or for the same reasons. He didn't yearn for more nights on the tiles. He just began to feel the experience was coming to an end.

"We always said we'd stop when we no longer had fun," says Eric. "I think a couple of us began to realise the fun was getting less.

"I went to a concert in Edinburgh recently – Bill Wyman's Rhythm Band. Georgie Fame was in it as well. I watched them carefully on stage and I could see they were enjoying themselves. But I still wondered, Why are they doing it? Going on the road again at the age of 60, when they've done it all before.

"With us, in our small way, doing little tours for the last three years, it's all been new to us, something we never did first time round. Now I think we've done it."

While Eric and Len were deciding quietly to themselves that they'd had enough, Pete made a more formal announcement, telling the others in May 2000 that he was packing it in.

They'd been invited to various upcoming events, such as August in Liverpool. They'd already agreed to play there, at Quarry Bank, their old school, a true trip down memory lane, but Pete said hard cheese, he wasn't going. Much to the disappointment of the others.

He'd had enough. The fun was over being a Quarryman. Just as John had said, all those years ago, he now wanted a divorce.

# 25

# Quarrymen At Quarry Bank

And then Pete changed his mind. He would turn up after all for the Quarry Bank School gig on Saturday, August 26, 2000, but that would positively be his last performance. The others sighed with relief, or just sighed. Pete is known for blowing hot and cold, getting into moods, for which John used to hit him over the head. None of the other Quarrymen today would go as far as that, being grown up, or pretending to be, and also being in some ways quite in awe of Pete, a very strong, sometimes unpredictable, character.

In the programme for Liverpool's Beatle Week 2000 it said Pete had been "thinking of quitting the band due to the late nights and heavy drinking . . . and this could be their last ever appearance." It then said the group had agreed to Pete's demands – "for more late nights and heavy drinking". Ha ha. But true, as we know. And also true, possibly, maybe, that this would indeed be their last public appearance. So catch them while you can.

Beatle Week was organised, once again, by Cavern City Tours. In the three years since The Quarrymen had turned up for the Cavern's 40th birthday, Cavern City Tours had greatly expanded. The company was now employing 100 full-time staff, all the year round, to run Beatles tours, clubs, shops, events, publications. They had just got planning permission, and the funding, for a £9 million 120-bed hotel to be built beside the Cavern Club – to be called A Hard Day's Night.

Over 250 different bands had been booked to perform during Beatle Week 2000 – almost all of them look-alike or play-alike groups from all over the world, including the USA, Japan, Argentina, Sweden, Venezuela, Germany, Brazil and Britain. Amazing to think that there are so many full-time musicians, far too young to have ever seen The Beatles live, who are today playing Beatles music in countries where The Beatles never went. I found myself studying the programme for ages, looking into the faces of these young Japanese or Brazilians, most of them wearing Beatles wigs, Beatle boots or even the full Sgt. Pepper outfit.

There were also dozens of exhibitions, lectures and flea markets spread around 28 different venues. They had block booked almost all the hotel bedrooms in Liverpool. Over 150 foreign journalists had asked for tickets. It had grown so much in recent years that, like the Edinburgh Festival, it now had its own Fringe.

"It's one of Britain's best-kept secrets," said director Bill Heckle. "The rest of the world knows more about Beatle Week than the people at home." For the all-day street festival on the Monday, which was August Bank Holiday, they were expecting a crowd of some 250,000.

I had agreed to give a little talk on the Sunday about The Beatles, my first appearance at a Liverpool Beatle Week. My talk was at the Adelphi Hotel and that was where I was booked in.

Pete, Eric and Rod were booked into the Thistle Hotel, down by the Pier. Colin and Len, living in Liverpool, didn't need a hotel. Eric had come from Edinburgh with his wife Relda, and Rod from Uxbridge with his partner Janet. Pete had materialised from somewhere abroad. Since selling out, Pete had spent a lot of time travelling, proving very hard to get hold of.

The Adelphi was totally packed with Beatles fans from all over the world. Beatles music, live and recorded, could be heard in every corridor, every corner, every lift. In every public room there were Beatles events going on, all day long.

In the main room, 90 different stalls had been set up to sell Beatles souvenirs – photographs, magazines, records, books, toys, clothes, old and new, genuine, replica, fake and bootleg. One stall, Solely of Liverpool, was selling Beatles suits and Beatle boots, made 'by their original tailors, from the original patterns and lasts, using the best material, quality leather, hand-finished in Italy'. I noticed the prices were given in both US dollars and pounds, indicating where their main market lay. Beatle suits, collarless, were $500 or £325. Original Chelsea Beatle boots were $140 or £89.95.

I could have spent hours at the stalls, as I do love Beatles rubbish, sorry, souvenirs, but I could hardly move, hardly breathe, so I went to look for some fresh air. Outside on the pavement, queues stretched round the block. Bewildered foreign fans, clutching leaflets and maps, were trying to work out how to get in, how to get tickets and most of all, what the hell was going on.

It was a sort of hell, if you didn't happen to be a Beatles fan. The Adelphi, once the pride of Liverpool, where the quality gathered for its Palm Court elegance, was even more creaking and tatty than I remembered it. Its ancient lifts took forever and my bedroom was dark and ugly. It also happened to be an incredibly hot weekend – so the lifts and internal corridor were fetid, the crowds sweating and heaving. Yet during my 24 hours there, everyone I met, or was forced up against, or pushed my way past, was unfailingly polite and good-natured. They were just so pleased to be there. No nasties, no drunks, no louts, no bad behaviour. But the crowds, my dear, the crowds.

I had intended to catch the shuttle bus from outside the Adelphi which was running all day taking fans to Quarry Bank School, where The Quarrymen were going to play, along with fourteen other bands. But fortunately, when I rang Pete at his hotel to check he had turned up, he said he had his own car and would pick me up, outside the Adelphi, at 12.30.

All heads turned when Pete drove up. Yes, quite a few recognised him, being Quarrymen fans, but mostly they were staring at his car – an Aston Martin in British Racing Green which had cost £150,000. His number plate was also pretty flash, SHO 10.

As we drove off, I told him I'd recently asked a Japanese-speaking friend about John saying he had learned the word Shotton in his Japanese lessons, that day Pete turned up to see him in New York. This expert said that there was no Japanese word exactly like Shotton – the nearest he could think of was 'sho-do' which means calligraphy, the art of handwriting. John might well have learned that word and been playing with it in his head. Just as you have to play with Pete's number plate to get the joke. On the other hand, the second part of Pete's surname, ton, means pig or swine in Japanese. Pete quite liked that. He had often heard John say, "You swine, Shotton."

Quarry Bank School is no longer called Quarry Bank. It's a comprehensive, an amalgamation of several schools, now called Calderstones. I'd never been there before, even when writing my biography, which I should have done, tut tut, but I instantly recognised the main entrance – not from photographs but because it was exactly like the main entrance to Carlisle Grammar School. Same dusty, greying sandstone blocks, same portico, same high windows, same Victorian Gothic architecture. Like Tesco or Safeways today, there must have been a central style set down for the nation's pre-war grammar schools. As I examined the main entrance, I told Pete that at CGS only the masters and prefects were ever allowed to use it. "Same at Quarry," he said.

Inside, I recognised the smell, a mixture of polish and teenage sweat. In the entrance hall, two vintage wood and metal desks had been laid out as exhibitions for Beatles fans, each ink-stained and carved, of the sort John Lennon would have sat in. They looked much older and smaller than I remembered, more Victorian Dame School, but of course in the Fifties we were still crammed into such desks, sitting in line, reciting in unison, being rapped over the knuckles for every mistake.

The front hall seemed quite clean, if worn, but when I wandered down a few corridors, I found walls dirty, paint peeling from the windows, everything in a very poor condition. Schools have it hard these days, forced to find so much of their own finance, but I hadn't realised things were this bad.

Outside, in the grounds, it was much more cheerful and pleasant. The school still has lots of green grass and flowerbeds, as it always had, being a suburban school.

At the edge of the main school field, an open-air stage had been set up, where The Quarrymen were going to perform. Inside, in the main hall, there was a second stage, where other groups were playing. An indoor cafeteria was doing good business and about 20 stalls were selling the usual Beatles stuff.

The sun was hot and people were lying on the grass, eating and drinking and having picnics, while listening to the bands playing. I sat down with Len and his wife Sue for a while. She'd brought a rug and a proper picnic hamper. Len was lying flat out, a typical pose, while stuffing his face. I don't think I'd seen Len not lying down or not eating, yet he remains so thin. Sue was tempting him with further goodies, feeding him like a baby.

With them were their two glamorous blonde daughters. Jane had just graduated that week from the London College of Fashion. She had been on the short list of 10 for Young Fashion Designer of the Year, but hadn't won. She had expected a First and had been slightly disappointed to get only a 2.1. All the same, pretty good. She had paid her own way through college, she said, working as a waitress but, even so, she'd ended up with debts of £5,000. A lot of her fellow students were from abroad, from wealthy families. "I think most of them get better treatment than we do. The College needs their money."

The other Quarrymen eventually arrived. Pete's son Matthew and his children had also turned up, Skye aged 10 and Jordan, seven. As The Quarrymen wandered round, they were constantly being recognised by Beatles fans and asked for autographs or photographs.

I estimated that by now the total crowd was about 3,000, over half from abroad. I talked to three American women in their late thirties from California who said they were in a group of 80 Americans on a 10-day Beatles tour. They had been to Hamburg, visiting the clubs where The Beatles had played, and been to London for Abbey Road. Liverpool was the highlight. The ten days was costing her $2,700. I also talked to groups from Brazil, Venezuela, Mexico and Japan, all of them on similar package Beatles tours.

The age range was broad, with lots of children and parents, with an average age of about 40. I saw few oldies, i.e. around 60, the age of The Quarrymen themselves. I didn't meet one local person, from the Liverpool area. The nearest was Widnes. But quite a few had come from London, Glasgow and Birmingham.

They all seemed kind, gentle people, not pushy or hustling each other or the bands, not like football fans who, when they spot one of their heroes, can turn demanding or aggressive. Ordinary working people, I would assume, rather than the professional classes, but able enough to afford to be there, pay their travel, hotels, entrance fees and lash out on all the souvenirs. None of it cheap. Being a Beatles fan, going to all the conventions, becomes a way of life, their pastime and hobby. No more pathetic or sad than collecting stamps or following football. I collect Beatles stuff, love their music dearly, yet I had never had the urge to attend such a gathering before. But I would do it again, if it was handy.

I asked each of The Quarrymen about the crowds, the people who come to such gatherings, and they said this was nothing compared with the States. Over there, they were bigger, noisier, more enthusiastic, but yes, they were still basically the same sort of people. Meaning what? "Uncomplicated people." That was what one of them said, but didn't want to be quoted, not wishing to give offence. Len, who loves all Beatles fans, wanted to be quoted as saying, "They are all kind and big-hearted."

A great many of the fans that day were wearing some sort of Beatles items of clothing – picture T-shirts, badges, caps, boots, even whole Beatle suits. Some were in Sixties style generally – girls in mini skirts with Vidal Sassoon haircuts and thigh high boots. A TV crew from Sky was filming the crowds and the bands live.

Scattered around the field were some of the groups, waiting to go on stage. A band from Japan called Beetles were in full 1963 Beatles outfits – tight-fitting grey suits, thin black ties, Chelsea boots and mop tops. Their hair looked real, not wigs. They were lolling against a school wall, drinking Coke and eating sandwiches, having their photographs taken by fans, waiting their turn.

One of them spotted Pete Shotton and shouted out his name, nudging the others. They had looked a bit bored, a bit haughty even, while posing for fans, but the minute they saw Pete, their jaws dropped, their mouths opened. They rushed over and asked for his autograph, handing him some of their flyers for him to sign. Pete said he had met them before, at some US Beatles convention. They were pretty good, he thought, as a cover band. But to them, Pete was far more than a look-alike. He was the real thing, someone genuinely connected to The Beatles.

I grabbed one of their glossy flyers which gave details of their British tour. They had started the week before at the Edinburgh Festival, playing at the Queen's Hall. In Liverpool, they were playing at the Cavern Club, as well as Quarry Bank School. They were all from a town called Kurayoshoi. Their flyer contained a personal message, in Japanese and English, from its Mayor, congratulating them on being invited to play at Liverpool. He felt proud of them "because their activity is loved by so many of the citizens".

The Quarrymen were not due on till 3.30. Around 2.30, they started looking for somewhere to have a quick practise, but failed to find a room or space empty. Colin looked very disappointed but the others just shrugged, deciding not to bother. Rod gave each of them a printed list, done on his computer, of the running order of their numbers for their 60-minute performance. I noticed the print was enormous, but then, when you get to 60, old eyes are not as good as they were.

Things were running late, as they usually do, but the moment it was announced that The Quarrymen were the next band on, all the people who had been sitting on the grass or strolling around immediately stood up and moved forward, trying to get as near the stage as possible. I was caught out by this sudden rush, and had to use both elbows to get near them.

I had watched The Quarrymen many times so far on video, listened to their CD tapes, but never seen them live, not even in Cuba, so I wanted as close up a view as possible.

Rod started off with some chat, saying this was the school that he, Pete, Eric and John had all gone to; in fact he was now looking across at what was Woolton House, where their house meetings used to be held. Pete took over, explaining who everyone was, how they had started, and that he would be on washboard. He held up his little metal thimble for all to see. "It's very good for safe foreplay."

He explained that they were the original Quarrymen, the group which John had formed, then later Paul had joined. "But eventually, we got rid of John and Paul and George . . ."

The audience, even the ones who must have heard some of these jokes before, all laughed loudly. Cameras and videos were whirring, people jostling to hear and capture all the introductory chat and jokes.

"Now we're going to annoy you with some music," said Pete. Then they went into their first number, 'Mean Woman Blues'.

60 Minutes: PAGE 1

1: MEAN WOMAN      G

2: Rod "Skiffle"
ROCK ISLAND LINE      G

3: Pete: "Who we are, how started"
THAT'S ALL RIGHT MAMA      G
   1  2  1234

4: Len:original 1957sound,instruments,
1 mike, play in bath, rock influences
BLUE MOON      G      1  2  123

5: Pete: Liverpool Sailors welcome
MAGGIE MAY      C
verse 1 Rod solo come in on "Maggie"
on F Chord in verse 2

6: Eric: "Learning guitar"
LOST JOHN      G      1  2  123
    COME IN ON "LONG" ON G

---

60m  PAGE 2

7: Len: Cavern 40th, brick in wall etc"
I FORGOT TO REMEMBER      D
   1234 12

8: Eric: "6 July Woolton 1997, Queen,
Blair, Paul McC, Yoko
BLUE SUEDE      G

9:Rod: dif get words, Paul meets John
COME GO WITH ME      G
   1  2  1234

10:Pete: "How Paul joined"
ALL SHOOK UP      G
1 2 1234

11: Rod: St Peter's Recording, S130,000
bought by EMI, put it out, royalties
PUTTING ON THE STYLE    C
   1  2  1234

---

60m PAGE 3

12:Len/Colin: P Phillips and Danger
DANGER      G
   1234  12

13:Rod:Leadbelly, Seeger, Paul warmup
MIDNIGHT SPECIAL      G 1234 1
    come in on "morning"

14: Eric: CD, Holland, N Yk, Chicago,
Dublin, Vegas, Vancouver CUBA
DON'T BE CRUEL      D
   1  2  123

15:Rod: As played by Paul and thanks.
TWENTY FLIGHT      G

SPARE: to go before 20-Flight Rock:
HAVE I TOLD YOU LATELY    D
start on "told"

Rod's running order for The Quarrymen's 60-minute performance at Quarry Bank School, August 26, 2000, with some notes for their spontaneous chat between numbers, all of it done in large print for old eyes.

They played their usual skiffle songs, such as 'Rock Island Line', plus some Elvis numbers like 'Blue Suede Shoes', all the songs they used to play, back in 1957 and 1958. There were no Beatles numbers, except 'In Spite Of All The Danger', the song Paul wrote which was recorded by The Quarrymen.

In between the songs, they told stories. Rod and Pete were the main talkers, plus bits from Eric and Len. Colin said nothing on this occasion. In their 90-minute set, Colin does get to talk.

It all seemed nice and impromptu, mates enjoying themselves together. Nothing was written down, but they had told most of the stories before, though as usual there were some jokes, observations, interruptions which were new. One of them complained about an echo on stage. Another said he couldn't hear any echo. "Where do you get the *Echo*?" "At any news-agent," said Pete. A purely Liverpool joke, which would have been point-less in Las Vegas. Nor would the phrase "Give it some welly", which I clearly heard Pete tell Colin.

They teased Colin sitting silently at the back which, of course, is the role of drummers. When he came in heavy on a number, someone said, "Hurrah, Colin's got his second wind."

"I hope the breeze isn't blowing this way," said Rod, holding his nose. All very schoolboyish, but the audience loved it. Len could be heard moaning that his legs were getting tired with standing up.

A woman aged about 35 climbed up onto the side of the stage during one number while they carried on playing. At a Beatles concert, such things could not have happened, as the stage was ringed with security guards. Was she going to kiss Len, stop him feeling tired? Could it be a streaker? The woman went up to Pete, as he scraped his washboard, and placed a tie around his neck. It was black with yellow stripes. It took me a while to realise the significance, though there is a well-known photo of John with Yoko, wearing the same tie. A Quarry Bank School tie, of course. Very apt.

Rod said they would be selling copies of their CDs after their perform-ance, but alas there would be no refunds on their entrance fees. All low key and nicely self-deprecating. After their final number, the audience cheered and cheered, demanding an encore, and of course they obliged.

I talked to as many people afterwards as I could. The ones who had never seen then before said they were hugely impressed. They had expected a feeble, amateur group, which would not have disappointed them, as it was seeing them in the flesh that mattered most, but they were surprised and delighted by the quality of their playing. Those who had

seen them before, at other Beatle occasions, said they were always enjoy-
able, always a highlight.

"The look-alike groups are great, from Japan, Brazil or wherever," said
an American woman. "I love listening to them, but really, they are now all
so good, they sound much the same. The difference with The Quarrymen
is they talk. The cover groups don't, as they can't speak English. And of
course The Quarrymen have something to talk about which no one else
has. It's all fascinating. And I just love their accents . . ."

For almost two hours afterwards, The Quarrymen signed autographs
and posed for photos, especially when they lined up outside the front
entrance to the school. Janet, Rod's partner, was selling their CDs and
photos from a small table she had set up.

I met a beaming, rather overweight, American woman who had just
managed to get Pete's autograph. She had been at their New Jersey
concert in March, which Pete had missed through having 'flu, much to
her disappointment. In New Jersey, she'd got the autographs of the others.
Now she had Pete's to complete her collection. "I'm just so excited . . ."

Back in the Adelphi Hotel, I was asked by a TV crew to do a 10-minute
interview for a documentary film about Pete Best. Seemed a strange
request, till I discovered that the director was Roag Best, Pete's younger
brother. I last met Pete Best 33 years ago, when he was working in a
factory, slicing bread for £18 a week, still feeling depressed at being
dumped by The Beatles, just as they were about to be famous. Today, said
Roag, Pete tours the world all the time, with his own group. Roag is his
road manager.

Then, in the dealers' hall, one of the 90-odd stalls turned out to be John
Duff Lowe's, selling special, limited edition reproductions of the 'In Spite
Of All The Danger' record. Not a repro you can play – just to hang on the
wall to look at. With it, for the price of £80, you got a CD of Duff talking
about his Quarrymen memories. I listened to it later and it was very interesting. As was his accent. Far more BBC, standard English than the other old
Quarrymen.

Duff today is still living in the West Country and still in finance. I got
the impression, from some people, that Duff would have liked to have
been asked to join The Quarrymen, but the others had felt it should be
limited to the original members.

★　★　★

That evening, I went over to the Thistle Hotel to join The Quarrymen for
dinner. Len in the end didn't turn up, as he was far too tired, nor did Colin

as he was having a birthday party for one of his daughters. So it was Eric, Pete and Rod, plus Rod's partner Janet.

Three ex-Quarry Bank School, so lots of Quarry memories came out. Mostly about masters. None worth repeating. They all remembered how Pete used to squeak when convulsed with laughter. He did it once when they were all at Woolton cinema, along with John, watching a Jerry Lewis film. Pete doubled up then sank to the floor where he rolled under the seats in front while John and the others kicked him and pushed him, to make him roll further, till the management came and chucked them all out.

Towards the end of dinner, I asked for their best memories of the last three years. I was assuming that their performance at Quarry Bank that day would be their last ever, so I was attempting a summing-up.

They all thought that Cuba had been the most interesting experience, visiting a Communist country, one they would not have seen but for The Quarrymen. Rod said it had reminded him of the tour parties he used to take to Eastern Europe.

Eric had been mugged in Cuba, which I hadn't known about. During a break in their performance, he and Len had popped outside, into a side street, to have a fag. As they smoked, someone grabbed Eric's watch and specs. A passer-by ran after him and managed to retrieve Eric's specs. Eric had to rush back into the hall and so never managed to thank the person or give him a tip.

The Bottom Line Club in New York had probably been the most exciting, though Las Vegas was also pretty good, and of course appearing coast to coast on ABC TV, that had been amazing. They all agreed that Derby, their first gig, was the worst.

Rod said one of his funniest memories happened on Vancouver Island. "The audience had been brilliant, all loving it – then suddenly at the end, they all ran out, without us giving an encore. We didn't know what the hell had happened, or what we'd done wrong. It was only later we realised we were on an island and they'd all rushed to catch the last ferry."

They all laughed, which brought out more stories. It was clear that they had enjoyed themselves these last three years. What a shame it was now going to end. Or was it? Although Pete had come to Liverpool after all, and not let the others down, it still appeared that this would be the end, for him at least.

"Come on, Pete," I said. "Watching you on stage, you can't say you were not enjoying yourself today." Yes, he admitted, he had been.

"And talking to the fans, posing for photos, you were charm itself, not someone pissed off and fed up and hating it." That was probably true as well.

"And here you are, together, no fans or Beatle people asking dopey questions, eating and drinking and reminiscing, ready to carry on for, well, quite a few hours yet."

"Yeah, it has been good today. And I'll tell you what I've been thinking. Before we finish, I would like to go to Japan. Someone from Japan today was asking if we fancied it. He said he could fix a tour for us. We've never been there. Could be fascinating. You know how the Japs always love us . . ."

"Guess what I was asked about today," said Rod. "Someone in Venezuela wants to invite us. We might be able to fit it in with a trip to Brazil as well. We've never done a South American tour."

Nor did The Beatles, of course. So why not? If they can take care not to have too many engagements, too spread out, avoid long drives and early mornings.

So, it was agreed. The Quarrymen live on, for the moment anyway.

We all packed up at 11 o'clock. They went straight to bed, except Eric, who wandered round for a while, having lost his specs.

Even Pete went straight to bed, despite his complaints about no one wanting to stay up and do the town with him. Well, it had been a tiring day, for chaps of a certain age . . .

# 26

## Colin Today

Colin's front door was open when I arrived and I could see that he was hoovering the hall. "Oh, you shouldn't have bothered," I said, "not for me."

He was getting rid of some dogs' hairs, not in my honour, but because he is always keen to have his soft furnishings in good condition, being in the business. The hairs had been left behind by one of his daughters who had been visiting with her two Bassett hounds.

Colin and his wife Joan are still in the same two-storey terraced house near Penny Lane which they bought for £2,400 in 1965. I guessed it must be worth about £150,000 today, being in a quiet street, near a park, in good condition with quite big rooms, but he thought more like £70,000. This is Liverpool, not London.

We sat in his front room on a very comfortable three-piece suite, which he had made himself. He is grey-haired, thin and wiry, looks fit and healthy, if slightly apprehensive about the world at large.

On top of his television I admired a clock in the shape of a set of drums. It was given to Colin by his sister on his 60th birthday in 1998. He went across to demonstrate its tricks, pressing a button which resulted in a drum roll and an American voice saying, "Good morning." The voice gets on his nerves, so he has that bit permanently switched off, but the clock itself works well.

He is still a self-employed upholsterer with a modest business and minimal overheads. He rents two rooms at the back of a carpet shop owned by a friend, Paul, in the village of Frodsham, near Runcorn, a half-hour drive away. It would have been more convenient to find somewhere local, but when he employed staff and rented a bigger space, he was based at Runcorn. He had built up a local custom, so it seemed sensible to stay in the same area when he scaled himself down into a one-man firm. His customers are mainly in North Wales or Cheshire. He does quite a bit of travelling, to inspect jobs, then bringing back the sofa or chair to his workshop, if they accept his estimate. His speciality is re-upholstering suites – a sofa and two armchairs – for which he charges between £600 and £800. He has orders three months ahead.

"I don't make a fortune, but it's not a bad living. I have a couple of good contacts in Chester and Knutsford who send me work. I only have to worry about myself. I can go home early if I want, or take a day off. No, I don't find it lonely. I can go and speak to my friend who has the carpet shop at the front. I also have a woman called Barbara who comes in a few times a week to do some sewing for me. I quite enjoy it. I wouldn't know what to do with myself, if I wasn't working.

"It's not as physically hard as it used to be. You don't get blue teeth any more. Horse hair has gone out. Now it's foam and a staple gun. The worst thing that happens now is that you shoot yourself in the fingers. Oh, we've all done that."

Joan came into the room, bringing a tray of coffee and biscuits. As his 'aunty', and a couple of years older, she must have seemed much more mature, back in 1958. Now they look the same age. She said Colin is a workaholic. And he can never sit still. No matter whose house he's in, he'll be fiddling with his hands down the back of sofas, feeling the upholstery. "He gets withdrawal symptoms if he's not at work."

One of the things she suggested to him, when he was having his minor nervous breakdown over his business, was that he should have some outside interests. He'd never really had any in the last 30 years or so. So he got a season ticket for Liverpool FC and goes each week to watch them, along with his brother-in-law.

Joan works part time for Meals on Wheels, in the kitchens. She has always had some sort of job, since their two girls were aged around seven or eight. They are now in their early thirties. Christine, the younger, is married and lives in Glasgow where she works as an archivist. Alison is still in Liverpool, living with her partner Gary and working as a nursery nurse. No grandchildren, so far.

The Quarrymen, regrouping when they did, came at a good time for Colin, providing a perfect outside interest. If it had happened two years earlier, when he was in the throes of his business disaster, he would have refused, point blank, to even contemplate joining them. "I couldn't have coped."

But by 1997, settled into self-employment again, it provided excitement as well as an outside interest. Who would have thought that a jobbing upholsterer, aged 62, would today be jetting off to Las Vegas and New York, being met in stretch limos, mobbed by fans? Must have amazed the neighbours when they heard.

"They don't all know. Flo and Roy over the road, they know. And a few others. It amuses them, really. When I meet them in the street, they say, 'Where are you off to now, Colin? Chicago or what?' "

Joan approved of The Quarrymen coming back into his life – but it hasn't provided much in the way of fun and excitement for her. She flew with them on their first foreign trip to Amsterdam, when they played at Utrecht. And was sick all the way. She tried it again when they flew to Dublin, in case it was a one-off bad experience. The same thing happened again. Sick all the way, and terrified. So that was it. She decided not to fly anywhere again and has therefore missed out on their five trips to the USA, a country she would dearly like to visit, if only she didn't have to fly.

Colin has enjoyed all the trips, except perhaps the first one to Derby. "That was a damp squib. So few turned up and we didn't go down all that well. Since then, we've had good crowds and people have liked us, on the whole.

"I think we do know our limitations, what we can and can't play. It happened by chance that at the Woolton anniversary all they wanted us to play was 1957 skiffle music – and we've stuck to it ever since. We don't play Beatles music. There wasn't any then, was there? But we couldn't anyway. You have to be musicians, which we're not. Well, I'm not. We stick to our Fifties acoustic sounds and tunes, just as we used to play them. Which I think is good."

Would he like the group to carry on?

"Yeah, I would, but not any more 10-day tours. A long weekend, out Thursday, back Tuesday, that would suit me best.

"That first USA trip was so exhausting. It was our fault, really, allowing them to book radio interviews for us in places hundreds of miles away when we were still jet-lagged. It meant getting up at six and driving six hours in a van. That was hellish. It made us all very, what shall I say, snappy with each other."

Despite being an old hand now, with around 40 appearances in the last three years, he is personally still as nervous on stage as he ever was. Joan knows this, how he feels, and suspects that some of the others are probably a bit nervous as well. She never watches them play. She might go to an event in Britain with Colin, but while he's on stage, she'll go for a walk rather than watch. She worries she'll make Colin even more nervous.

"Sue, Len's wife, she does enjoy watching them. She loves it all. I just get nervous on their behalf. It seems to me that none of them are really relaxed."

"I'm the weak link, you see," said Colin. "I make most noise, so if I make a mistake, it's obvious. With three guitars, if one hits a wrong note, you won't quite hear it.

"At our Quarry Bank gig, I started on the wrong beat when we got to 'Midnight Special'. I was too slow – but I couldn't change, once I'd started. That's why I'd wanted a rehearsal beforehand. When you haven't played for four months, you do forget what you did last time. All I needed was a few minutes, to go over the beginning and end, but we couldn't manage it.

"It's the beginning of each number, that's the most worrying. When it's 'Be Bop A Lula' coming up, I'm thinking now, How does it begin? How did we do it last time? I usually wait for Len to start, then follow him. The end is not so bad. When it just sort of happens to come to an end, that's the end . . ."

Colin's nervousness on stage often results in him not being able to sleep the night before, which in turn stops him eating. But, apart from all that, he does like it, does enjoy playing and travelling with the others.

He is not in it for the money, as none of them are. But Colin, like Len, has to take into consideration loss of earnings when they are away or travelling.

"Probably overall, since we got together again, I've lost more money than I've earned. We could make more. There was a guy in the States who said if we came for three months he could fix a gig every day and we would make a lot of money.

"But it's not about money. It's about having fun. And about having an interesting experience, something I could never have imagined happening to me.

"It's most amazing in the USA. They really do stand in line and queue for hours for our autographs. When we played the Bottom Line in New York, there was one old man who was there when we went in to rehearse in the morning and was still there in the evening. I reckon he must have stood outside that door for about eight hours, just for us. And he didn't even see the show. As I was signing his autograph book, he said he was now off to get the last train home. Amazing . . ."

Colin played his old, original, Quarrymen drums for their first public reappearance at the Woolton Fete. Since then, he has used whatever has been available. "It was bad enough carting them around in the old days, getting on and off buses. I'm not starting that again. In those days, I just used to shove them under the stairs, then go and sit on the top deck with the rest of the lads. When I came down, there was usually someone who'd put a pram on top of them. That was hell, getting them out."

It means the quality of the drums available can vary enormously. He doesn't know what they're like till he starts, especially if they haven't had a rehearsal. "That was probably why our Derby appearance didn't go down so well. The first I'd played their drums was when we played the first number. I hadn't realised how loud they were. Pete turned round and glared at me . . ."

So where is the original set of drums? Still on top of his wardrobe. Could I see them? He looked hesitant, but eventually agreed to go upstairs and get them while I sat tight.

They were wrapped in old plastic carrier bags which he carefully opened and then assembled all the bits for me on the carpet. There was a largish bass drum, a snare drum, a small tom-tom, then one loose cymbal which was meant to clip onto the bass drum. A Broadway set, which cost him £34.19.6 back in 1956. He also brought down two original pairs of drumsticks, with red tips, all very worn in the middle.

The drums were yellow, which surprised me, as in the famous photo they all look white. "They were white. They've just gone yellow and a bit wrinkled with age." As we all have, Col.

I could see the maker's name, John Gray and Sons, but no sign of The Quarrymen logo on the skin of the bass drum. "It was never painted on," said Colin. He just used to cut out paper letters and stick them on with Sellotape. When they fell off or faded, he cut out more letters.

"Charlie Roberts made me some good letters once, out of fluorescent orange paper. I had them a long time.

"It was Charlie Roberts I gave the copy of 'In Spite Of All The Danger' to. He was a printer working at Littlewoods pools. I then forgot all about it. I never knew he'd handed it on to Duff Lowe. I met Charlie's wife at the Woolton Fete and she told me she nearly melted it down. There was a fashion at one time for melting down old vinyl records and making lamp shades."

Duff Lowe was therefore the lucky one who ended up with the record and sold it to Paul McCartney. But Colin's part in making the record was acknowledged when, in 1996, the Beatles got round to their *Anthology* albums and TV programme.

"I got this call one day from someone at Apple. They told me they were thinking of using the original recording of 'In Spite Of All The Danger'. It might or might not be used, and I might or might not be in it, but anyway they would like to offer me a fee. What did I want? I said I didn't know, did I? Whatever they thought was a fair price. They said £500. That seemed fine by me. I couldn't really be bothered at the time. I was up to my eyes in business worries. So I said yes.

"I later happened to speak to Rod and he said I was mad to accept a one-off fee for anything. I said I didn't even know if I was on the recording. My memory could have played tricks. But when I heard it on the radio, I could definitely tell it was me on drums. Rod said he would find me a lawyer. Apple were furious, when this lawyer gets on to them. They said I'd made a verbal agreement with them. They played hell."

Colin was, in the end, offered a much bigger sum, which he was happy with and accepted – though he signed an agreement never to reveal it.

I asked if he would ever sell his drums. He won't have a lot of money when he retires from upholstery, and it would help with his pension.

"I didn't keep them for that reason. It was just because I'm a bit of a squirrel. I knew I'd never use them again, but I didn't want to get rid of them. I did offer them to someone in Liverpool with a Beatles shop, to put on display. But the person was worried about their safety. And then the shop closed.

"I don't think they're worth a lot. Rod did speak to Sotheby's about them. They thought no more than £3,500. That was what a set of Ringo's drums had fetched, ones he'd played when he was with Rory Storm."

Colin also has two original copies of Quarrymen photos taken by Charlie Roberts at Roseberry Street and given to Colin afterwards. One of them has never been published. (Until this book.) And he has one of The Quarrymen visiting cards. "I've been told they're worth £4,000. No, £4,000 each. Even for the little card. Incredible, isn't it?"

Apart from all the fun and foreign travel, the last three years have given him a glimpse of what it must have been like to be a Beatle.

"I can see why The Beatles, at their young age, sometimes went off the rails. They all must do, these young pop stars, what with the drinking and the drugs and women. I can understand it now, what the temptations and dangers must be like. And we've only had a very little bit of their adulation.

"I can also understand why they gave up touring. In fact I don't know how they stood it for 10 years. We've only done it off and on for three years, and I've found it knackering. No, I don't envy them, the sort of life they led."

But what about their success and fame? Surely a bit of that might have been nice?

"I wouldn't have wanted their sort of fame. I wouldn't have enjoyed it. I am not a jealous person anyway. I just get on with my own life."

OK, so what about the money?

"Well, I suppose I would have liked to have ended up with a little more in life, after all these years of work.

"Not for me. For my daughters. I would like to be able to give them some money towards a house, help them get a place of their own. That would have been nice . . ."

# 27

# Len Today

Len and his wife Sue are also still in Liverpool, in the house not far from Woolton which they bought on their return from New Zealand in 1988. They have a Jack Russell called Charlie and a singing canary in a cage and have recently been joined by their older daughter Ruth, a very lively and attractive 27-year-old, whose marriage has just failed. She is living at home again, about to do a computer course.

Robert, their eldest, who went to university at Lampeter, is now a teacher in a large comprehensive in Shropshire, second in charge of the English department. Jonathan, the former punk, is now a landscape gardener in Bournemouth. He has a daughter Laura, aged nine, from a previous relationship. She is Len and Sue's only grandchild, so far. Jane, 24, the one who graduated from the London College of Fashion, is planning to open a dress shop.

Their house is nicely artistic, if a bit bashed at the edges. Len lies on the sofa in his socks, curled up like a teenager. He is as relaxed, laid-back as ever. Sue says she has never met anyone as relaxed in her life. "If the bomb went off, I don't think Len would notice." All the other Quarrymen are very fond of Len. Impossible to argue with or be upset by Len as he floats through life, smiling and being pleasant. "If Len was any more laid-back," says Pete Shotton, "he'd be a floorboard."

Len is still working in the day centre, looking after handicapped people, singing with them, playing with them, taking them on outings. His salary is £17,000 a year. Sue never complained during the years Len dragged her and their daughters round the globe, or when he was continually losing or throwing up his job. "I would always do anything to keep Len happy," she says, smiling.

Len is lean and fit-looking, hardly any heavier or wider round the waist than he was as a teenager. He says his health has been fine for years. His teenage meningitis does not seem to have left any mark, though Sue says that for many years, after they first met, he always seemed to be ill, mostly complaining about his throat. He did smoke, but says he has now given it up.

Like Eric, he has a fine head of hair, all intact and surprisingly blond, for his age – 60 on January 6, 2002. He denied at first that he did anything to it, despite a few give-away suspicious-looking streaks. He smiled and said well, he might help it along a bit, but he didn't dye it.

Sue still works as a night nurse in an old folks home. She is no longer a churchgoer, though she believes in God. Len still goes to church most Sundays.

"Some years ago, in the Seventies probably, long before he died, I wrote a letter to John. It was about God. They all seemed interested in God at the time. I've always had a faith. Never lost it."

So what happened to the letter, Len?

"Oh, I wrote it. But I never posted it. Can't remember why . . ."

As The Beatles progressed, he admired their success from afar, but was never a real fan of their music. He always preferred Elvis. He didn't have any Beatles records in the house, till his daughters started buying them. They have always been quite proud of the fact that he used to play with them. So is Sue. She now deeply regrets that during her religious phase she burned his Quarrymen photos.

Today, Sue has moved the other way, sometimes embarrassing Len by telling total strangers about his Beatles connections.

They were recently in Yorkshire, visiting the Brontë museum at Haworth, when Sue heard some American tourists talking about music. Sue went over and said to them, "Do you know who that is?" They didn't, of course. So she pointed over at Len, her blond 58-year-old husband. Still no recognition. By which time Len was trying to hide, pretend he wasn't with her.

"It's Len Garry," she explained, "one of the original Quarrymen." By chance, all of the Americans had heard of The Quarrymen. And one could even recall Len's name. Sue was thrilled, lapping up the reflected glory.

She always enjoys watching Len play and has followed the group on almost all their tours, to the USA and Cuba.

Len, of course, has loved every moment of being able to sing and play in public. At long last, doing what he always wanted to do.

He enjoys the attention from Beatles fans and also Beatles experts, some of whom ring him up from all over the world, wanting a quote or an opinion.

"We had 10 little Japs in this room the other week," says Len. "Outside they had this massive satellite aerial. Dunno what it was all for, just some

TV programme. No, it's not a drag. I don't mind them. And the money can be quite good. We got £150 expenses from that lot. Not bad, was it?"

One result of being a born-again Quarryman was that Len was encouraged to write his own book, give the world the benefit of his own personal story.

"It all came out of meeting someone in Canada. I got talking to this bloke who makes a living as a Ringo Starr look-alike. He then introduced me to another Canadian, who happened to have a little publishing firm. He suggested I should write my memories. I thought people must be bored to death by all these Beatles books by now, but he talked me into it."

*John, Paul And Me, Before The Beatles, The True Story Of The Very Early Days*, by Len Garry, was published by CG Publishing of Toronto in 1997. It came with a CD of Len and Pete visiting Mendips, John's old house, and giving their Lennon memories. What they say is interesting, but you can hardly hear it for traffic noises. The book itself is good and nicely written, apart from some liberties with recalled, not to say fanciful, dialogue.

Did someone help you with it?

"No, I wrote it all by myself. And I enjoyed doing it. I've always been able to spell. I think I got that from my father, being in the print."

Sue went upstairs to get his original manuscript. I was amazed to see how beautiful it was – 200 handwritten pages, in ink, absolutely immaculate, with hardly any corrections.

Len might appear rather lacking in energy at times, with his laid-back attitude to life, but he did pass the Eleven Plus for a very good grammar school, and he did spend many years in an architect's office where neatness and clarity is vital.

Apart from personal memories, the book contains some good material on the background to skiffle and on the history of Calderstones Park, where he and John and Pete and the gang used to hang out. He got daughter Ruth to take photographs of the park and of the tunnel where he and John used to take girls. All in all, an interesting production for Beatles fans, if, of course, you can get a copy.

As with so many small-scale publishing houses, he didn't actually get paid for his efforts. He received no advance in the way of money – just 300 copies of his book which, over the last three years, he has sold to fans at Beatles events. They are now all gone. People ask him all the time for copies, but he has none.

He is pleased the fans liked his book, but he is most pleased when they say they like his singing. "When people come up to me afterwards and say, 'Hey, you've got a good voice, Len,' I'm thrilled."

The Quarrymen don't pretend to be better than they are, but they can get a bit hurt if they are rubbished or put down, even if they shrug and smile it off.

With Len, as the lead singer, there is part of him that would like to play in a better group, to develop and move forward, but he pauses to choose his words carefully in order not to give offence to the others, which, of course, he never would.

"No, I'm not criticising them at all. If we were slick and professional, we wouldn't be The Quarrymen, would we? We make the sound we made 40 years ago. That's what people come to hear.

"But, well, it is a bit restricting, having to do what we did back in 1957. Now and again, it can be a bit embarrassing. We do have a few stupid songs that I hate singing.

"Don't get me wrong, I love it. I'm proud to be the lead singer of The Quarrymen. In a sense, I've taken John's place. So that's an honour. But it's not what I want to do."

What would that be, Len?

He curls up even further, almost disappearing into the cushions. "I'd like to sing with a big band. That would be my fantasy. If I ever had the money, I'd hire some really good musicians, get all the best gear, go into a top recording studio and make a record of me fronting a big band. That's my dream. You have to have dreams. Otherwise you might as well pack up.

"But I don't have regrets about my own life. I've got a wonderful wife. I wouldn't change my Susie for anyone. And I've got four healthy kids. You have to count your blessings, haven't you?"

Long pause.

"On the other hand, if you sit around counting your blessings, you'd never move on, would you?

"I suppose it would be nice to have a bit more money for things like travel. But at least I'm in a job I enjoy doing. I'm glad to be out of architecture. All those meetings and arguments used to do my head in.

"My only regret in life is that I didn't make more of the talent I do have. I'm not saying I'm as talented a singer as John and Paul. Of course not. But you do have to have self belief. I suppose I didn't have self belief when I was young, when it mattered, or at least I didn't do enough about it.

"It's nice being in The Quarrymen today, but I would have liked to have made it in my own right. We are doing it on the back of The Beatles. I realise that. I'd prefer it if it was my talent that mattered, not my connection with John and Paul.

"It's funny how these things work out. One day a lad called Pete, a friend of a lad called John, says to another lad called Paul, 'Will you join our group?' Then he cycles off.

"Three people, one question, one simple answer. And that's it. That's what happens in life . . ."

# 28

# Eric Today

Eric Griffiths lives in Edinburgh, far removed from his Liverpool roots. John would have been most amused to find out he had become a senior Civil Servant, the sort who gets invited to Royal Garden Parties, as Eric did in 1988, though, of course, he did have those early years at sea and in dead-end jobs. Looking at his solid lifestyle today, his house and general interests, it's hard to believe that from time to time he pops off round the world to play in an elderly skiffle group.

His home is in the affluent suburb of Colinton in a modern three-storey town house in an exclusive cul-de-sac. He plays golf on Wednesday and Friday afternoons and tries not to devote more than two or three hours a day to his business interests.

He's stockier than he was, looks fit and healthy enough, with a crinkled face which might eventually make him look like W.H. Auden, plus the most unlikely looking mop top of thick brown hair. All real, he says, no fiddles, no colouring. In America, after gigs, people are always asking him if it's a wig. His reply is to say he'll give them 50 dollars if they can pull it off.

He still smokes, as he did as a teenager, though not as many, so he says. He did look rather embarrassed when he asked if I minded if he had a quick drag. "It's your house," I said, though I was worried about his immaculate decor and pristine furnishings. His wife was out at the time.

From his own accounts, he was as precocious and rebellious at school as John and Pete, a bolshie teenager at home, yet he turned out to be a solid, suit-wearing member of the middle classes. Only the quick, Andy Capp drags on his fag indicated traces of his former life.

He has been married to the same wife, Relda, for 36 years, with three grown-up sons, all now left home, all doing sensible jobs. Their eldest, Timothy, 31, went to Dundee University and is now an accountant, working for the Royal Bank of Scotland. Matthew went to Edinburgh University to read pure chemistry, then changed subjects and university and is now working in computers. Daniel didn't go to university, but is

*The Lord Chamberlain is*

*commanded by Her Majesty to invite*

*Mr. and Mrs. E. R. Griffiths*

*to a Garden Party*

*at the Palace of Holyroodhouse*

*on Thursday, 30th June, 1988 from 4 to 6 p.m.*

*Morning Dress, Uniform or Lounge Suit*

working for a stockbroker. All live in the Edinburgh area, none is married, none has children.

Eric and his wife could make more money, could expand their dry-cleaning business, but he has no desire to maximise his assets. He prefers to enjoy life and live comfortably, with the minimum of aggravation, though while he still owns his shops, there will always be staff problems and passing worries. He has a lot of capital equipment tied up in the shops, so he has to keep a watchful eye on them and his staff, which now and again annoys him and he wonders why he ever got mixed up in dry-cleaning.

Having built up the business, however small, wouldn't he like one of his sons to take it over?

"Two of them have expressed an interest, but I wouldn't let any of them get involved. I've enjoyed it, but I think they can do better in life than dry-cleaning . . ."

It was thanks to his sons, encouraging him, that he went off to that Cavern reunion, otherwise he would never have rejoined The Quarrymen. It was always a passing fad anyway, playing skiffle. Unlike Len with his singing and Rod with his banjo, he never thought about music again, once it came to an end.

He never showed much interest in what happened afterwards to The

Beatles. Even today, he has only one of their albums in his house. So he thought. He went off to look for it and came back with *The Beatles – 1967–70*. It still has the sticker on it saying '85p off'. Perhaps that's really why he bought it.

He never liked their early stuff much, like 'Twist And Shout' or 'She Loves You', finding them too noisy, too shouty, too much influenced by American music. Personally, he preferred Neil Diamond or Simon & Garfunkel. But he enjoyed 'Penny Lane' and 'Strawberry Fields' for the memories of Liverpool they brought back. He liked John's music best after he'd left The Beatles, when he wrote songs like 'Wheels' and 'Woman'.

Apart from that moment on board ship in 1963, when he heard 'Please Please Me' and told some of the cadets, he has never revealed to other people that he once knew them. He wasn't keeping it secret. Just couldn't see the interest, for him or anyone else.

"I suppose I could have contacted John, had a chat with him about old times. As you get a bit older, you do think back to your roots. But I never did. Once someone becomes famous, there's a barrier set up. You don't want to break it down, in case it looks as if you're only doing it because they've become famous. It was only ever a passing thought, which soon went out of my mind."

Over those years, when he himself was struggling, before finding his feet and his niche in the Civil Service, surely he must have felt some pangs of jealousy at their success?

"Hand on heart, I never felt any envy when I heard about how well they were doing. I knew I could never have been at their level musically, so I didn't identify with them or feel 'but for events, that could have been me'. The only reaction I ever felt, when I switched on the TV and there they were, was amazement. It just struck me as fantasy, what they had achieved."

How about their money? Would a bit of that not have been nice at certain times?

"No, not really."

Their fame, then. Would that have amused you?

Eric thought longer about this. "I suppose a bit of their fame might have been an interesting thing to have had in life, but I certainly would not have wanted the lifestyle and pressures that go with it."

The women then, young girls panting for you. Surely that would have been fun? By your own admittance, you were a goer in your youth.

"You mean having groupies? No thanks. Girls who go to such extremes are prostituting themselves for a very small piece of fame."

Looking back at the life he has led, he says he has enjoyed it all, well, most of it. He has no regrets about those years in the navy, they were fun, taught him a lot, and he often looks back at them. It was exciting joining the Civil Service, being promoted to the Scottish prisons, starting with a blank sheet, achieving so many things, till his career came to a halt and he felt he was standing still. But he pulled himself out of all that. Family-wise, there have been no real disasters.

"I'm happily married with three sons who have done OK."

Then he paused, thinking. "They now say I was too strict on them when they were young. I wasn't aware of it, but I suppose I'm reaping that now. They open up to Relda and tell her more things than they tell me. Then she tells me. On the other hand, this just might be the role of most fathers."

Given his lack of interest in The Beatles, never boasting or letting slip his connections with them, it was surprising that he agreed to rejoin The Quarrymen.

"It was because I enjoyed seeing them all again, that was the only reason. I agreed to the Woolton Fete because it was a way of keeping in touch."

Eric bought a guitar for Woolton, for the first time in 40 years, which cost him £100. When other invites came in, he then traded up and now has a £300 Seagull guitar.

He is still in two minds about the future of the group, and whether he wants to continue.

"With us, in our small way, doing little tours for the last three years, it's all been new to us, something we never did first time round. Now I am beginning to think we've done it, had that experience. But I'll probably go on, as long as the others want to."

When Relda came home, I asked what she had thought about Eric rejoining The Quarrymen. She was surprised, in some ways, as he had never talked much about them, even when they were first going out together in the Sixties. "I only discovered he'd been in The Quarrymen when I saw a photograph of them in a Liverpool paper.

"But I was all for it. When he went to that reunion in 1997, I thought, Why not? He might enjoy it."

And since then?

"Well, there have been pluses and minuses. I did enjoy going with them to Cuba, Dublin and Holland. I didn't go on any of the US trips. They were on the move all the time, so it wouldn't have been much fun."

And the minuses?

"The frustration Eric shows when things like visas don't come through on time and have to be picked up at airports. It does cause niggles between them . . .

"It can also be a bit embarrassing. There was recently a bit about Eric in the Scottish papers, in the *Scotsman* and the *Edinburgh Evening News*. After the Liverpool Beatles Week, and all the John Lennon 60th birthday events, more people seem to know about The Quarrymen. In the Scottish papers they go on about 'The Boy From Scotland' which, of course, he's not, or 'Launderette Chief and The Beatles' which is embarrassing."

How?

"Well, it can look as if they are just these ageing people, trying to be pop stars. The papers also get things wrong. One reporter wrote that Eric had always regretted not staying with The Beatles. Which, of course, is totally untrue.

"I would never tell anyone Eric was in The Quarrymen but now, of course, friends and neighbours are finding out.

"I don't mind if they go on, playing occasionally. As long as they can agree on things and don't have any hassles."

Eric has acquired one memento from the last three years which has pleased him. While in Chicago, a Beatles fan came up to him and said he must be pleased that his name had been sung by John.

Eric had no idea what he was talking about. Even when the fan explained, Eric still wasn't clear, not having the knowledge of bootleg tapes which all true fans have. These are the out-takes from Beatles recording sessions, when they were simply messing around or jamming or trying out something new, which still mysteriously and illegally appear on the market. The fan said he would send Eric a copy, so he would hear for himself what it was all about.

Eric went to get the tape. He fiddled with his music system for some time, as if not sure how it worked, and eventually played it to me.

It sounded like an excerpt from a full recording session, from the late Sixties, but they are clearly just mucking around as they get ready to play whatever it was they were going to record next. They start making up words and music as they go along, singing or playing things at random, being silly, till the serious work begins.

"Why don't you put it on the phone," sings John, for no apparent reason, except perhaps a half-reference to Paul's "Why Don't We Do It In The Road".

Then John starts singing out the names of people – starting with names from their teenage or school years – "Billy Turner", "Ivan Vaughan", "Eric Griffiths".

Paul joins in, singing out other names, like Russ Conway, John Lennon. John adds, "Mary Whitehouse, Richard Nixon."

You can hear them all laughing at their own silliness, which is funny, but also a bit eerie, hearing those random names from their past, such as Ivan Vaughan and Billy Turner. Ivan died of Parkinson's Disease in 1993. Billy had a heart attack and died in 1993. But Eric is still with us.

He played it back again and smiled at the mention of his name.

"It does prove I did know them . . ."

# 29

## Rod Today

Rod lives with Janet in a small terraced cottage in Uxbridge, Middlesex, about 10 miles from London, with his computer, his musical instruments and his windsurfing boards. His two children from his first marriage are now grown up but he still sees them. Sophie went to the University of Kent at Canterbury and works in computers. Jonathan went to Southampton University and is in finance.

Rod, as befits an ex-head boy of Quarry Bank, is an organiser – or a bit of a fusser, according to Pete. He organises much of the life and itineraries of The Quarrymen today as well as keeping scraps and memorabilia from his own life, such as school certificates and reports, programmes and documents from his Cambridge years, cuttings and accounts of The Quarrymen, both past and present.

On the hall wall, as I entered, I noted some copies of the well-known photos of The Quarrymen from the Fifties, taken at the Roseberry Street celebrations and the Woolton Fete.

"The Roseberry Street photos have a strange history. They were taken by Charles Roberts who was a mate of Colin's. It was Charlie's mum who was organising the celebrations. Charles had a camera and took the first known photo of The Quarrymen, the one with John at the mike in his check shirt, Eric smiling on his guitar, Colin grinning on drums, an earnest Pete Shotton on the washboard, Len pounding the tea chest. I'm at the back, as usual, strumming my banjo, a bit obscured, as usual, but looking very serious.

"Many years ago, when I was still living in Liverpool, I called at Colin's house with my own camera to copy the two photographs I knew he still had, given to him by Charlie. They were just a few inches across, with crinkled edges. I wanted to have copies for myself.

"Some years later, I was looking at The Quarrymen photos in one of Mark Lewisohn's books, and I realised one of the photos I had was different from his. That's the one not published, till now. What's specially interesting to me is that it shows my face. On the other Quarrymen photos you can only ever see the top of my head or the back of my neck. Over the years, I've had to put up with a lot of leg-pulling from friends and family, saying that it isn't really me, I wasn't really there.

"I later tracked down Charles Roberts, who still lives in Woolton, to see if he had any more shots. He told me he had nothing – not even any of the negatives. He had taken them to the chemist in 1957 to have them printed, but when he returned to collect his prints, he was told the shop had been burgled. All the negatives had gone. I was pleased to give him back an admittedly poor copy of his original.

"The Woolton Parish photo was taken by Geoff Rhind, still a friend of mine. He was at Sunday School and Quarry Bank with me, John and Pete. He had his little Kodak at the fete and captured The Quarrymen.

"His photograph has been reproduced thousands of times – but it's almost always seen cropped. They do that so you can get a closer look at John. What you don't see is all the children around, watching us perform on the platform. Most of them get cut out, but in the original, there are a lot more, including some Brownies. One of the boys watching is Peter Radcliffe – father of Paula Radcliffe. You know, the runner, captain of the British women's team in the 2000 Olympics."

Well, what do you know. Rod does, of course, know a lot, but he doesn't lecture you, doesn't tell it like a teacher. It just sort of floods out, rather hesitantly, almost apologetically, in case you might know it all anyway, or not be interested.

The other bit of interesting, and now well-known, memorabilia from that 1957 Woolton Fete is the tape recording done by another ex-Sunday School friend, Robert Molyneux, who lived opposite Rod in King's Drive.

"I never knew till it came up for auction at Sotheby's that he'd tape-recorded us."

On the day of the auction, Rod was rung by Radio Merseyside who played him a bit of it down the phone. "It was Donegan's 'Putting On The Style'. John's voice was unmistakable – but the rest of us sounded as if we were singing at the other end of a drainpipe."

Nevertheless, it went for £70,000 and was bought by EMI for their archives. Rod and Len later wrote to them, suggesting that with modern equipment they could isolate John's voice, which was quite clear, then re-record the backing using the remaining Quarrymen, playing their original instruments.

Nice try, Rod.

"Yes, but it didn't work. I got a courteous letter back saying the recording was of very poor quality, but they would bear my suggestion in mind.
I know lots of fans would love to buy a copy. And so would I.

"In 1997, when The Beatles were doing their *Anthology*, they recorded
'Free As A Bird' using John's old voice. I've often wondered if my Quarrymen suggestion had been picked up by someone . . ."

The sale of the old Woolton tape recording reminded Rod that Colin
Hanton's next-door neighbour, Geraldine Davies, had once recorded
The Quarrymen on her Grundig when they were rehearsing at Colin's
house.

He tracked her down and was excited to hear she still had her old tape
recorder in the attic, plus some old tapes. There was even an old tape still
in the machine, on which she remembered recording The Quarrymen,
just after Paul had joined them. Alas, when it was played back, she had
recorded something totally different over it, thus destroying the original.
"What a tragedy," says Rod.

Rod collects and files anything to do with the history of the old Quarrymen, and is archivist of their modern incarnation, with his own website
which covers Quarrymen activities. But he does have several other interests. He still plays his bluegrass guitar, which he much prefers to skiffle.
With a friend, he plays a jazz rhythm guitar in a duo. "Skiffle is pretty
unsophisticated music. Basically, you just strum chords in skiffle. In bluegrass, you do get to play proper bass runs."

He used to do a lot of karate and is still very keen on Aikido, a Japanese
form of martial arts. But his major interest, which takes up even more time
than The Quarrymen, is windsurfing. Because of his stubbly grey beard,
you don't at first quite realise what a wiry, athletic figure he is.

As a student, he joined the sailing club at Cambridge, then in the
Eighties, when windsurfing came in, he moved on to that, as it was easier
to transport a board than a boat. He introduced Janet to it when they met
and they'd recently come back from windsurfing on Lake Garda in Italy.

Rod races on what's called a longboard, which has a dagger board, as
opposed to the short board, which has none. The longboard goes very fast,
up to 20mph, in very rough seas ". . . and frightens the living daylights out
of you".

In 1999, Rod was the first vet – meaning anyone over 50 – home in the
national series. The year before he was 41st in the World Masters champ-
ionships, for anyone over 35, which at the age of 57 was pretty good. He is
involved in the BSA, the Board Sailing Association, while Janet is
Vice-Commodore of the Queen Mary Sailing Club.

"The attraction to me is the wonderful feeling of it just being you and the wind and the water. All your troubles just fade away . . ."

You haven't got troubles, have you, Rod?

"No, not really. I've always gone through life believing the bottle is three-quarters full."

Given your life over again, would you like to have been a full-time professional musician?

"It was always what I would have liked to have been in an ideal world, but at the same time I knew it couldn't really ever happen. The music I like best is not popular. But yes, it would have been nice to have been a full-time musician.

"It would have been a very selfish ambition, though. The rest of your family has to suffer. When I used to take my two children to bluegrass festivals, they would have to sit around for hours and wait, often in the rain, for me to get my 30 minutes of playing. In the end they said, 'Please, no more festivals.' When I dragged Janet to them, she felt much the same.

"I now also realise that the life of a musician is much harder than you think. All that travelling, all that humping stuff around, is very exhausting. If we had roadies like The Beatles had, that would make life a bit easier for us."

During The Beatles' rise to fame, he says he never felt envious of their fame and success and money. "I haven't gone through life crying for 15 minutes every morning because I might have been a Beatle. I've got no regrets about my own life.

"I was never, in fact, a Beatles fan – for the simple reason that I've never been a fan of anybody. I have never tended to believe that the sun shines out of anyone's orifice.

"But with age, and playing all sorts of music, I have come to appreciate how good their tunes are. Their strength is in their unpredictability. As a musician, so much of what you play you can tell what's coming next. With so many Beatles' tunes, you can't even predict the next chord. They do spring brilliant surprises. Oh, I can't think immediately of examples. I never can, when asked that sort of question. But let's say I like very much 'If I Fell'.

Rod still loves playing in The Quarrymen, though he would like them to expand their repertoire a bit, perhaps move from 1957 into 1958, even 1959, and play a few more rock numbers.

Janet is all for him playing in The Quarrymen. She managed to make one of their US trips, plus Cuba, which she loved. "From when I met Rod, he has been playing in some sort of group, so that's just him.

"I do get a bit nervous when I watch them playing, worrying if one of them will make a mistake, but I enjoy being with them. You meet so many different sorts of people. In America and Europe it's very different from here. Foreign fans always know who's who and everything about them. In Britain, people are not as interested."

What does Rod think about the future of The Quarrymen?

"I remember spending hours on the phone with Colin in 1997, and with Eric, trying to persuade them to play with us. I said I couldn't guarantee anything, but I predicted we would get a trip to the USA at the very least. So I must have been fairly optimistic. But I didn't think we'd get this far. It's been incredible the countries we've been to since 1997. If anyone had told me, I would not have believed it. We've been extraordinarily fortunate. The bands I've played with would have given their back teeth and most limbs to have had the chances we've been handed virtually on a plate.

"Now, I do think we will continue. We could be bigger, do more events, but perhaps three or four big gigs a year, plus the odd weekend, that will be enough for us. I could do more personally, as I only do the odd hour lecturing at Brunel, but we have to fit in with Len's job and Colin's and Eric's businesses."

Does he think Pete will back out again, as he did in early 2000?

"I hope not. I think he'll stay with us this time. This is based on something he said to me after Liverpool. 'I missed you, you bastards . . .' "

# 30

## Pete Today

Pete today lives abroad, going here, there and everywhere, as the mood takes him. He might pop over to Majorca to sail his 60-foot, eight-berth yacht. Or perhaps head off to Las Vegas for a spot of gambling. He'd been there recently for a long weekend, taking Ruth, Len's daughter, who also likes a bit of gambling. Pete today is a single man, after three marriages, but it was all very proper. He was giving Ruth a break, after the collapse of her marriage.

I arranged to see him in Dublin. This appeared to be his main residence at the time, though Pete moves in mysterious ways, making it hard to work out what he does or where he does it. He keeps his phone numbers and mobiles very private. His daily life is also very unusual, rarely surfacing before one o'clock, sometimes staying up all night.

"I've always done that. I like the night better than the day. It's so peaceful. Nobody bothers you. At 17, when I was a police cadet, I used to meet up with Billy Turner at midnight, after he'd taken his girlfriend home and after I'd taken mine home. We'd go to the Blue Angel or just sit on a park bench till four in the morning. Doing nothing, really."

He can be very funny and amusing, tells a good story, is very generous and thoughtful. He can also be rather volatile, get upset, even angry, then just as quickly calm down again. He pulled out of helping on this book twice, then came back in again.

Then, of course, he said he was leaving The Quarrymen. He appeared to be back in again when we met in Dublin, judging by the fact that he was talking of taking bass guitar lessons. "I'm fed up plucking that stupid fucking washboard and looking like an idiot. I want to stand up front and play a proper instrument."

He was also talking about taking motorbike lessons. He'd signed up for a residential course, planning to buy a super bike and zoom along the country lanes of Ireland like a sixty-year-old teenager, indulging his fantasy. (Which he did, for three days, then gave up.)

Despite all his millions, Pete has not changed much, as the other Quarrymen observed. Still the same jaunty walk, still a Scouser, without any of the gloss which affluence often bestows. A stranger would scarcely take him for a multimillionaire, not by his appearance or manner, unless, of course, he was in his Aston Martin.

He always says he was very shy and embarrassed on stage as a boy with The Quarrymen – though there again, Len says Pete always struck him as a confident person. On stage now, he is by far the most relaxed and confident, the most polished and fluent, even more than Rod, the Cambridge graduate. Pete, of course, has graduated through the hard school of business. He did become a chairman of the board, in charge of himself and his surroundings.

I can see how John liked Pete so much. And also why he hit him over the head with his washboard in 1957. He is unpredictable, can be a bit wild, a bit moody, but always entertaining. I judged him wrongly that time, when John told me he'd let him have £20,000 for a shop, thinking he'd waste it. I'm sure at Apple they also underestimated him, assuming he was just John's mate, therefore no good at management and would never get the boutique open on time.

The house where he was staying was on the south side of Dublin, in a fairly run-down street. His little block was modern, set back from the road, behind a high security fence. He was sharing a three-bedroom apartment with a friend, Kevin, a computer expert, who had worked with him at Fatty Arbuckle. Kevin still seemed to be working with him, as Pete's PA, helping on various business deals, and also looking after a Quarrymen website. (They have two – Rod does the other.) Staying with them, while I was there, was Pete's son Matthew, aged 33, who lives in Cheshire. He also works with Pete.

On the Saturday night, I went with Pete to a very swish restaurant, Locks, over the Grand Canal. It was a humid summer's evening and the young waitress was mopping her brow. "It's so hot," she said. "Then take your clothes off, love," said Pete. It wasn't really very funny, nor was it lascivious, but it made me smile, enough to order another bottle. And we hadn't even started eating yet.

Over dinner, he talked quite a lot about John, revealing the nickname John once gave him – Peen. What did that mean, Pete?

"It was short for penis. A penis is long and thin with a red head and has white stuff coming out of the top – just like me. Oh Christ, don't write that down. It's too embarrassing. No one knows that. If The Quarrymen find out, I'll get slaughtered."

He remembered watching television with John, in John's favourite little room at Kenwood, curled up on the sofa, and how weird it was to be sitting with John when John and the other Beatles suddenly appeared on the screen.

"John would say, 'It's not me, it's Micky Mouse.' He did look upon The Beatles as not him, as a fictional creation."

I asked him if he ever paid back the money John had let him have for the shop in Hayling Island, which got him started in business.

"Of course I fucking did. I took out an endowment policy to pay it all back, with no interest, because that was the agreement."

It came to £29,000 in all, as he'd borrowed another £9,000 for the fashion shop, the one he had to close. When John died, Yoko inherited everything, as his widow. It naturally took some time to sort out and understand the thousands of documents and deals which John had left behind – and Pete's little policy was not one of the mega ones. But eventually, Pete did hear from Yoko's representatives – who said she wanted the full amount. "Her people even wanted to know if there was any interest as well, but my lawyers could prove that John made it clear he never wanted any interest. But I paid all the loan back."

One of the things Pete did, after John died, was write a book about him in 1983. This was at a time when Pete had yet to begin his restaurant career and was still wondering what to do next in life. As he had known John for over 30 years, he thought he should get down some of his memories.

"I went to America with a brief synopsis. I didn't have an agent. I just tried to sell it on my own. I met people at McGraw Hill and someone there began talking about an advance of $500,000. I should have grabbed it. But nothing was ever written down – and it all fell through. I then went to see Doubleday, had talks with them. While I was talking to them, Sol Stein of Stein and Day came along and offered me $52,000. I was impressed by his enthusiasm and his love for The Beatles, so I took it.

"I did try to write the book myself, but soon realised it was harder than I thought, so I found an American writer who had written a book about The Beatles, Nicholas Schaffner. He was a nice bloke and I liked him, but I don't think he understood my Liverpool sense of humour. I shared the money with him 50-50. I just spoke into a tape recorder. He knocked it into shape.

"The book came out, but we only got one quarter of the advance – $13,000, which I shared with Nick. I wrote endless letters asking for the rest of the money, demanded statements, a copy of the accounts, but heard nothing. So in the end I got an American lawyer and began to sue them. But it never came to court – because Stein and Day packed up. So that was it. I never got any more money. I made a big mistake, choosing the publisher I did.

"Perhaps some time I'll bring it back into print, put more in. At one time I made a list of 100 Beatles songs which I knew about, created when I was around. I wrote out the list about 20 years ago. Not sure where it is now. I think Matthew has it."

After dinner, I asked how he explained his sudden and late success as a businessman. "Delegating," he said. "And common sense. But I'll tell you one thing about common sense. It's not very common . . ."

He is now interested in helping other people, the way John had helped him to get started. He's recently been eating in an Indian restaurant in Dublin and been impressed by the young Indian struggling to run it. He has now set him up in an Indian takeaway and delivery service. "Dublin is wide open for such things, the sort London has had for years."

He was also still making money on his own account. There was a new computer business which Kevin was working on and also a property idea he'd had which Matthew was running – buying 'off plan' apartments. This means acquiring properties not yet built, still at the drawing-board stage. He had sent Matthew round the UK looking for high-class two-bed flats in new luxury blocks being built over water – either the sea, a river or a canal, it didn't really matter. "You can never build on water, so I reckon it pays to be near it." They ended up with sixteen flats, from London's Docklands to the Isle of Man.

Is Matthew going to find tenants and collect rents?

"Oh no, we'll sell every one, the moment it's complete. You only have to pay a proportion up front, when it's off-plan. The rest is not paid till it's finished – and that's when we sell. We've sold most already, and made a good profit."

He had, of course, been smart in his timing, as property prices had boomed the moment he began buying. He says it wasn't luck. He looked at mortgage rates, the relationship between earnings and what mortgage companies will lend you, and estimated that the ratio was such that prices would still go up, before they came down again or steadied. I think that's what he said. Sounded clever anyway.

He still believes, as John always maintained, that he and John got none of their cleverness from Quarry Bank School. In fact, he feels they had a bad education – that they were let down by the school, not the other way round.

"They just wanted to absorb you, like a sponge. You got your five 'O' levels or whatever, then they soak you up, into the system. It still goes on. This way of defining intelligence is all wrong. All they're doing is producing bricks to place in a wall – bricks marked bank manager, architect, solicitor, car mechanic. Yeah, I lump them together. A mechanic does have to work hard to become a mechanic. When a new car comes out, he has to read the manual, learn all about it, but all he's doing is learning stuff – just the way a doctor or lawyer has to. I don't call that intelligence. It's just absorbing information.

"Most mechanics are like most professors – as boring as shit. A lot of doctors I have met have been the most stupid people I've ever come across. They have the least common sense and the most prejudice . . ."

Ah, it took me back, back to the Sixties, listening to The Beatles. We'd also finished two bottles of wine, which was helping things to flow along. The Beatles, at the time of setting up Apple, did believe that most people could do most things, without the need for formal academic or professional qualifications, if they were given the chance, and if they put their minds to it.

Any other wisdoms to pass on, Pete, now you are a man of mature years?

"You have to acquire wisdom for yourself. You can't pass it on. Youth is wasted on the young in that they can't learn from it at the time.

"Youth can be a fucking pain in the arse, but that's how we progress. Each generation has to question what the previous generation did or thought, but that's how we develop. Otherwise, the human race would stagnate, then die out."

Was John the most interesting human being he'd ever met?

"No. I've met a lot of one-offs in my life, people with great insight and an irreverent sense of humour. I've known a lot of people who've made me laugh. Those are the sort I like best.

"John, of course, was one. He didn't take life too seriously. Nor do I. It puts a spring into your step, when you meet such people with the same views."

I asked if he thought he might marry again, but he didn't think so. He did live with a woman for about a year, after the collapse of his third marriage, but not any more.

"I tell you who I liked the look of. That Heather Mills, the girl who lost her leg. I saw her on an Esther Rantzen show. I can even remember the date – March 2, 1998.

"I was so overwhelmed by her story, her terrible accident, then devoting

252

her life to that charity, that I told myself that when my money comes through, for I was selling the business at the time, I'll track her down and give her money for her cause. But that bastard Paul McCartney got to her first . . .

"Just joking about Paul. Good luck to him. No, I haven't seen Paul for many years. Don't suppose I will again."

Looking back at his own life so far, what did he think of it – good, bad, middling, could have been better?

He paused to think. "Thanks to knowing John, I've had a most interesting life, more than normal people. I've seen things, done things most people never do. It's been incredible at times.

"I've had some very good friends in life, who have helped me a lot when I needed it . . ."

He paused again, as if in the middle of a thought. But?

"But personally, I've had a lot of pain in life, a lot of difficulties . . ."

Because of the three marriages?

"Because of me, really. It's been exciting, but not very happy. I would say on the whole I haven't been very happy in life. I've had to put up with me . . ."

Meaning what?

"People have loved me, but many have found there was a limit to their love. They thought they could put up with me, but in the end they couldn't. I can hardly put up with myself. I always begin to crave freedom. I hate being put in a cage. I hate being tied down to anything or anyone.

"It doesn't make me happy, being like that. I can become depressive, have ups and downs. I know all that . . .

"Look, you're an arsehole. Will you stop this fucking conversation. I thought we were going to talk about John."

OK, let's get back to John.

"All I really have to say about him is that I knew him from when I was six, he went on to be thought special by millions of people all round the world, but to me he was always just my best mate. Now fuck off . . ."

# End Bit

All the way through, I was thinking of The Beatles. Not their fame, their millions, their achievements, but their ordinary, domestic lives over the last 40 years, of daft analogies, of trivial comparisons between them and The Quarrymen.

The five Quarrymen are still with us, as I write. One Beatle has gone. That was the direct result of being a Beatle, though there again, a madman, a terrorist, a chance accident, a deadly illness, can finish any of us off, at any moment. All the same, five blokes who have known each other between 40 and 50 years and are still up and around, none with any serious illness or injury or debilitations, that's pretty good. But then we are all living longer, healthier lives. Even men, the less fortunate sex when it comes to longevity.

Only one of the five never left home. One left and returned. That means there are just two out of five living in Liverpool, where it all began. We all move around more these days, so we are told.

One has been married and divorced three times. One married and divorced and is now with a new partner. But three out of five have been happily married to one woman all their lives. Better than the national average, and much better than The Beatles. Three out of four Beatles got married and divorced. Second time round, they married a foreigner. Paul did as well, when he married Linda.

As for children, the four Beatles between them had nine children – which works out at 2.25 each. (Let's not get into children born out of wedlock or we could be here for hours. At one time in the Sixties, The Beatles had a solicitor working almost full time, sorting out the claims and allegations.)

The five Quarrymen have totalled 12 children between them which works out at 2.5. About the same rate. (No, I didn't ask about love children, but today, if they are attracting groupies aged around 59, they are unlikely to have many.)

Is Rod Paul? When the Beatles were beginning, Paul was the charming, organised one who wrote letters to journalists, kept in with managements, tried to get the rest of the group organised. Rod does a lot of that for The

254

Quarrymen today. But he says that's through his background. In his working life, he has worked in marketing while in the travel trade, and played in other groups for many years. He knows how the world works, what's expected from managements and media and audiences.

Is Pete John? He is the stroppy one, the original one, who can't be taken for granted, who has his own view on the world. His talents, like John, were not recognised for a long time. In the case of Pete, a very very long time.

Eric is a bit like George, rather serious and solemn, with his own strong opinions. Len and Colin can be seen as Ringo figures, laid-back and unpushy, but also amusing, philosophical, who worry more than they might appear, certainly in the case of Colin. Ringo did worry, which was why he was the first to say he was leaving The Beatles.

It was interesting to chart the individual lives of The Quarrymen, watching their ups and downs, the changes that happened in their working lives. This, too, is a sign of our times, now that so many people have a variety of jobs and careers.

Unlike most of us, they had a change of life very late in life, a sudden and remarkable experience which came their way, offering an insight into the nature of being a celebrity. All on a modest scale, but a real experience nonetheless. For them, it's been like living twice, with a gap of forty years between the two lives.

Will they go on, performing as Quarrymen in their sixties? Age doesn't seem to be a handicap for those who have always performed, such as Cliff Richard or The Rolling Stones. But even if The Quarrymen pack up now, they will always have had this unexpected bonus, simply by once knowing somebody who later became famous.

If they do carry on, and you have a chance to catch them, do so. There is firstly The Beatles' connection. Even if they are mere marginal notes in Beatles history, they will always be of interest to true Beatles fans. There is also a social and musical interest, for those of a certain age who remember the age of skiffle and expected, perhaps hoped, never to hear it again.

But mainly the enjoyment is enjoying their enjoyment, watching and listening to them doing something they never expected to do again.

# Appendices

## APPENDIX A
### ORIGINAL QUARRYMEN PERFORMANCES

John Lennon, Pete Shotton, Eric Griffiths, Rod Davis, Colin Hanton and
  Len Garry became part of a schoolboy skiffle group, formed some time
  in 1956, exact date unknown.
First Performances: also pretty unknown. In the early months, they
  played in each other's homes, at friends' parties, St. Peter's Youth
  Club, Quarry Bank School dances.
Earliest appearances any of them can remember: Lee Park Golf Club,
  some time in late 1956 or early 1957. No fee.

### Public Performances: for which some sort of record exists:

*1957*

*June 9*: Empire Theatre, Liverpool
  Audition for Carroll Levis discovery show. Did not win.
*June 22*: Roseberry Street, Liverpool
  Street party, playing from the back of a coal lorry. Not invited back.
*July 6*: St Peter's Church Fete, Woolton
  Paul meets John for the first time.
*August 7*: Cavern Club
  No Paul. Gone off on a scout camp.
*October 18*: New Clubmoor Hall, Norris Green
  Paul's first appearance with The Quarrymen. Very nervous.
*November 17*: Wilson Hall, Speke
  First of several known appearances. Wilson Hall was where John was
  regularly chased by Teddy Boys.
*November 16*: Stanley Abattoir
  No, not during working hours. Entertaining slaughtermen and wives at
  their evening soiree.
*November 23*: New Clubmoor Hall
  A return appearance. Must be doing something well, or very cheaply.
*December 7*: Wilson Hall

## 1958

*January 10*: New Clubmoor Hall
*January 24*: Cavern Club
*February 6*: Wilson Hall
Possibly the first time George Harrison met them.
*March 13*: Morgue Cellar Club
Opening night of new club, soon to close as a bit of a dump.
*December 20*: Upton Green
Party for George's brother's wedding.

## 1959

*January 1*: Wilson Hall
*January 24*: Woolton Village Club
Sometime in mid 1959, The Quarrymen cut their first record in the back room of a house in Liverpool owned by Percy Phillips.
Some time later, Colin Hanton left the group. Pete, Eric, Rod and Len had already left, sometime earlier.
John, Paul and George went on to become Beatles. The other five original Quarrymen went out into the world.

### APPENDIX B
### THE RE-BORN QUARRYMEN

*January 16, 1997: Cavern Club*

All five – Pete, Eric, Rod, Len and Colin – met up again for the first time in almost 40 years for the Cavern's 40th anniversary. It was a private party, but they got up on stage, pretended to play, despite having drunk too much.

## Public Performances

## 1997

*June 5*: Woolton Church Fete, 40th anniversary party
First time playing together again.
*November 9*: Derby
Beatles Convention, Derby Playhouse.

*1998*

*April 11*: Utrecht, Holland
  Beatles Festival, Vredenburg Muziek Centrum
*July 1–10*: US Tour, New York and East Coast
*July 2*: Foxwoods Casino, Connecticut
*July 3*: Private party on the Hudson River, upstate New York
*July 5*: American picnic at Boscobel, overlooking West Point
  Later that day, on stage with Pete Seeger at Peekskill, NY
*July 6*: Bottom Line Club, Green Village, New York
*July 7*: Visit to Shea Stadium where they played cricket followed by a spot
  on ABC coast to coast TV news
*July 9*: Avalon Theatre, Easton, Maryland
*August 14–16*: USA, Chicago Beatlefest at Hyatt Regency O'Hare
*November 7*: Dublin Fan Club of Ireland, Olympia Theatre
*November 25–30*: Cuba, Havana. Third International Beatles Conference

*1999*

*January 22*: USA, Las Vegas Palace Station Casino
*January 23*: Canada, Vancouver Island, Tidemark Theatre, Campbell
  River
*January 24*: Canada, Vancouver, Vancouver East Cultural Centre
*January 25*: Canada, Vancouver, Vicki Gabereau TV show
*July 6*: Liverpool, Cavern Club
*August 22–30*: USA
*August 26*: USA. Johnny D's, Cambridge, Mass.
*August 27–29*: USA. Orlando Beatlefest
*October 9*: Belgium, Mons. Beatles Day
  Pete ill with flu.

*2000*

*March 24–26*: USA, New Jersey, Metro Beatlefest
  No Pete.
*August 26–27*: Liverpool Beatle Week
*August 26*: Quarry Bank School
*August 27*: Liverpool Institute of Performing Arts
*September 30*: Channel 4 TV, *The Real John Lennon*
*October 9*: Liverpool. John Lennon's 60th birthday celebrations, Royal
  Court Theatre

*December 10*: London, concert to mark 20 years since John's death at the Palace Theatre – their West End debut.

*2001*

*May*. Launch party for the book, *The Quarrymen* . . .

## APPENDIX C
### USEFUL BOOKS, CONTACTS, ADDRESSES

### Beatles books which cover The Quarrymen years

*The Beatles*, the authorised biog by Hunter Davies, new, updated edition, published by Arrow. Still fantastic.

*The Complete Beatles Chronicle* by Mark Lewisohn, Chancellor Press, 1992. Jolly useful work by leading Beatles Brain.

*The Beatles Off The Record* by Keith Badman, Omnibus Press, 2000. All the stuff they said, back in the Sixties.

*The Beatles Anthology* by The Beatles, Cassell, 2000. Beatles own account of themselves. Good pix, some good, if oldish, quotes.

*The Day John Met Paul* by Jim O'Donnell, published by Hall of Fame Books, USA, 1994, Penguin UK, 1996. Audio version, read by the one and only Rod Davis, Scorpion Publications, 1997.

*John Lennon: In My Life* by Pete Shotton and Nicholas Schaffner, Stein and Day, New York, 1983, Coronet, UK, 1984. (Out of print.)

*John, Paul And Me Before The Beatles* by Len Garry, CG Publishing, Toronto, 1997. (Out of print.)

### The Quarrymen's CD

*John Lennon's Original Quarrymen Get Back – Together*
Recorded in Liverpool in 1997, the original line-up, minus John of course, playing 15 rock and skiffle numbers from their 1957 repertoire, in the original style – with tea chest bass and washboard. The nearest thing to the sound that gave birth to The Beatles. Available from Scorpion Publications, PO Box 616, Uxbridge, Middx UB8 2YP. Tel. 01895 847504 or by email: davispain@compuserve.com

### Quarrymen websites:

www.quarrymen.co.uk

http://ourworld.compuserve.com/homepages/davispain
  (This site features soundclips from The Quarrymen's CD and contains
  up-to-date news about the Quarrymen's activities)
http://www.arrakis.es/~alcr/indexi.htm
  Internet comic book history of The Quarrymen and The Beatles
  (Spanish and English versions)

## Tours:

Cavern City Tours, 10 Mathew Street, Liverpool, Merseyside, L2 6RE,
  tel. 0151 236 9091. For tours, events, annual Beatle week.
Forthlin Road Tours, to Paul's old house, run by National Trust, tel.
  0870 9000 256.

## APPENDIX D
## A PERSONAL ADDENDUM FROM ROD DAVIS
### ABOUT JOHN'S GUITAR

I was in the USA in August 1999 with The Quarrymen and phoning
home. I was astounded to learn that John's guitar was coming up for sale at
Sotheby's. The guitar was the one he was playing in Geoff Rhind's famous
photo; a Gallotone Champion, actually the second guitar he had ever
owned, the first one being an Egmond like the one George Harrison is
playing in the photo on page 25 of *From Yesterday To Today* published by
Time Life.

As an inveterate haunter of junk shops I had often wondered what had
become of John's guitar. I had played it frequently myself and could still
recall the way my fingers smelled of smoke afterwards as John was in the
habit of parking his still burning cigarette stub on the end of the first string
where it stuck out of the tuning peg.

But the problem was, how to recognise John's guitar among all the
hundreds, or more likely thousands, of Gallotone Champions which were
snapped up by skifflers way back in 1957. Here I had an advantage. On
one occasion, it may even have been at St Peter's Church Hall, John had
broken a string and in the process had also skinned the edge of his index
finger, probably as a result of playing too hard, don't forget we had no
amplifiers! He handed the guitar to me to replace the string and took my
banjo to play the next number. I noticed that a fine spray of blood droplets
from John's cut finger had gone through the soundhole of the guitar and
had landed partly on the label (Guaranteed not to split!) and partly on the

wood above the label. If I ever found a guitar in a junk shop I was sure I could tell if it was John's or not!

When The Quarrymen returned from the US, after playing in Boston and Orlando, I contacted Sotheby's who very kindly invited me to examine the guitar. They said they were in no doubt that it was John's because it had come originally from his Aunt Mimi with a letter from her to that effect! I did, of course, mention the bloodstains but in the circumstances it was quite clear that this was John's guitar. After John's death she could no longer keep it in the house and had given it away to a disabled boy so he could learn the guitar. From him it passed to a young girl, also disabled, and it was her guardian who was putting the guitar up for sale to secure her future.

It was a big thrill and a great privilege to see and hold the guitar again. Mimi had had it restored somewhat with the intention of presenting it to John. She had even mounted on the machine head a little brass plate which he had originally given her bearing her famous quotation, "The guitar is all very well John, but you'll never make a living out of it." Then came the moment I looked inside for the bloodstains. Yes, they were clearly visible when you knew what to look for. Sotheby's had noticed the marks but had simply thought it was discoloration due to the ageing of the wood. I pointed out that the same marks were also found on the top part of the label, but not on the bottom part of the label nor on the wood beneath!

With the guitar came an apparently unused guitar tutor printed in 1958 with, tucked inside, a picture of Lonnie Donegan cut from a magazine. There was also an old leather briefcase which contained another newspaper clipping with photos of various film stars including Brigitte Bardot, John's favourite.

In the briefcase was a collection of 78rpm records which had also come from Mimi. They were 'Heartbreak Hotel'/'I Was The One', 'All Shook Up'/'That's When Your Heartaches Begin', 'Hound Dog'/'Don't Be Cruel', 'Got A Lot O' Living To Do'/'Party', 'I Don't Care If The Sun Don't Shine'/'Blue Moon', 'Jailhouse Rock'/'Treat Me Nice', all by Elvis, Buddy Holly's 'Peggy Sue'/'Everyday', Little Richard's 'Lucille'/ 'Send Me Some Lovin' ', The Goons' 'Ying Tong Song'/'Bloodnok's Rock And Roll Call' and Lonnie Donegan's 'Cumberland Gap'/'Love Is Strange', 'Lost John'/'Stewball' and 'Alabammy Bound'/'Don't You Rock Me Daddy-o'.

This, for me, was like opening a time capsule, this was the music which influenced us in 1957 and, of course, John was a big fan of The Goons, as we all were. I was particularly interested in the records as in 1957 I had bought from John his copy of 'Rock Island Line' for two shillings and sixpence. It had been badly chipped around the hole in the centre where John had carelessly slapped it on the turntable. In fact, the hole was so damaged my father stuck a bit of plastic over the hole and re-drilled it so it would not slide about when played. Some of these records were damaged in the same way. I would have liked to have restored this record to the rest of the collection! The Quarrymen still play 'All Shook Up', 'Don't Be Cruel', 'Blue Moon' and 'Lost John' in our current stage show.

Sotheby's kindly allowed me to take some photos holding John's guitar, but alas I was not allowed to tune it up and try to play it. It is possible that the neck might have collapsed and as it eventually went for £140,000, my own neck would have been in a sling. At the auction itself, which was held at the Hard Rock Café in Piccadilly, the eventual purchaser was a Beatles fan from New York, who was absolutely delighted that he had been successful. The collection of records made £750.

All in all an extraordinary find for Sotheby's, and so now I have one less guitar to look for when trawling the junk shops.

### APPENDIX E
### ANSWERS TO QUESTIONS

You must know them all, having read every word of the book, but here they are.

*Multiple Choice, page 78*

1, Pete; 2, Pete; 3, Eric; 4, Len; 5, Len and Colin; 6, Eric; 7, Colin; 8, Rod; 9, Rod; 10, Eric.

*Quotes To Come, page 134*

1, John; 2, Len; 3, Colin; 4, Len; 5, Pete; 6, Pete; 7, Eric; 8, Pete; 9, Colin, 10, Rod.